LEADING IN PRAYER
A Workbook for Ministers

LEADING

A Workbook

IN PRAYER

for Ministers

Hughes Oliphant Old

WILLIAM B. EERDMANS PUBLISHING COMPANY
GRAND RAPIDS, MICHIGAN / CAMBRIDGE, U.K.

© 1995 Wm. B. Eerdmans Publishing Co.

255 Jefferson Ave. S.E., Grand Rapids, Michigan 49503 /

P. O. Box 163, Cambridge CB3 9PU U.K.

Printed in the United States of America

02 03 04 05 06 07 08 09   11 10 9 8 7 6 5 4 3

Library of Congress Cataloging-in-Publication Data

Old, Hughes Oliphant.
    Leading in prayer : a workbook for ministers / Hughes Oliphant Old.
      p.   cm.
    Includes index.
    ISBN 0-8028-0821-2 (pbk.)
    1. Prayer. 2. Public worship. 3. Prayer—Reformed churches.
    I. Title.
    BV226.043 1995
    264′1—dc20   95-21725
                                    CIP

Dedicated to
Charles Ainley Hammond

Contents

Acknowledgments

What started this book was the conversations I had with some of my younger colleagues out in Indiana. It must have been about 1975 when the youth revival had brought many capable, well-educated young men into the ministry. Several in particular seemed to be quite interested in my research into the history of Christian worship. We often got together and talked about leading worship in our different Churches. There was Stuart Robertson, pastor of the Federated Church in Brookston. He had recently graduated from Trinity Divinity School in Chicago and he knew his Bible very well. He was interested in the way I used the biblical prayers as patterns for my leading of public prayer. He offered to type up my handwritten prayers. Further conversations stimulated by that project got the manuscript off the ground. There was Pat Johnson, pastor of the Baptist Church in Pine Bluff. We used to get together for breakfast on Mondays and talk about how things had gone on Sunday. One time he asked me to write out for him a few brief directives on what should be treated in the different prayers in the service. Again this led to quite a bit of discussion about what his congregation expected of him and what Scripture taught about public prayer.

Then there was Joe Bell, pastor of Grace Chapel, a recent graduate of Southwestern Baptist Seminary in Fort Worth, Texas. He, too, got into the conversation with his constant questions about the theology of prayer.

When I came to the Center of Theological Inquiry back in 1985, Tom Summers, then a student at Princeton Theological Seminary, took on the job of putting these bits and pieces of a manuscript onto the computer. Again this sparked quite a bit of discussion. He had studied under Tony Campolo at Eastern Baptist and he had a strong sense that worship should be reformed according to Scripture. Then Rob Redman at Fuller Seminary used a draft of this evolving work in teaching a course for the doctor of ministry program at Fuller. He carefully reported the reactions of his students and they were worked into the manuscript. Finally, Professor James Kay of Princeton Theological Seminary read over the proofs for me and advised me on a number of unresolved questions. All the way along, conversation with my colleagues has shaped this book every bit as much as my pastoral experience and my historical research. To these partners in thought and brothers in prayer I wish to express my highest appreciation.

A number of classic prayers and hymns have been quoted in this work.

Because it is essentially a pulpit book it reflects the liturgical books used by the congregations I have served over the years. *The Book of Common Worship* (Philadelphia: Board of Christian Education of the Presbyterian Church in the United States of America, 1932) has served as the source for the text of the Apostles' Creed, the Lord's Prayer, the Words of Institution for the Lord's Supper, several prayers, especially those of Henry van Dyke and Louis F. Benson, and several of the Benedictions and Ascriptions. Some of these have been slightly revised, especially when the language seemed too archaic for my congregation.

Several collections of prayers have been most helpful in supplying translations of material from the ancient Church, the continental Reformers, and other classic texts. The following especially should be mentioned: *The Macmillan Book of Earliest Christian Prayers,* edited by F. Forrester Church and Terrence J. Mulry (New York: Macmillan, 1988); *Liturgies of the Western Church,* edited by Bard Thompson (Cleveland: World Publishing Company, 1961); *Liturgies Eastern and Western,* edited by F. E. Brightman (Oxford: Clarendon Press, 1896); and Charles W. Baird, *The Presbyterian Liturgies* (photolithographic reprint, Grand Rapids: Baker Book House, 1957). For the English translation of the Communion Prayers of the *Didache* I am indebted to Kirsopp Lake, *The Apostolic Fathers* (Cambridge: Harvard University Press, 1965). The *Apostolic Constitutions* I have quoted from the *Ante-Nicene Fathers,* volume VII. Two Prayers for Illumination are quoted from John Wordsworth's *Bishop Serapion's Prayer-Book* (reprint, Hamden, Connecticut: Archon Books, 1964) and from Gottfried W. Locher, *Zwingli's Thought: New Perspectives* (Leiden: E. J. Brill, 1981).

My colleague at the Center of Theological Inquiry, S. T. Kimbrough, has been a constant inspiration on the subject of hymnology in general and the work of Charles Wesley in particular. It was he who pointed me to the excellent collection of Wesleyan hymns found in The Classics of Western Spirituality volume entitled *John and Charles Wesley: Selected Writings and Hymns,* edited by Frank Whaling (New York, Ramsey, and Toronto: Paulist Press, 1981).

Hymns that I mention in this book or quote, partially or in full, are often among those that one can find in the hymnals of several different denominations. Those that I have consulted most frequently are *The Hymnal* (Philadelphia: Presbyterian Board of Education, 1933); *The Pilgrim Hymnal* (Philadelphia: The Pilgrim Press, 1972); *The Presbyterian Hymnal* (Louisville: Westminster/John Knox, 1990); *Rejoice in the Lord,* edited by Erik Routley (Grand Rapids: Wm. B. Eerdmans Publishing Co., 1985), and *Trinity Hymnal* (Philadelphia: Committee on Christian Education, Orthodox Presbyterian Church, 1961).

In quoting the Bible I have used the Revised Standard Version, recognizing that more recent translations will probably be preferred by many. My use of the RSV reflects no more than the fact that this verison was in use in the congregations I served at the time the prayers were composed. In spite of my best intentions, however, the fact is that I often revert to the language of the old King James Version when I pray. I have not tried to make all these allusions and quotations conform to one version. With so many versions of Scripture today that seemed unrealistic.

Appreciation is expressed to Hope Publishing Company for permission to quote Michael Perry's hymn, "The God of Heaven." Fred Anderson has given permission to quote two of his metrical psalms from his collection, *Singing Psalms of Joy and Praise* (Philadelphia: Westeminster Press, 1986). Likewise Christopher Webber has graciously let us quote a selection from his *A New Metrical Psalter* (New York: Church Hymnal Corporation, 1986).

Introduction

When I was a rookie preacher, there was nothing I found quite so difficult as leading the congregation in prayer. I loved to preach, and I felt fairly confident about how I was supposed to do it, but leading in prayer was a much more awesome task. I knew what prayer was supposed to be. To pray was to enter into the holy of holies, to ascend Mount Horeb and stand there in the full force of the storm and yet hear the still small voice of calm. I knew I was not up to that.

As a boy, one of the pastors whom I regarded as a particularly holy man was Morgan Phelps Noyes, pastor of Central Presbyterian Church in Montclair, New Jersey. With the admiration that only a boy can have for a mature man, I noted the solemnity with which he approached prayer. I knew that was the way it was supposed to be done. It was only years later that I realized he had written a very good book on preparing prayers for the service of worship. I could have used that book if I had known about it, but then I had much more, the living memory of a great minister of the Word of God leading the congregation in true worship. I had very early in life gotten a sense of what public prayer could be.

My first church was rather demanding on their green young minister. The members were not about to come to church to hear the minister read someone else's prayers. They could read, too. They had books of prayers at home. John Baillies's *A Diary of Private Prayer* was in great favor at the time. It was not, of course, that they thought there was anything wrong with reading the classic prayers of the Church in public worship. It was more that they expected a time during which their minister would lead them in prayer. They considered that an essential part of the pastoral office. It was all right to have a unison prayer of confession or a litany on special occasions, but if their pastor did not devote a considerable portion of the time set aside for prayer to leading that congregation in that time and place, with all its sins and supplications, all its particular needs and special joys, into the presence of the Eternal, then that minister was neglecting a very important part of the job.

On both sides of my family, there was a strong tradition that prayer makes a difference. My father had been nourished in a small Southern town on the banks of the Mississippi River, where his family had for generations provided fuel wood for the river boats on the run between Memphis and St. Louis. When my father was four years old, my grandmother was left a widow with three small boys to raise. Her witness that prayer changes things was unshakable. My father was a great storyteller. The stories of his youth were always vivid and entertaining. Sometimes they were very serious, and I realize now that in my father's stories his faith was communicated. Only with reflection do I understand what they really meant. Yet they were very entertaining. Tom Sawyer had nothing on my father. They went fishing in the same river; they lived in much the same kind of small river town and had many of the same kind of adventures. In fact, I sometimes have a hard time keeping straight the stories Mark Twain told about Tom Sawyer and the stories my father told about his own youth. There was one important difference, of course. Tom Sawyer had been taught about prayer by the Enlightenment. It was the backwoods version of the Enlightenment, but it was the Enlightenment nevertheless. You remember the story. God cannot really be depended upon to provide fishhooks when fishhooks are needed. My father had been taught about prayer in the Southern Methodist Church, and he firmly believed in prayer. His family had lived by prayer. That was clear from so many of the stories. They had a solid spirituality based on prayer and the Methodist hymnal. Prayer was an experience that was lived every day. No other argument, no philosophical consideration, could stack up against that. The tradition that was handed on to me was that prayer was pretty potent.

From the other side of my family, I received quite a bit of tradition about prayer, too. Grandfather Chambers was a prayer warrior. The story was that his wife would often awaken in the middle of the night to discover that he was no longer in bed. The first place she would check for him was in the closet, where he had more than likely fallen asleep while reciting psalms. He is supposed to have known the whole book of Psalms by heart. His sister, Aunt Margaret, who lived in New York City, was no less a champion of prayer. She was devoted to foreign missions and other worthy causes, *une grande dame* of New York society. About her it is told that at the age of ninety-six she was asked to convene with prayer a meeting of the Daughters of the American Revolution. She must have prayed for half an hour, but that notwithstanding, for years after her prayer was remembered as the outstanding event of the convention. The way it was always put was that she had the gift of leading in prayer, and it was understood very clearly that the gift of leading in prayer was a very significant spiritual gift.

It was a heavy weight on my young shoulders, placed firmly there by the laying on of hands, to develop that gift. I knew that my congregation expected its minister to lead them in prayer, and I knew pretty much what that meant, but I really did not have much of an idea how one went about developing that gift. So it was that from my very first weeks of service in the ministry, I began to devote myself to fulfilling the awesome role of leading my congregation in prayer. I knew that prayer had to become for me the intense personal experience it had been for my grandmother, who as a widow had sent up constant prayer to the throne of grace. I knew it had to have the discipline of my great-grandfather Chambers, who prayed through the psalter every week and read through the Bible once a year.

So I set to work. How did one learn to pray? I started to pray the Psalms and the prayers of Scripture. Saturday mornings I set aside to prepare the prayers for Sunday. One of the things I found most helpful was to take a psalm and attempt to rewrite it in contemporary English. I had a good course on the exegesis of the Psalms in seminary, and I was aware of the different psalm genre. More and more I studied the Psalms as examples and patterns of prayer. I became more and more aware of how the Psalms had been prayed all through the history of Christian worship. Then I began to study the prayers of the Protestant Reformers. I became interested in how Luther, Calvin, Knox, and Baxter recast the prayers of public worship at the time of the Reformation. After five years of this kind of study, the subject had become so fascinating to me that I decided I wanted to do graduate work in the history of Christian worship. The preparation of prayers for public worship had become one of my favorite ministerial tasks.

When I finished my graduate work and came back to this country, I took a church in Indiana, and there I continued my discipline of carefully preparing prayers for public worship. By that time I had some new ideas, and the congregation had been established only a few years before, so there were no long established traditions. The members were really rather good about letting me develop things the way I thought they should be done. While some of the prayers in this book go back to my first pastorate in Atglen, Pennsylvania, and while some were written for First Presbyterian Church in Trenton, New Jersey, where I have worshiped since the fall of 1985, most of them come from my thirteen-year pastorate at Faith Presbyterian Church in West Lafayette, Indiana.

The reason I have wanted to publish these prayers is that I have found studying the prayers of other ministers very helpful in my attempt to learn how to lead the congregation in prayer. I have no objection if some other minister were to use the prayers I have written, but that is not what they were written for. These prayers were written for a very specific congregation at a very specific time (though the names of people prayed for—those who are not public figures—have been changed). What I would hope is that other ministers might use these prayers as I have used the prayers of the *Apostolic Constitutions* and the *Genevan Psalter*. Sometimes I have simply used the classic prayers of the past as I found them, but more often I have revised them, abridged them, or rewritten them in a more contemporary idiom. I publish this book much in the same spirit as Matthew Henry published his *Method of Prayer* or Isaac Watts published a similar sort of volume a generation later. I mean it as a source book for ministers who conscientiously want to prepare themselves to lead their congregations in prayer. Perhaps even more, I see it as a workbook. It is printed with ample margins so that those using it can insert what is more pertinent to their own time and place.

Another aspect of the minister's preparation to lead in public prayer is the preparation and preaching of the sermon. A study of John Calvin's prayers shows that the Reformer of Geneva maintained a strong dynamic between Word and prayer just as he did between Word and sacrament. He prepared for preaching by prayer. The Prayer for Illumination asked for the inspiration of the Holy Spirit in opening up the Scriptures, and then the sermon concluded with a call to prayer that those things treated in the sermon become matters of prayer. The exposition of Scripture was expected to open up concerns about which the Church would need to pray. Perhaps the sermon suggested matters for repentance and supplication, or perhaps it suggested matters for thanksgiving and dedication. Hundreds of the prayers that Calvin offered after his sermons have been preserved. They all show how the subjects treated in the sermon became concerns of the prayers that he led after the sermon. As time has gone along I have learned that leading in prayer and preaching are complementary. The preparation of the sermon and the preparation of the prayers go hand in hand.

The Art of Leading in Prayer

Just as there is an art to preaching, so there is an art to leading in prayer. A passage of the New Testament that teaches us quite a bit on the subject of leading in prayer is the account in the book of Acts of the prayer of the earliest Christian community (Acts 4:23-31). Peter and John, having been arrested for healing a cripple and preaching in the Temple, were warned by the authorities not to preach in the name of Jesus. They were then released and went to find their friends, who were gathered for prayer. The group began its prayer with psalms. That would have been the normal thing for a group of Jews to do when they assembled for prayer. The text tells us that "they lifted their voices together to God and said, 'Sovereign Lord, who didst make the heaven and the earth and the sea and everything in them. . . .'" This would seem to indicate that the whole group sang together Psalm 146. To sing Psalms 145 to 150 was how devout Jews of the time commonly began the order of morning prayer, and the words of Scripture here are a quotation from Psalm 146:6.

Surely, another psalm that these early Christians prayed was Psalm 2, several verses of which are quoted by our text. This psalm speaks of the kings of the earth setting themselves against God's anointed Christ. The prayer then goes on to interpret the psalm:

> For truly in this city there were gathered together against thy holy servant Jesus, whom thou didst anoint, both Herod and Pontius Pilate, with the Gentiles and the peoples of Israel, to do whatever thy hand and thy plan had predestined to take place. And now, Lord, look upon their threats, and grant to thy servants to speak thy word with all boldness, while thou stretchest out thy hand to heal, and signs and wonders are performed through the name of thy holy servant Jesus (Acts 4:27-30).

At this point, some individual must have begun to lead the prayers. Perhaps this person was Peter or John. What is interesting about this story is the way the traditional prayers were elaborated to fit the problem of the hour. The psalms were prayed by the congregation as they always were and yet the one who led in prayer elaborated the themes of the traditional psalm in a way appropriate to the situation. The one who led in prayer elaborated the traditional prayer.

In the early centuries of the Christian Church those who led in worship were expected to know the traditional forms of prayer and yet at the same time be able to extemporize on these forms. Those who led Christian

4   INTRODUCTION

worship led prayer in much the same way that the typical rabbi of the time led in prayer. A rabbi knew what prayers belonged to the service of worship. He knew that there were to be benedictions before and after the *Shema*. He knew that there were to be the Eighteen Benedictions and what the traditional themes of these prayers were supposed to be, but he was also free to formulate these prayers in a fresh and original way. Most people saying morning or evening prayer at home in private or with their families would simply repeat the prayers as they memorized them, but at the synagogue the elders of the congregation, or any rabbis or scribes who were present, would extemporize on the traditional text. This gave variety and freshness to public prayer. The themes were traditional but the variations were original.

It is in this light that we understand a number of statements in the earliest records of Christian worship. The *Didache*, for instance, gives a number of texts for the prayers of the service of worship, but then tells us that prophets are free to pray as they wish. We hear much the same thing from Justin Martyr and then from Hippolytus at the beginning of the third century. Leading in public prayer was obviously one of the spiritual gifts that those who led in the ancient Church's public worship were expected to cultivate. There were as yet no set prayer texts that every minister was expected to follow word by word, but there were definite traditions as to how the prayers were supposed to go.

For many generations American Protestants have prized spontaneity in public prayer. I hope it will always be so. One has to admit, however, that the spontaneous prayer one often hears in public worship is an embarrassment to the tradition. It all too often lacks content. It may be sincere, but sometimes it is not very profound. One notices sometimes that the approach to prayer that these prayers reveal is immature, if not simply misleading. Spontaneity needs to be balanced by careful preparation and forethought. It needs to be supported by an intense prayer life on the part of the minister. One must be well experienced in prayer to lead in prayer. One can hardly lead if one does not know the way oneself. Spontaneity has to arise from a profound experience of prayer.

The Puritans were masters at prayer. They were intense in subjecting themselves to the disciplines of private prayer, and in public prayer they were both well prepared and fervent. Richard Mather, one of the earliest ministers of the Massachusetts Bay Colony, was renowned for maintaining vigorous disciplines of prayer. He conducted morning and evening prayer with his family each day and in addition spent time in his prayer closet. On Sundays his public prayers were greatly prized by his congregation. They may have lasted almost as long as the sermons, but somehow his congregation realized that in these prayers they were passing beyond the veil of temporal experience.

The praying of the minister, like the minister's preaching, is not something done merely privately. It is rather something one does as a minister of Christ, in the name of Christ. Leading in prayer is one of those ministries that the minister has been sent to perform, one of those services to which the minister has been called and set apart. William Perkins, a most distinguished Puritan theologian of the late sixteenth century, taught that the Christian minister, like the prophets of ancient Israel, had two functions.

First was preaching and teaching the Word of God to the people of God; second was presenting the needs of the people before their God. Perkins liked to show the importance of the prayer ministry of the prophets such as Moses, Elijah, and Jeremiah. As Perkins saw it, prayer was a prophetic ministry that demanded the same gifts of discernment and inspiration that preaching demanded.

Puritan ministers prepared themselves to lead in public prayer by the disciplines of private prayer, but they also prepared themselves by studying the prayers of Scripture. They paid very close attention to the teaching of Christ and the Apostles on how we are to pray. They collected examples from the great heroes and heroines of prayer such as Abraham, Moses, Hannah, Elijah, and Esther. One of the most important guides in this kind of study was Matthew Henry, who today is famous for his commentary on the whole Bible. In his own day he was equally famous for his *Method of Prayer*, a book intended to help ministers prepare to lead in public prayer. It was expected that during the week the minister would begin to think of the prayer to be led on Sunday. In this way the prayers were "conceived," as they liked to say. Public prayer was not left to last-minute inspiration; the typical Puritan minister expected that the inspiration to lead in prayer would begin well beforehand and that that inspiration should be cultivated. All week long the minister "waited upon" the moving of the Spirit. This did not mean that the prayer would be written out and then read, although notes might be made during the course of the week. It meant rather that well before Sunday morning began the ministers would already be meditating on the prayer concerns that they intended to present.

One who in our own time has spoken particularly well on the subject of leading in prayer is Dietrich Bonhoeffer. In his devotional classic *Life Together* he has written several pages on saying our prayers together. He has spoken with great sensitivity of the dangers of leading in prayer and the responsibility of doing it nevertheless. What Bonhoeffer has written on the subject is something everyone who leads in prayer should read, because Bonhoeffer is right: To lead in prayers is an awesome task, but a task from which the minister may not shrink.

The Language and Imagery of Prayer

There has always been a wide discussion of the language of prayer. Down through the history of the Church prayers have been offered in a great variety of languages and literary styles. Back in the days when the classical liturgies were beginning to be formulated, there was considerable variety in the matter. The Greek liturgies tended to be phrased in elaborate language. The Eucharistic Prayer of St. Basil recounts at length the mighty acts of creation and the whole history of redemption in rich language. Basil's prayers are filled with biblical imagery. On the other hand the Latin prayers of the Gregorian Sacramentary are much shorter, simpler, and more sober. We find much the same sort of contrast between the prayers of John Calvin and the prayers of Richard Baxter. Baxter, typical of his age, was profuse in piling one biblical image upon another, while Calvin was more simple and direct. Each age has its own taste. What seems beautiful and profound to one age will seem verbose and pedantic to another age. Such varying demands of style can even today be quite different from one congregation to another within the same city. Ministers themselves will develop their own styles as a natural result of their differing ministerial gifts.

As a seminary student I was always moved by the prayers of John Mackay. They were literate, cosmopolitan, and evangelical. On the other hand I remember an older woman in my first church, Gerty Pickle, who must have had no more than an eighth grade education, but who had a wonderful gift of prayer. She had the eloquence of Fanny Crosby. Her prayers were sincere and lyrical, hearty and sweet like the apple pies she baked for church socials. I could no more pray like Gerty Pickle than I could pray like John Mackay. To pray like such saints one has to be like them.

Some of these considerations have to do with literary style, but it is not about literary style that I want to speak. The more one can learn about it the better, but there are others far more qualified to speak about it than I. There are, however, certain considerations of language about which I have something to say. Prayer does have its own language, its own vocabulary, and its own imagery. This language is not simply a matter of style. Prayer, particularly Christian prayer, uses biblical language. Prayer has its own words like "Hallelujah" and "Amen." It has some styles that are peculiarly its own. The Bible provides a typology of prayer. This typology is an ingenious series of examples of how and why God's people are to pray. The Bible contains a vast number of paradigms for prayer and a thesaurus of words to handle the unique experience of prayer. All this inspires, encourages, and feeds our experience of prayer. Above all, there are two things involved here that go far beyond the matter of literary style. One is typology and the other is vocabulary.

Every kind of work, every profession, every craft has its own terminology and its own technical expressions, and so it is with prayer. Those who would learn the techniques of prayer must master this terminology. There is a distinct difference between supplications, confessions, and lamentations. How much our prayers are encouraged by realizing that lamentation, crying before the Lord, is an important part of prayer! There is a unique essence to psalms as opposed to hymns, which, if one is to pray with understanding, one must grasp. When we realize how often the saints of the New Jerusalem sing over and over again, "Hallelujah, Hallelujah, Hallelujah," we are encouraged to join that ever resounding hallelujah chorus.

One of the most characteristic features of Christian prayer is its typology. The Bible provides a distinct prayer typology as a means of explaining prayer, a means of showing how it works and of affirming that it does work. The biblical types of prayer are paradigms showing us how the experience of prayer unfolds. Prayer does not always unfold the same way and so there are different types that suggest different situations. The intercession of Abraham for Sodom and Gomorrah gives us a surprising picture of prayer. Moses' intercession on Mount Sinai is also an illustrative example of the nature of intercessory prayer. Yet the two are very different. The meditations of Job, the lamentations of Jeremiah, and the confessions of Ezra show distinctly different approaches to prayer. The whole story of Elijah is filled with intimations of the mysteries of prayer. From the three years of seclusion in the Brook Cherith, when the ravens brought him food each morning and evening, to the prayer contest on the top of Mount Carmel, Elijah was a man of prayer who had learned to hear the still small voice after the wind, earthquake, and fire. One even wonders if Elijah's transport into heaven in a fiery chariot is not intended as a type of prayer. Elijah's experience of prayer had a wide variety. In the New Testament Elijah is still recognized as a great example of prayer (James 5:17-18). Esther and Daniel have always been presented as heroes of prayer as well.

One must make very clear, however, that a type is more than just an example. This is particularly obvious when we consider David as the type of Christian prayer. The psalms of David were the prayers of Israel. This had to do with the whole understanding of the role of the king in the Old Testament. The king prayed for the people, and in the king's prayers were the prayers of the whole people. In the prayers of David, corporate prayer and private prayer flow together. The typology of prayer has a lot to do with the corporate nature of prayer. But there is more to it than this. David is one of the types of Christ, and therefore just as Israel prayed in David so the Christian prays in Christ. Earlier we spoke of the prayer of the Christians in Jerusalem reported in the Acts of the Apostles, and we noticed how much of their prayer was based on the psalms. The typological dimensions of the prayer in Psalm 2 are considerable. It spoke powerfully to those Christians of the way the kings of the earth would set themselves against the Lord and his anointed. In the Greek text it reads "against the LORD and his *Christos*." These early Christians prayed the second psalm because they understood it as prophetic of Christ. They understood that prayer as a foreshadowing of their own prayer, as prophetic of both Christ's humiliation and his exaltation. By praying that psalm they came to understand that the Church of Christ must share in both the sufferings and the glory of Christ. Because the psalm was prophetic it was encouraging. The type always has a promise of fulfillment in it.

It long puzzled me that the terminology of the Temple occupied such an important place in the language of prayer. Christian prayer clings to it just as it clings to the psalms. It is because of this typological dimension of Christian prayer that the imagery of the psalms and the worship of Solomon's Temple is so important to Christian worship. But there is a sort of double imagery here. The imagery of Solomon's Temple suggests the imagery of the heavenly Jerusalem. It is prophetic of eternity. Christians use this imagery to speak of the Christian hope, just as the book of Revelation speaks of heaven in the imagery of the Temple and its worship.

Much of Christian prayer has always been an elaboration of the psalms. We find this particularly to be the case with the prayers we find in the New Testament. Both the *Magnificat* and the *Benedictus,* the prayers of Mary and Zechariah in the first chapter of the Gospel of Luke, are Christian psalms. We find the same thing with the praise in Revelation. The hymns of the heavenly Jerusalem are a cultivation and consummate flowering of the hymns of ancient Jerusalem. The oldest collection of Christian hymns that has come down to us, the *Odes of Solomon,* is a series of elaborated psalms. Rendall Harris calls them "psalm pendants." Each one is the re-working of a particular canonical psalm.

In the same way, then, I have very consciously used the imagery of the Temple and the idiom of the psalms. Many of the prayers I have written are in fact reworked psalms. I have found it a good way of praying as so many have before me. I have intentionally joined my prayer to theirs.

While in general I have tried to avoid a discussion of styles, sometimes it is unavoidable. For example, one recurring characteristic of the prayer style is its meditative nature. So often I have noticed in reading prayer texts or listening to prayers in worship that the pace of their delivery is slow. There is often a great deal of repetition, particularly of such weighty phrases as "Praise ye the Lord" and "Have mercy upon us, O Lord, have mercy." The refrain is a constantly recurring feature of this meditative style. There are several other matters of prayer style that will come up in the course of our study, but for the most part I leave to others the question of literary style.

The Invocation

That the service of worship should begin with an invocation is a tradition dear to American Protestantism. There is a good reason for this. It is a profoundly biblical form of worship.

One notices that most of the psalms begin with an invocation. In many of the psalms, the invocation is very simple, as in Psalm 8:

> O LORD, our Lord,
>> how majestic is thy name in all the earth!

In other Psalms it is more elaborate, as in Psalm 113:

> Praise the LORD!
> Praise, O servants of the LORD,
>> praise the name of the LORD!

> Blessed be the name of the LORD
>> from this time forth and for evermore!

> From the rising of the sun to its setting
>> the name of the LORD is to be praised!

In fact, one might regard the whole of this psalm as one great invocation. Studying the psalms, one rather easily comes to the conclusion that from the standpoint of literary form, prayer normally begins with an invocation. This invocation names the God to whom the prayer is addressed. One might therefore define an invocation as a prayer that begins worship by calling on God's name. The Latin word *invocare* means to call upon, to appeal to, or to invoke in prayer.

That an invocation names the God to whom we pray is particularly clear from a psalm such as the seventh Psalm: "O LORD my God, in thee do I take refuge." For the most part, the Psalms invoke God by the tetragrammaton, LORD, which is God's personal name. This is the name that God revealed to Moses from the burning bush, the name that must not be used in vain and that in generations to come was never spoken except by the high priest when on the Day of Atonement he came out of the Holy of Holies and gave the Aaronic Benediction to the people. So sacred was that name! It was the name by which God was addressed in prayer.

The exceptions to this are mainly in Psalms 42–83, where God is invoked by the name "God." Much speculation has arisen over this fact, speculation that need not concern us here. For our purposes, it is sufficient to call attention to this fact as an indication that it is indeed significant by what name we invoke God. It might be quite acceptable to speak of God from time to time as the Great Originator, Universal Spirit, or Unmoved Mover, but God should not regularly be addressed by such names in prayer.

Jesus was also interested in the question of the name by which we are to invoke God. He himself invoked God by the name "Father," even more precisely, by a specific form of that name, "Abba." Jesus taught his disciples to pray, "Our Father, who art in heaven." This was an important teaching of Jesus on prayer. That Jesus should take the initiative to teach his disciples to invoke God as Father shows his consciousness of having messianic authority. Giving his disciples a new name by which to invoke God was one of those sovereign messianic acts that, like telling them to celebrate the Passover in remembrance of him and like establishing the first day of the week as the Christian Sabbath, demonstrates that Jesus had authority far beyond that of Moses.

The full daring of this innovation on the part of Jesus is made clear when, as we find it in the Gospel of Matthew, Jesus formulated a short invocation: "I thank thee, Father, Lord of heaven and earth . . ." (Matt 11:25). This was a striking departure from Jewish tradition. This invocation was normally recited as "I thank thee, LORD, Lord of heaven and earth. . . ." What Jesus did was to replace the tetragrammaton LORD with a new tetragrammaton, ABBA, or, as Matthew translates it into Greek, *Pater*, Father. Even today many Jewish prayers begin with essentially the same formula, "Blessed art thou, O LORD God, King of the universe. . . ." Allowing for different ways of translating the Hebrew, it is the same invocation used by Jesus — except that Jesus addressed God as Father.

There are a number of characteristic elements to a prayer of invocation. Most important is this naming of the God to whom we would pray. The prayers of Scripture do not show a great variety in the names by which God is invoked. There is a definite preference in the Old Testament for the tetragrammaton, LORD, yet we do find other names or combinations of names and titles. Psalm 22 begins with "My God, my God, why hast thou forsaken me?" Psalm 80 begins with "Give ear, O Shepherd of Israel. . . ." Psalm 92 begins with "It is good to give thanks to the LORD, to sing praises to thy name, O Most High."

When Psalms 97 and 99 begin, "The LORD reigns," we are probably to understand this as an invocation of God as King. In fact, at the time of Jesus, the prayer of the synagogue most often began with "Blessed art thou, O LORD God, King of the universe." It is still customary in the synagogue to invoke God as King. In the same way, God was often addressed, "O LORD God of hosts" or "O LORD of hosts," as in Psalm 84.

The God of Scripture is not the God of a thousand names. The inventing of glorious names for God is not regarded as an open field for human creativity. That Jesus should teach us to invoke God as Father was a messianic act of unique significance. In the Judeo-Christian tradition, it is God's prerogative to reveal his name.

The same is true with the name of the Messiah.

> For to us a child is born,
> to us a son is given;
> and the government will be upon his shoulder,
> and his name will be called
> "Wonderful Counselor, Mighty God,
> Everlasting Father, Prince of Peace."
>
> Isaiah 9:6

The Gospel of Matthew tells us that it was an angel of the Lord who directed Joseph to call Mary's child Jesus. The name that is above every name, the name to which every knee shall bow, is a name that God himself revealed.

Not only had Jesus taught his disciples to invoke God as Father, he also taught them to pray in his own name. Here we have the second focus of the Prayer of Invocation. Four times in the discourse in the Upper Room in the Gospel of John, Jesus repeats the promise that God will hear them if they pray together in his name. Christian prayer should be addressed to the Father in the name of Jesus. Again we read in the Gospels that Jesus promised us that whenever two or three are gathered together in his name, he will be in their midst. This promise has particularly had its effect on the prayers with which Christians have begun their services of worship. Wanting to claim the promise of Christ's presence with them as they came together, they have constituted their worship assembly in the name of Jesus. What would be more natural! An invocation, then, has a second function: It is a prayer that claims the promise of Jesus that when we meet together in his name he will indeed be with us.

Another important element in the Prayer of Invocation is the hallowing of God's name. The invocation should both call on God's name and hallow God's name. That this should be done is taught us by Jesus in the Lord's Prayer: "Our Father, who art in heaven, hallowed be thy name." We notice this again and again in the Psalms and the prayers of Scripture. In the invocation at the beginning of Psalm 105, we find a combination of the themes of invocation and praise.

> O give thanks to the LORD, call on his name,
> make known his deeds among the peoples!
> Sing to him, sing praises to him,
> tell of all his wonderful works!
> Glory in his holy name;
> let the hearts of those who seek the LORD rejoice!   Psalm 105:1-3

The hallowing of God's name surely includes the proclamation of the divine attributes, as in Exodus 34:6: "The LORD passed before him, and proclaimed, 'The LORD, the LORD, a God merciful and gracious, slow to anger, and abounding in steadfast love and faithfulness. . . .'" It would also include making known God's deeds among his people. This is why relative clauses beginning with "who" are so characteristic of prayer: "Our Father, *who* art in heaven," or

> Bless the LORD, O my soul; . . .
> *who* forgives all your iniquity,
>   *who* heals all your diseases,
> *who* redeems your life from the Pit,
>   *who* crowns you with steadfast love and mercy,
> *who* satisfies you with good as long as you live. . . .   Psalm 103:1-5

This proclamation of the attributes and blessings of God hallows God's name.

A fourth element we find in prayers of invocation is that the prayer claims God as *our* God. In the invocation from the Lord's Prayer, we claim God as "Our Father." So also in Psalm 46:1, "God is our refuge and strength," God is claimed as our God. The Puritans liked to say that in our prayers we should "own" God. This sounds a bit strange in modern English. What they meant by it was that in our prayers we should claim God as our God and confess ourselves to be his people. Matthew Henry in his *Method of Prayer* made a particularly strong point of this. It is this aspect of the Prayer of Invocation that leads many to call the invocation a "votum," that is, a vow of allegiance to God. This aspect of the invocation is particularly clear in that much beloved invocation from Psalm 124, "Our help is in the name of the LORD, who made heaven and earth" (v. 8). The same thing is happening when God is invoked as the God of Israel or of Zion. This claiming of God comes out very clearly in the Song of the Sea in Exodus 15:

> I will sing to the LORD, for he has triumphed gloriously;
>   the horse and his rider he has thrown into the sea.
> The LORD is my strength and my song,
>   and he has become my salvation;
> this is my God, and I will praise him,
>   my father's God, and I will exalt him.   Exodus 15:1-2

Another element frequently found in invocations is the petition that our worship be inspired by the work of the Holy Spirit and received through the intercession of Christ. Christian worship is Trinitarian. It is the work of the Holy Spirit in the body of Christ to the glory of the Father. True Christian worship, according to the teaching of Jesus, is worship that is in Spirit and Truth (John 4:24). Our worship is inspired by the Spirit, led by the Spirit, warmed by the Spirit, and purified by the Spirit. There is a major theological point to be observed here. Christian worship is part of the procession of the Holy Spirit from the Father and the Son. The pouring out of the Holy Spirit and the gifts of the Spirit are essential to the relationship of the persons of the Trinity. The unity of God is not static or self-contained but overflowing, ever seeking and ever moving. Worship is part of the Spirit's anointing of the Son and of the Son's offering up of the Spirit to the Father.

In the same way, Christian worship is worship that is in Christ. It is in Christ in the sense that true Christian worship is an act of the body of Christ. Our worship is in Christ in the sense that it is because of the sacrifice of Christ that we are able to pass through the veil into the Holy of Holies. It is for the sake of Christ that the Father receives our prayers (Heb 9:24). It is appropriate, therefore, that our prayers plead both the intercession of Christ and the inspiration of the Holy Spirit. This is implied by praying in the name of Jesus.

Finally, an invocation should conclude with a full Trinitarian doxology. And this should be a very prominent element in a prayer of invocation. The sealing of our prayers with a doxology is an old practice. The Lord's Prayer is sealed with the doxology, "For thine is the kingdom and the power and the glory." Since the Lord's Prayer is the prayer of Jesus, it would be redundant to conclude it "in the name of Jesus we pray. Amen." But evidently the earliest Christians ended all their other prayers in the name of Jesus. One of the earliest Christian prayers to be recorded ends with these words: "through the name of thy holy servant Jesus" (Acts 4:30). The earliest Christians normally prayed in the name of Jesus, and it was in the concluding doxology of the prayer that this was made clear.

Several remarks may be helpful on the subject of the literary form of the Invocation. At its most basic, the Christian invocation prays, "Father, hear us in the name of your Son." This is the core of the Prayer of Invocation and into this core certain themes are worked. We have mentioned a number of these themes: the hallowing of God's name, the promise of his presence, the claiming of God as our God, and so forth. This has to do with the content of the prayer, but in terms of outward literary form, we may look at the Invocation as having three basic parts: first, the naming of God, second, the request that he receive our worship, and third, the sealing of the prayer. For a theologian, literary form is one of those things that we must regard as "indifferent," or to use the Greek term made famous by Martin Luther, literary form is *adiaphora*.

Literary form does, however, help us to communicate and therefore is important. The minister of the Word has to lead in prayer so that the flock can follow. We all learned in our high school speech classes that an address should have an introduction, a body, and a conclusion. One can say this about prayers just as about sermons or any other kind of talk or presentation. It is good literary form if it helps us communicate.

One can say of all prayers that they should begin with an introduction. That introduction is the naming of the God on whom we call. A very simple introduction would be the calling out of God's name, "Father." It is not much more than this that we find in the Lord's Prayer, "Our Father who art in heaven, hallowed be thy name." The essential name on which Christians call is "Father." This essential name can be unfolded by those names and titles that God has revealed in times past: God Most High, God Almighty, LORD, Lord God of Hosts, Shepherd of Israel, God of Abraham, Isaac, and Jacob, Great God, Rock of our salvation, and several others. One can even unfold the name Father with some of those abstract philosophical names and titles, such as God Omnipotent, God Omniscient, God Omnipresent, which although not found in Scripture have won their place in Christian devotion. As time has gone along, however, I find myself preferring the names and titles that are specifically biblical. How elaborate one wants to become at this point is a matter of style. Your own personal style as a minister comes into play here and so does the style of the congregation. Congregations have their own styles, too, just as ministers do, and both need to be respected.

The main body of the Prayer of Invocation I see as the petition, "Hear us in the name of your Son." The relationship between Father and Son is the basis of the Christian approach to God. It is the basis of our being able to call on God and of our worship and service of God in general. There is an important theological point here. Christian worship has its logic in the doctrine of the Trinity. It is profoundly trinitarian. Our worship is part of the relationship between the persons of the Trinity. It is part of what sometimes has been called the inner trinitarian conversation. It is part of the homage of the Son to the Father. For this reason, therefore, we worship in the name of the Son. The relationship goes in both directions. Our prayer is part of the outpouring of the love of the Father to the Son. It is in Christ that we share in the fellowship of the house of the Father, that we sit at his table and are fed by his bread and share his cup. Our worship participates in the love of the Father for the Son and in the love of the Son for the Father. When we proclaim the gospel in Christ's name, baptize, and teach what he has commanded in his name, this is part of the obedience of the Son to the Father. But it is also part of the Father's glorification of the Son. In the ministry of preaching and teaching that we perform in Christ's name, Christ is glorified. Human hearts are changed and disciples are made of all nations — and thus the Father is setting all things under the feet of the Son, so that at last Christ is Lord of all. The Invocation, therefore, has as one of its cardinal concerns this relationship between the Father and Son. It is in terms of this that the other themes of invocation are worked into the prayer.

This being the case it seems to me a good thing to use variety in expressing this basic request that God hear us. When I started out I seemed to be overly fond of those courtly liturgical formulas such as "Grant unto us, we beseech thee," or "Deign to regard us with thy favor." I began to search out the language of Scripture for other possibilities and found that there were many ways of putting this basic petition. I began to realize that when Psalm 95 prays, "O come, let us sing to the Lord; let us make a joyful noise to the rock of our salvation" (v. 1), there is an indirect or implied request expressed to God, that he receive the worship of his people. It is the same way with Psalm 100, "Enter his gates with thanksgiving, and his courts with praise" (v. 4). This is not what people sometimes term a "call to worship," but a very reverential request that God receive us into his presence. We might call it reverent indirection.

In some of these psalms we find this principle at work. As a matter of respect, God is not addressed directly but indirectly, and the request is put indirectly. The request might be put in the subjective mood: "O that we might enter your presence." Or sometimes it is put in the jussive rather than the imperative: "Let our prayers be received into your presence." There is another way this reverent indirection is expressed that was particularly cultivated in the days of Jesus. The blessings, or *berakoth,* shaped by Jews of the time were masterpieces of reverent indirection. God was blessed for the gift of the Sabbath. This was a means of asking him to receive the Sabbath day worship of the synagogue. Instead of directly asking God to hear prayer, a typical Jewish *berakoth* blesses the God who hears prayer. We have a good example of this reverent indirection in the beautiful benediction by which the Apostle Paul begins his Epistle to the Ephesians.

Undoubtedly there will be those who will feel more comfortable with an open and direct style. That is much more consistent with our contemporary culture. I have tried that style, too, as some of the following prayers will indicate.

The conclusion of a prayer is, by a long tradition going back to the synagogue, called the "sealing" of the prayer. We have already spoken about this, but we need to develop it a bit more. I spoke of the fact that this sealing is done by a doxology. "For thine is the kingdom and the power and the glory" is the seal at the end of the Lord's Prayer. Another example of this sealing is found in the prayer of the Apostles in Acts 4:30: "through the name of thy holy servant Jesus." As time went on Christians normally sealed their prayers either in the name of Jesus or with a more elaborate trinitarian formula. There were two ways, then, of sealing Christian prayer. One can seal a prayer simply in the name of Jesus or with a Trinitarian doxology. Sometimes the Trinitarian doxology can be simple and sometimes more elaborate. The same is true with sealing the prayer in the name of Jesus. It has been my practice to use a longer, more festive Trinitarian doxology to seal the Invocation at the beginning of the service; in the Prayers of Confession and Supplication I usually seal the prayer in the name of Jesus in such a way that the intercessory ministry of Jesus is emphasized, and then in the Prayer for Illumination I seal the prayer very simply, "in Jesus' name we pray" or "through Jesus Christ we pray."

The prayers that follow are in two groups. The first thirty are Invocations that I have written for the usual Sunday morning service. Each prayer in this first group follows a short scriptural invocation or votum, either the one used in the Genevan Psalter, that is, Psalm 124:8, or Psalm 105:1-3 or Psalm 8:1. The second group of prayers is made up of six Invocations for the evangelical feast days. This collection reflects a very simple American Protestant approach to the celebration of Christian feasts. It allows for a celebration of Christmas, for a Christian celebration of Passover with a service on Maundy Thursday as well as on Easter Sunday, a celebration of the Ascension on the Sunday following Ascension Day, and finally a celebration of Pentecost.

Invocation 1 —————————

(based on the Lord's Prayer)

"Our help is in the name of the LORD,
    who made heaven and earth."
                         Psalm 124:8

Let us pray.

Our Father,
    you are in heaven
        high and lifted up
        higher than our highest thoughts.

Holy is your name;
    beside you there is no other!

You are God
    and you alone!
                         (Matthew 6:9)

Receive us into your Kingdom —
    the coming Kingdom —
    the Kingdom of your anointed Son Jesus
        whose name we bear.

Receive us,
    for we come to you in his name
        we pray in him and with him.

For yours is the Kingdom,
    and the power and the glory.
                        (Matthew 6:13)

    Father,
    Son, and
    Holy Spirit

One God, now and forever. *Amen.*

Invocation 2 ————————————

(based on Matthew 18:20)

"Our help is in the name of the Lord,
  who made heaven and earth."   Psalm 124:8

Let us pray.

O Father,
    majestic is your name!

  From the rising of the sun
      to its setting
          your name is to be praised,
      Merciful God,
      Gracious Lord.

Hear us in the name of your Son,

  For he has promised
      that where two or three of us
          are gathered in his name
      he would be with us
          and our prayer would be heard.

Hear us in the name of your Son,

  For he is the revelation of your wisdom,
      the outpouring of your glory,
      the incarnation of your mercy toward us
          and the whole human race.

To you be glory,
    all praise and honor,
        Father,
        Son, and
        Holy Spirit,
    one God, now and evermore. *Amen.*

Invocation 3 —————————

"Our help is in the name of the Lord,
   who made heaven and earth."

Psalm 124:8

Let us pray.

Our Father,
      rich in mercy,
      splendid in grace,
   wisdom and justice go before you;
   peace and righteousness
      are at your right hand.

Lord of heaven above,
   you are God and you alone.

Give ear to our prayer
   in the name of Jesus,
      for we would worship you in him.

   He is our Great High Priest;
   He is our intercessor and mediator.

Give ear to our prayer
   that we might serve you
      as a royal priesthood,
         your own people,
   for you are our God
      and you alone.

(1 Peter 2:9)

To you be all honor,
   all praise and glory,
      Father,
      Son, and
      Holy Spirit,
   One God for all eternity. *Amen.*

Invocation 4 ————————————

(based on the Prayer of Mary)

> "Our help is in the name of the Lᴏʀᴅ,
>   who made heaven and earth."   Psalm 124:8

Let us pray.

O Lord,
    we magnify you,
    we rejoice in you,
        O God our Savior!

You have regarded
        the low estate of your handmaiden,
            the Church in every age!

You have done great things for us,
        and holy is your name,
            O mighty God!

Remember your mercy to us
    in the name of Christ,
        for in him
            we plead the new and eternal covenant;
        for in him
            the promises made to Abraham
                have been fulfilled.

Remember your covenant,
        once again,
    as you have from generation
        to generation.

For yours is the Kingdom,
    and the power, and the glory,

        Father, ever blest,
        Son, ever praised,
        Holy Spirit, ever adored.

    One God, now and always. *Amen.*

Invocation 5

(based on the Prayer of Zechariah)

"Our help is in the name of the Lord,
    who made heaven and earth."   Psalm 124:8

Let us pray.

Blessed be the Lord God of Israel
    for he has visited
        and redeemed his people.   (Luke 1:68-79)

Blessed you are, O God,
    our redeemer, our Lord,
    for you have sent to us a Savior,
        the promised Savior of the
            house of David.

Save us in his name
    as you promised
        to those who have gone before us.

Save us in accordance with the covenant
    which you swore as an oath to Abraham
    which you established in the
        death and resurrection of Christ
    which you have written on our hearts
        through the indwelling of your Holy Spirit.

Blessed you are God Eternal

    Father,
    Son, and
    Holy Spirit

One God, now and always. *Amen.*

Invocation 6 ————————————

"Our help is in the name of the LORD,
  who made heaven and earth."   Psalm 124:8

Let us pray.

Blessed you are, O Father,
  Lord of heaven and earth.   (Matthew 11:25)

Father, most wise,
  intelligence beyond us,
   deepest mystery,
    and highest truth.

  O heavenly wisdom,
   perfect in simplicity!

Reveal yourself to us, O Father,
  in the name of your Son
   for to him you have delivered all things
   and no one knows you except in him.

Reveal yourself to us, O Father,
  in the name of your son
   for he is gentle and lowly in heart
   and we would take his yoke upon us
    and learn of him.   (Matthew 11:29)

For yours is the Kingdom,
  the power and the glory,

    Father,
    Son, and
    Holy Spirit.

  Forever one God. *Amen.*

Invocation 7 ———————

(based on John 4:22-23)

"Our help is in the name of the LORD,
who made heaven and earth." Psalm 124:8

Let us pray.

Father,
Lord of heaven,
dwelling beyond all place and time, (John 4:22-23)

Eternal and Infinite you are,
beyond our grasp and control.

Blessed is your name,
O Father, our Father!

Pour out upon us your Holy Spirit,
that we might worship you in spirit and truth.

Pour out upon us your Holy Spirit,
that though we cannot see you,
we might know you in our hearts.

Pour out upon us your Holy Spirit
that your truth be indwelling,
a fountain of living water welling up
to eternal life. (John 4:14)

To you be all praise

Father,
Son, and
Holy Spirit,

Eternally one God. *Amen.*

Invocation 8 ———————————————

(based on John 17)

"Our help is in the name of the Lord,
    who made heaven and earth."

Psalm 124:8

Let us pray.

Father,
    all glorious
        in every age,
        in eternity,
    glorious in our time,

It is in your Son
    that we behold your glory
        in his crucifixion suffering for us
        in his resurrection victorious
          and alive for us.

(John 17:1)

Holy Father,
    keep us in your name,
        that we be one as you are one with the Son
          and the Son is one with you.

Keep us in that name into which
    we have been baptized.

Keep us in the sacred bond of the covenant,
    that in the name of your Son,
        we might enter into your eternal glory.

(John 17:11)

For all glory,
    all grace and truth are to you!

        Father,
        Son, and
        Holy Spirit

Three persons, one God, all glorious, forever. *Amen.*

Invocation 9 ————————————

"Our help is in the name of the LORD,
    who made heaven and earth."
                                             Psalm 124:8

Let us pray.

Father,
    your name is exalted,
        honored in every land,
        praised in every tongue.

    Your name is praised above the heavens,
        adored by heavenly hosts.

    You are our Lord and God.

Hear our prayer, our Lord and God,
        for it is you whom we would worship,

    in the name of your Son,
    your only begotten Son,
    your well-beloved Son.

Glory be to you, God Most High,

    Father Almighty,
    Son all-beloved,
    Spirit all-pervading,

    One God, now and forever. *Amen.*

"Our help is in the name of the LORD,
    who made heaven and earth."   Psalm 124:8

Let us pray.

Father,
    gracious LORD,
    righteous, merciful God,   (Luke 22:42; Psalm 116:5)

Father,
    full of care for all your children,
        hearing our voice and supplication,
        saving us in distress and anguish,
    by your will, alone,
        all things come to pass.

Hear our prayer
    in the name of Christ,
        who in all things was obedient
            to your will,
        who took the bitter cup
            of suffering for us.   (Luke 22:42; Psalm 116:13)

Hear our prayer
    for the sake of his sacrifice.

Father, to you be praise.
    Son, to you be adoration.
        Holy Spirit, to you be glory.

        One God, now and forever. *Amen.*

"Our help is in the name of the Lord,
    who made heaven and earth."   Psalm 124:8

Let us pray.

Father,
    our rock of refuge,
    our strong fortress of salvation,
        steadfast you are;
        faithful you are.   (Luke 23:46; Psalm 31:2)
Almighty Father,
    you alone are our God.
        From you we came in the beginning,
        and to you we return in the end.

Receive us, O Father,
    in the name of your Son.
        It is in him that we come to you,
            in his offering up of his Spirit,
        that Holy Spirit that is both his and yours.   (Luke 23:46)
In Christ's sacrifice alone
    we come to you.

Receive us to yourself, O Father.
    Into your hands we put ourselves,
        in our worship and in our work.

For to you be all service,
    all praise and proclamation,

        Father,
        Son, and
        Holy Spirit.

One God, forever and ever. *Amen.*

Invocation 12 ———————————————————

"Our help is in the name of the Lord,
    who made heaven and earth."   Psalm 124:8

Let us pray.

"Sovereign Lord,
    who didst make the heaven and the earth and the sea
        and everything in them,"   Acts 4:24

O God our Creator,
    hallowed is your name,
    blessed forever!

Create in us your new creation.
    After the image of Christ renew our lives.
    Create us one people, the body of Christ.

Create of us a people to serve you,
    a people to serve your purposes
        and your glory.

Create in us your new creation.
    Stretch out your hand to heal,
        that signs and wonders be performed.

"Through the name of thy holy servant, Jesus,"   Acts 4:30

    to whom with you, O Father,
        and the Holy Spirit,
        one God, forever,

    be all praise and glory. *Amen.*

Invocation 13 ————————————

(based on Ephesians 1:3)

"Our help is in the name of the LORD,
   who made heaven and earth."   Psalm 124:8

Let us pray.

Blessed you are, O God and Father
   of our Lord Jesus Christ,
   you who have blessed us in Christ
   with every spiritual blessing.

Blessed you are, our God and Father,
   who have destined us in love
      to be your sons and daughters
         in the person of your Son, Jesus Christ.

Who have freely bestowed
   your grace upon us
      in your beloved Son.

Who have made known to us
   in all wisdom and insight
      the mystery of your will,
   the plan to unite all things
      in Christ.

Who have sealed us with the promised Holy Spirit,
   the guarantee of our inheritance.

Blessed you are O God,

   Father,
   Son, and
   Holy Spirit.

One God, forever and ever. *Amen.*

"Our help is in the name of the LORD,
    who made heaven and earth."   Psalm 124:8

Let us pray.

Blessed God and Father, you are
    praised above
        by all the heavenly host,
    praised in the Church
        by your people.

Blessed God and Father,
    who have given us your Son
        that we might be your sons and daughters.
    We bless you
        because in him
        we have been blessed again and again.

Hear us now
    as we come to you
        in the name of your Son,
    for we are his people,
        his Church.
    We are called by his name.

Hear us now
    in our generation,
    that we might inherit the blessing,
    that we might be united to your Son
        by faith,
            and know the mystery
            and fullness of time.

Blessed you are, O God,

        Father,
        Son, and
        Holy Spirit,

    ever three persons, ever one God. *Amen.*

"Our help is in the name of the LORD,
who made heaven and earth." Psalm 124:8

Let us pray.

Blessed you are, O God and Father
of our Lord Jesus Christ.

By your great mercy
we have been born anew
to a living hope
through the resurrection
of Jesus Christ. (1 Peter 1:3)

To your name be all praise,
glory and honor.

Blessed you are, our God and Father
and blessed is your Son Jesus Christ,
our Lord and Savior.

In him be our inheritance,
imperishable, undefiled,
and unfading.
In him be our worship, our adoration,
and our service to you.

Blessed you are, O God and Father.

To you belong praise,
glory and honor,

Father,
Son, and
Holy Spirit.

One God and only one,
now and always. *Amen.*

Invocation 16 —————————————

(based on James 1:17)

"Our help is in the name of the Lord,
  who made heaven and earth."   Psalm 124:8

Let us pray.

Father of lights,
    with whom there is no variation
        or shadow due to change,
    from whom comes down
        every good and perfect gift.
    Your name is holy
        and wondrous altogether.

Father of lights,
    changeless in your mercy,
        invariable in your grace.
    Your name is glorious
        and blessed altogether.

Receive us in Christ, the Light of the world,
    God of God, Light of light,
        very God of very God.

Bring us into your presence,
    that we might become radiant in your service,
    lights in this world,
        reflecting the light of eternity.

To you be all radiance,
        O Father of lights,
        O Son, Light of light,
        O Spirit, burning fire within our hearts.

    One God, now and forever. *Amen.*

O give thanks to the Lord, call on his name,
>   make known his deeds among the peoples!
Sing to him, sing praises to him,
>   tell of all his wonderful works!
Glory in his holy name."

Psalm 105:1-3a

Let us pray.

Father,
>   whose glory is ever above us,
>   whose mercy is ever with us,
>>   and whose everlasting arms are ever underneath us,
>   holy, holy, holy
>>   is your name!

Hear us, Father,
>   for we gather together in the name of Jesus,
>>   your only begotten,
>>   well-beloved Son,
>   that in him
>>   we might recognize your presence,
>   that in him
>>   we might see your glory.
Hear us, Father,
>   we have been too long
>>   in our far country.
>   Receive us again
>>   in the name of Jesus.

To you, O Father,
>   together with the Son
>   and the Holy Spirit,
>>   One God from all eternity and to all eternity,
>   Be glory, wisdom, power,
>>   and dominion evermore. *Amen.*

Invocation 18 ——————————

"O give thanks to the Lord, call on his name,
    make known his deeds among the peoples!
Sing to him, sing praises to him,
    tell of all his wonderful works!
Glory in his holy name."   Psalm 105:1-3a

Let us pray.

O Father Most High,
    whose dwelling place is beyond the heavens,

O Lord Incomparable,
    far beyond our loftiest thoughts,

Gather us together in the name of Jesus
    whom the angels adore as the
        Son of the Most High,
    for his name is above every name.

Lead us in our worship,
    that all that we do might be
        undertaken at your bidding,
            filled with your grace,
            directed by your wisdom,
                informed by your truth, and
            accomplished to your glory.

Through Christ, our Lord,
    whom with you and the Holy Spirit, O Father,
        we constantly bless and glorify.

One Eternal God, age after age. *Amen.*

Invocation 19 ————————————

(based on 1 Peter 2:5)

"O give thanks to the LORD, call on his name,
    make known his deeds among the peoples!
Sing to him, sing praises to him,
    tell of all his wonderful works!
Glory in his holy name."   Psalm 105:1-3a

Let us pray.

O Eternal and Everlasting Father,
    God most glorious,
    God most exalted,
        whom we have come to know
            in Jesus of Nazareth,
        the rock of our salvation,
        the cornerstone,
            chosen and precious in your sight,

Bring us together in the name of Jesus,
    that in him we might be a spiritual Temple,
    that founded on him we be built
        together as living stones;
    that in him we offer to you
        the spiritual service
            of praise and thanksgiving,
            of proclaiming your work,
            and of sharing your gifts.

All glory be to you, O Father,
    and to the Son,
    and to the Holy Spirit.

One God forever and ever. *Amen.*

Invocation 20 ────────────

"O give thanks to the Lord, call on his name,
    make known his deeds among the peoples!
Sing to him, sing praises to him,
    tell of all his wonderful works!
Glory in his holy name."
Psalm 105:1-3a

Let us pray.

Almighty God, O heavenly Father,
    whose presence is an eternal peace,
    whose dwelling is an everlasting glory,

Lord who rules over earth and heaven,
    we bow before you in this place,
        confessing with our hymns and prayers
            the name of Christ,
        whom we acknowledge as Lord indeed.

Grant to us
    your blessing and your presence,
    your Word and your peace,
        that our worship be that worship
            which is in Spirit and in truth.

Through Jesus Christ our Savior,
        whom with you, O Father,
        and the Holy Spirit
we always worship and adore.

One God forever and ever. *Amen.*

"O give thanks to the Lord, call on his name,
 make known his deeds among the peoples!
Sing to him, sing praises to him,
 tell of all his wonderful works!
Glory in his holy name."   Psalm 105:1-3a

Let us pray.

Almighty God,
Most Gracious Father,
 whose love is constantly ready to receive us,
You are God,
 God alone,
 our God!

We come before you in humility,
 troubled by how often we ignore you,
 troubled by how we have failed
  our neighbors,
  our family,
  and our friends.

Receive us in the name of Jesus
  your Son,
 that we be renewed by your grace,
 that we be established in
  faithfulness toward you,
 that we be restored in the love
  of family and friends.

For to you, O God Almighty,
 be all glory,

  Father,
  Son, and
  Holy Spirit.

One God, now and forever more. *Amen.*

"O give thanks to the LORD, call on his name,
　　make known his deeds among the peoples!
Sing to him, sing praises to him,
　　tell of all his wonderful works!
Glory in his holy name."　　　　　　　　　Psalm 105:1-3a

Let us pray.

Father,
God of all consolation,
　　patient, long-suffering,
　　whose love is revealed
　　　　in the sacrifice of your Son,
　　whose well-beloved Son
　　　　we behold as the Lamb of God.

Have mercy upon us,
　　for the sake of that most precious Lamb.

Have mercy upon us,
　　for we behold the Lamb of God,
　　　　who takes away the sin of the world.

Have mercy upon us,
　　in the name of the Lamb,
　　　　who was slain and lives forever more.

To you, O Father, be all glory,

　　and to the Son,
　　　　who offered himself,

　　and to the Spirit,
　　　　the all-consuming fire.

One Redeeming God.

　　　　Forever. *Amen.*

Invocation 23 ————————————

(based on the story of the Prodigal Son)

"O give thanks to the Lᴏʀᴅ, call on his name,
    make known his deeds among the peoples!
Sing to him, sing praises to him,
    tell of all his wonderful works!
Glory in his holy name."   Psalm 105:1-3a

Let us pray.

Father,
    faithfully waiting for us,
        graciously reaching out to us,
    whom we have come to know
        in Jesus Christ,

We gather together in the name of your Son,
    that from him
        we might know of our welcome,
    that with him
        we might make the journey
            to our true home,
    that in him
        we might serve you throughout eternity.

Therefore,
    we pray in his name,
        and in the power of his Spirit,
    ever rejoicing in your glory, O Father.

One God Most High,
    forever and ever. *Amen.*

"O give thanks to the LORD, call on his name,
 make known his deeds among the peoples!
Sing to him, sing praises to him,
 tell of all his wonderful works!
Glory in his holy name."   Psalm 105:1-3a

Let us pray.

Father,
 most kind,
 most generous,

We come to you as your children,
 because we need you
 and want to be with you.

We come to you as our Lord and God,
 because we are in awe of you
  and worship you.

We come to you in the name of Jesus,
 because you have promised to be with us
  when we gather together in his name.

All glory be to you, O Father,
 and to the Eternal Son,
 and to the Holy Spirit.

 One God, forever and ever. *Amen.*

"O Lord, our Lord,
    how majestic is thy name in all the earth!"   Psalm 8:1

Let us pray.

Father, most blessed,
Almighty Lord, Creator of heaven and earth,

Because of your splendor and greatness,
    we praise your name.

Because of your mercy and grace,
    we love your name.

Because of the salvation promised to us in Christ,
    we gather in your name.

Seal us, therefore, in the name of Jesus.
    Stamp the reality of the risen Christ
        within our hearts.

Write his name upon our foreheads,
    the name of the Son upon whom your favor rests,
        that in him we might be your sons and daughters as well.

To you, O Father, be all glory,
    and to the Son, the only begotten,
        the well-beloved,
    and to the Spirit, welling up within us.

    One God forever more. *Amen.*

"O LORD, our Lord,
    how majestic is thy name in all the earth!"   Psalm 8:1

Let us pray.

Most Gracious Father,
    who from all eternity have searched us out
        that we might know you,

Receive us in the name of Christ,
    that we might be his disciples
        and hear his Word,
    that we might celebrate
        his mighty acts of redemption.

To you, O Gracious Father,
    enthroned above,
and to the Son,
    incarnate in this world below,
and to the Spirit, dwelling within our hearts,

Be all glory now, and again and ever again. *Amen.*

"O Lord, our Lord,
how majestic is thy name in all the earth!"   Psalm 8:1

Let us pray.

Father, ruler of earth and heaven,

We bow before you in this place,
for you are all glorious, all wondrous,
all holy.

We worship you, O God, our Father,
confessing with our hymns and prayers
the name of Christ, your Son,
whom we acknowledge as Lord indeed.

Grant to us
your blessing and presence,
your Word and your peace,
that we be witnesses of your truth,
the reflection of your image,
the ambassadors of your Kingdom,

O Sovereign God,
all glorious, all wondrous, all holy.

To God be the glory ever on high,

to Father,
to Son,
to Holy Spirit.

Ever one God, for ages and ages. *Amen.*

Invocation 28 ——————————————————

(based on the parable of the Wedding Feast)

"O Lᴏʀᴅ, our Lord,
    how majestic is thy name in all the earth!"   Psalm 8:1

Let us pray.

Father,
    Almighty and Eternal Lord,
    King and Sovereign of all ages,
    God and Father of our Lord Jesus Christ,

You have sent out an invitation.
You have prepared a great feast,
    that at last we might enter
        into the palatial courts of your presence,
        into the royal mansions of ebony and ivory.

Even on this day
    you have gathered us together
        in the name of Jesus.
    You have invited us to the wedding feast.
    You have brought us to the banqueting house.

Kindle our spirits now,
    most gracious Lord.
Renew us in the beauty of holiness,
    that we be radiant in your presence.

All glory be to you,

    O Father,
    Son,
    and Holy Spirit.

    One God forever and ever. *Amen.*

"O Lᴏʀᴅ, our Lord,
how majestic is thy name in all the earth!"   Psalm 8:1

Let us pray.

Father,
God on high,
O Ancient of Days,
from everlasting to everlasting.

In the name of Jesus we would come before you,
ever mindful of the love of Jesus,
which he poured out to death for us,
ever mindful of the resurrection of Jesus,
which has given us new life.

"Blessing, and honour, and glory, and power
be unto him that sitteth upon the throne,
and unto the Lamb

forever and ever." *Amen.*   Revelation 5:13 (KJV)

"O LORD, our Lord,
    how majestic is thy name in all the earth!"   Psalm 8:1

Let us pray.

    Father,
    Almighty and Eternal God,
        whose glory is revealed in the person of your Son,
           our Savior and Lord,

    In the name of your Son
        we would worship and serve you this day.

Claiming the sacrifice of your Son
    we would stand before you
        as redeemed people,
        justified and sanctified
           by faith in your Son.

Rejoicing in the resurrection of your Son
    we would enter into a new
        and holy life,

    walking in the ways of your Son
        all our days,
           and
        delighting in the Day of his coming.

All glory be to you, O Father,
    and to the Son,
    and to the Holy Spirit.

    One God forever and ever. *Amen.*

"'Behold, a virgin shall conceive and bear a son,
and his name shall be called Emmanuel' . . .
God with us."   Matthew 1:23

Let us pray.

Father, Most High,
    you have given your Son Jesus
        to be born of the Virgin Mary,
        to inherit the throne of David,
        and reign over your Kingdom forever.   (Luke 1:32)

Father, faithful God,
    ever faithful to your promises.

    We bless you for the birth
        of your Son, Emmanuel.
    We bless you
        because you are with us.

Grant that through Christ your Son,
    born to Mary, child of our humanity,
    "the first-born of all creation,"
    we, too, be born from above,
        inheriting through faith,
            the covenant promises of the
            children of God,
    that we, too, know you as our Father
        and love you as your children.

All praise and honor be to you,
        O Father,
        Son, and
        Holy Spirit.

One God, forever and ever. *Amen.*

" 'Behold, a virgin shall conceive and bear a son,
and his name shall be called Emmanuel' . . .
    God with us."

                                          Matthew 1:23

Let us pray.

Father,
    all wise from everlasting.

We bless you for your Word,
    the Word
        which was from the beginning,
    the Word which has always
        been with you,
    the Word
        which shares your divinity,
    the Word
        made flesh, dwelling among us.

Grant that we might behold in him your glory,
    that in that Word
        we might hear you,
    that in that Word
        we might speak to you,
    that in that Word
        we might meet you.

To the name of Christ, your incarnate Word,
    be all glory,
        as to you, O Father,
        and the Holy Spirit be all praise.

One God forever and ever. *Amen.*

"Christ, our paschal lamb, has been sacrificed.
Let us, therefore, celebrate the festival."   I Corinthians 5:7-8

Let us pray.

> O Lord God Most High,
>> Eternal Father,
>>> Everlasting Lord,

> In the name of Christ
>> we come to you,
>>> that in him we might keep this feast.

>> His blood has been put on the doorposts and lintels of our hearts.

>> The Paschal Moon has risen;
>>> and the time has come to move out.

> O God, most compassionate, most gracious,
>> open for us a way,
>>> that we might pass out of the evil
>>>> that besets us.

> All glory be to you, O God,

>> Father,
>> Son, and
>> Holy Spirit.

>> One God, forever and ever. *Amen.*

(This Easter Invocation was put together at the request of an Eastern Orthodox family that for several years provided three basses for our choir. Without the ancient antiphon, "Christ is risen, indeed!" they felt it was not quite Easter. So they taught us all that when the minister proclaimed, "Christ is risen!" the congregation should roar back, "Christ is risen, indeed!" When that family moved on we all felt it was a good thing to keep on doing this.)

Christ is risen!
> CHRIST IS RISEN, INDEED!

"O give thanks to the LORD, for he is good;
> his steadfast love endures forever!"

Christ is risen!
> CHRIST IS RISEN, INDEED!

"Hark, glad songs of victory
> in the tents of the righteous:
'The right hand of the LORD does valiantly,
> the right hand of the LORD is exalted,
> the right hand of the LORD does valiantly!'
I shall not die, but I shall live,
> and recount the deeds of the LORD!"

Christ is risen!
> CHRIST IS RISEN, INDEED!   Psalm 118:1, 15-17, with antiphon

Let us pray.

O Father, Eternal Lord,
God Almighty.

> In the name of him who is the resurrection
>> and the life,
> we come to worship you,
>> for Christ is the first born from the dead,
>> the first fruits of those who slept.

> As his disciples this day,
>> we would proclaim the gospel of his
>>> resurrection.

This is the day the Lord has made;
we rejoice and are glad in it.

This is the Lord's Day!
All praise be to you!

Christ is risen!
CHRIST IS RISEN, INDEED!

To you be all glory,
Father,
Son, and
Holy Spirit.

One God forever and ever. *Amen.*

Christ is risen!
CHRIST IS RISEN, INDEED!

THE INVOCATION

"The LORD says to my lord:
    'Sit at my right hand,
till I make your enemies your footstool.'
    'You are a priest for ever
        after the order of Melchizedek.'"   Psalm 110:1, 4b

Let us pray.

Father, O God Most High,
    who dwells in the highest of heavens,
        we praise you!

Father, O Lord Most Exalted,
    beyond our thoughts and imaginations,
        we praise you!

We celebrate the victory of your Son
    who has overcome death
    and saved us from the power of sin!

We rejoice in his exaltation!
    Our Great High Priest
        has gone before,
        has entered into the
            Holy of Holies,
        and opened up a way for us to follow.

In his name
    we, too, would enter
        into your eternal presence,
    for he is our priest forever
        after the order of Melchizedek.

To him be all praise,
    together with you, O Father,
        and the Holy Spirit.

One Lord, the same in every age. *Amen* and *amen.*

"Ascribe to the LORD, O heavenly beings,
    ascribe to the LORD glory and strength.
Ascribe to the LORD the glory of his name;
    worship the LORD in holy array."   Psalm 29:1-2

Let us pray.

Father, Lord of Heaven,
    who sent forth your Spirit
        to brood on the face of the waters,
    who poured out your Spirit
        upon the Apostles in the Upper Room,
            flashing forth in flames of fire
        that the Church might come alive
            in spirit and truth.

Pour out upon this congregation,
    gathered in the name of Christ,
        that same Spirit,
    that we might come alive in holiness,
    that we might become brilliant in purity,
    that we might catch the fire of righteousness.

To you be all glory, Eternal God,

        Father,
        Son, and
        Holy Spirit.

One God, from the very beginning,
    even now,
        and as long as time shall last. *Amen.*

The Psalms as Prayer

Praying the psalms together has long been one of the most cherished traditions of Christian worship. As a matter of course Jesus and his disciples would have sung the psalms together as part of saying their morning and evening prayers. The Apostle Paul on more than one occasion encouraged the early Christians to sing psalms, hymns, and spiritual songs as part of their worship (Eph 5:19; Col 3:16). The Epistle of James does the same thing: "Is any among you suffering? Let him make supplications. Does any among you rejoice? Let him sing psalms" (James 5:13, my translation). The first Christian hymnal, the *Odes of Solomon*, put together about the end of the first century, is a collection of some forty psalm pendants or paraphrases. Athanasius, the great fourth-century church leader, tells us in both his life of Saint Anthony and his letter to Marcellinus about how Egyptian Christians prayed the psalms. John Cassian, who did so much to establish Christianity in Southern France, gives another vivid picture of the psalm piety of the ancient Church. For centuries the monks of both the Eastern and Western Churches prayed through the whole Psalter week by week. In fact, that is the heart of the famous Rule of St. Benedict. Benedict arranged a system for praying through the whole Book of Psalms in the course of a week. For fifteen hundred years this basic plan for psalm prayer has been elaborated, reformed, and embroidered.

The Protestant Reformation was no less devoted to the praying of the psalms. Some of Luther's first liturgical reforms were his German psalm versions. "A Mighty Fortress Is Our God" is only the best known of several metrical psalms and psalm paraphrases that he produced. For Luther it was very important to provide the common people with versions of the psalms that they could sing in their own language. The Protestants of Augsburg were among the first to respond to Luther's challenge. As early as 1531 they were able to publish a psalter with at least eighty-five metrical psalms. Many of these psalms were produced by the Reformers of Wittenberg and elsewhere, but a good number were written by Jakob Dachser, the greatly respected associate pastor of St. Ulrich's Church in Augsburg. With considerable enthusiasm the Reformers of Strasbourg took up the task of providing the Christians of Germany with psalms that they could sing in their own language. As early as 1537 the *Strasbourg Psalter* was able to include vernacular versions of all one hundred and fifty psalms.

The French Reformation produced a particularly fine psalter. Clement

Marot, the leading French lyric poet of the sixteenth century, wrote a magnificent collection of French metrical psalms. Although we do not yet know how he obtained them, the Reformer John Calvin immediately put Marot's psalms to use in the worship of his congregation of French refugees in Strasbourg, and shortly afterward when he returned to Geneva he was able to have them adopted by the Reformed Church of Geneva. Calvin gave a great deal of attention to developing the *Genevan Psalter*. He employed the services of the best poets and musicians of his day in order to make the *Genevan Psalter* a classic. While Marot only produced metrical versions of about half the psalms, the job was ably completed by Theodore Beza, who had won a reputation as a competent poet even before he began his career as a theologian. For generations the French Huguenots were characterized by their psalm singing.

Before long the *Genevan Psalter* inspired psalters in the Netherlands, in Scotland, in England, and even in Massachusetts. The Dutch psalter was particularly loved. In the Netherlands organ building had developed into a highly refined art. Peter Sweelink, the greatest of Dutch organists, provided the psalter with brilliant psalm settings. The psalms were so important in the devotional life of the Dutch Reformed Church that it was not at all unusual for people to know the whole metrical Psalter by heart. In seventeenth century Lutheran Germany the unsurpassed psalmodist was Heinrich Schütz, who produced numerous psalm versions. Some of these were elaborate choral settings that presented the psalms in all the elegance of high baroque style. While these psalms were written to be sung in the court chapel of the Duke of Saxony, Schütz also composed much simpler settings for the *Beckworth Psalter*.

In the eighteenth century much excellent psalmody was produced. The English Congregational minister Isaac Watts penned some of the finest hymns of the English-speaking world, but even more beloved were his psalm versions, which were very free versions of the psalms. Some people insisted on calling them psalm paraphrases rather than metrical psalms, but particularly where the Great Awakening made its influence felt Watts's psalms became the favorite psalter. A generation later Charles Wesley gave us a complete set of psalms. They resembled Watts's psalms, but also had the characteristic devotional insights of Wesleyan hymnody.

At the end of the nineteenth century the singing of metrical psalms lost popularity. The metrical psalms were thought of as terribly old-fashioned and lacking in poetic elegance. Some circles argued for psalm singing in a sort of stick-in-the-mud legalistic way that only hastened the demise of the practice. One by one the leading Protestant hymn books dropped their collections of psalms. In other circles responsive reading of the psalms was offered as a substitute for singing the sacred texts. This became very popular for a while, but then abuses set in. The editors of a number of hymn books took the opportunity to show their creativity by abridging the texts of longer psalms and expurgating lines that offended the Victorian sense of propriety. Psalms were sometimes spliced together or whole new compositions were drawn together by gathering verses from anywhere in the Bible to develop some particular theme. The connection between responsive reading and the Psalter almost disappeared.

Since the Second World War there has been something of a revival of psalmody. The French religious community of Taizé has popularized the singing of French psalms in worship. Set to contemporary music by Father Joseph Gelineaux, these psalms are clearly an attempt to restore liturgical chanting. When a religious community has the time and the ability to learn to chant, these and other similar attempts at a revival of chanting can indeed be very beautiful. Quite different but much more usable are the psalm versions of various groups of "Jesus people" and charismatics that began to appear in the early 1970s. In addition to this, modern biblical scholarship has given us a fresh look at the Book of Psalms. From many different quarters we are being encouraged once again to take up the psalms and pray them as the people of God have for some three millenia.

Responsive Readings

Why should we have a responsive reading of the Psalter in the Sunday morning service? Responsive reading is not, we must admit, a form of psalm prayer recommended by any antiquity. In the form we are accustomed to, it only goes back to the nineteenth century. Responsive reading of the Psalter, whatever its origins may be and whatever abuses it may have suffered, is most certainly an effective way of praying the psalms in public worship. When a full-length psalm, or several shorter psalms, are used as a responsive reading, these texts greatly increase the element of praise and prayer in the service. The generous use of psalms and canticles in a service of worship emphasizes the doxological nature of what we are doing. When there are several hymns of praise and thanksgiving, an anthem, a number of doxologies at appropriate places, and a responsive reading of the Psalter in the service, then there is no question but that we have gathered together to praise God. Adoration and prayer should be the prevailing tenor of any worship assembly, and use of a responsive reading of the psalms helps us maintain that emphasis.

A generous use of the psalms in worship, either as responsive readings, as anthems, or sung in metrical versions by the whole congregation, has a very important theological principle behind it. Prayer is in the final analysis a gift of God, a divine work in the human heart. As the Apostle Paul tells us, prayer is the voice of the Holy Spirit crying out within us (Rom 8:15-16; Gal 4:6). We pray the psalms because they are the prayers of the Holy Spirit. We find the same thing in the Acts of the Apostles. When the first Christians gathered for prayer and sang the psalms together, they were very much aware that the psalms were the prayers that the Holy Spirit had given them through the mouth of David (Acts 4:25). It is very clear in Luke's report of this prayer service, which no doubt resembles very closely the prayer services that occurred on a daily basis in the primitive Church of Jerusalem, that not only had the early Christians spoken to God in that prayer but that God had spoken to them in that same prayer. The psalms spoke to the Church in prayer.

This was nothing new. It was not a recent discovery or some novel theological construction on the part of first-century Christian enthusiasts. God's people had prayed the psalms for centuries because the psalms were the Lord's song. When the Jews were taken as captives into Babylon they were asked to sing the sacred music of their temple services, and they replied, "How shall we sing the LORD's song in a foreign land?" (Psalm 137:4). The psalms were in a very special way the Lord's song. Israel had experienced this for centuries. When the faithful had wanted to pour out their hearts to God, when they sought God's consolation and guidance, they prayed the psalms, because when they did, they discovered that

> By day the LORD commands his steadfast love;
>> and at night his song is with me,
>>> a prayer to the God of my life.   Psalm 42:8

The psalms were God's songs, the prayers given to God's people by God's own Spirit, that is, the Holy Spirit. We as God's people today pray the psalms because in them God speaks to our hearts so that in our hearts we may speak to him.

One of the best reasons for using a responsive reading of the psalms is that it acquaints the congregation with the actual language of the psalms, which even in translation is often beautiful and powerful. Yes, even in most of the standard English translations the flow and rhythm of the psalms comes out very clearly. One senses their poetic music when they are read responsively. This rhythmic speech is like poetry, but yet, at the same time, something quite different from poetry. It is unique. Psalmody is not just religious poetry; it is something distinct, something all its own. This is particularly brought out when the psalms are read responsively.

The regular use of a responsive reading of the psalms has a significant teaching dimension. It keeps the simple text of the psalms before the Church Sunday by Sunday. In the course of time, when these psalms are used again and again, the congregation gets to know the biblical language of prayer. Public prayer should always have a pedagogical function. To be sure, it should demonstrate how we are to pray when we pray in smaller groups and when we pray alone. But there is another pedagogical function beyond this, and it is perhaps even more important. Our public prayer should teach the language of prayer. Public prayer should lead private prayer. A responsive reading of the psalms is only one way of doing this, but it is an important way of doing it.

Responsive reading of the Psalter should be presented as prayer and praise. It should not be presented as the Old Testament Lesson. To be sure, the psalms are Scripture, but when the psalms are read responsively in public worship they function as prayers or hymns of praise. For the most part I have usually chosen psalms of praise and thanksgiving for the Sunday morning service. Psalms of lamentation and confession I have usually left for the weekday prayer services. It is because the psalms are the divinely inspired hymns of praise that they should be the core of Christian praise. All the other praises that Christians present to God are interpretations and elaborations of these fundamental hymns of praise that God has given to us.

Further, the responsive reading of the Psalter should not be confused with the call to worship. Recently there has been a trend to use a very short responsive reading of a few psalm verses as a sort of call to worship and to drop the responsive reading. In fact one frequently gets the impression that these responsive calls to worship have taken the place of the Psalter. No significant amount of psalmody is apt to be found elsewhere in these trendy services. This is unfortunate, because it means that the beauty of the whole psalm usually disappears in the effort to keep it short. Beside that, these collages of dismembered psalm verses usually concentrate on the theme of being called to worship, and since not much from the psalter appears elsewhere in the service, many other themes of praise are omitted. The themes of praise are rich and varied. That is one of the things we learn from the psalms. These short responsive calls to worship hardly accomplish this purpose. The responsive reading is the place for a full development of our praise.

Which psalms should be chosen for use at the Sunday morning service? While in principle I want to agree with those who have considered it an important spiritual discipline to pray through the whole Psalter over a stated period of time, I would insist that this is not a discipline for all Christians. Many of the psalms are difficult for the Christian to appropriate, and it is far easier to pass over those psalms at the Sunday service. They can be used by groups in which they are less likely to be a stumbling block. But once I have decided which psalms can be used without an extensive explanation, my first concern is to choose a psalm of aspiration or adoration. For the Sunday morning service my rule of thumb is to use the prayers of praise and thanksgiving that are fairly easy for the congregation to follow. Those that I use most often are

Psalm 16	Psalms 99, 100
Psalm 18	Psalm 103
Psalm 19	Psalm 104
Psalm 24	Psalm 107 (dividing it)
Psalms 33, 34	Psalms 111, 112
Psalms 46, 47, 48	Psalms 113, 114, 115
Psalm 65	Psalms 116, 117
Psalms 66, 67	Psalm 118
Psalm 68 (omitting	Psalm 119 (dividing it)
some verses)	Psalm 136
Psalm 72	Psalm 138
Psalm 73	Psalm 139 (omitting some
Psalms 84, 85	verses)
Psalms 86, 87	Psalm 145
Psalm 96	Psalms 146, 147
Psalm 97	Psalm 148
Psalm 98	Psalms 149, 150

There are psalms of lamentation and confession that should be used regularly in the Sunday morning service because they express such an important part of our prayer, emphasizing to us that crying before the Lord is a legitimate part of our worship. Having said this, I would want nevertheless to emphasize that worship on the Lord's Day is above all a celebration of Christ's resurrection and a commemoration of our hope of eternal life. Lamentation and supplication should therefore be a secondary theme. One might say that it has its legitimate place in the worship of the

Lord's Day because it is an anticipation of the Christian hope. The following psalms, because they move from supplication to thanksgiving and affirmation, are therefore quite appropriate to the Lord's Day service.

Psalm 22	Psalm 51
Psalms 25, 26	Psalm 80
Psalm 27	Psalm 90
Psalm 37	Psalm 91
Psalms 42, 43	Psalm 102

Another consideration for psalms to be chosen for responsive reading is their length. Some psalms that are particularly significant for Christian devotion, such as Psalms 8, 23, 100, 117, 121, and 150, are too short for use in responsive readings. In some cases one of these psalms can be coupled with the preceding or following psalm. We have done this with, among those in the list above, Psalms 100, 117, and 150. On the other hand, some short psalms are best treated as choral anthems or sung as metrical psalms, for example, Psalms 1, 2, 8, 23, 67, 93, 121, 122, 130, 132, 134, and 137.

Still other psalms are greatly beloved because of a single verse, yet the remainder of the psalm is too difficult for use without a long explanation. One thinks, for example, of Psalm 55, which as a whole is a difficult psalm and yet some of its lines are very beautiful: "O that I had wings like a dove! I would fly away and be at rest," or a bit further on, "Cast your burden on the LORD, and he will sustain you; he will never permit the righteous to be moved." Felix Mendelssohn wrote a beautiful anthem on this second text for his oratorio *Elijah*. Another example would be the opening lines of Psalm 63:

> O God, thou art my God, I seek thee,
>   my soul thirsts for thee;
> my flesh faints for thee,
>   as in a dry and weary land where no water is.
> So I have looked upon thee in the sanctuary,
>   beholding thy power and glory.
> Because thy steadfast love is better than life,
>   my lips will praise thee.
> So I will bless thee as long as I live;
>   I will lift up my hands and call on thy name.   Psalm 63:1-4

And one thinks of the opening lines of Psalm 141. The psalm as a whole is not too edifying but these lines are marvelous:

> I call upon thee, O LORD; make haste to me!
>   Give ear to my voice, when I call to thee!
> Let my prayer be counted as incense before thee,
>   and the lifting up of my hands as an evening sacrifice!
>   Psalm 141:1-2

Generally speaking responsive readings should use whole psalms. They should be long enough to give the congregation time to get into what is being done. Psalms can be combined particularly if they stand next to each other in the canonical Psalter. In fact a number of psalms already seem to be arranged in the Bible in pairs or series. For example, Psalms 111 and 112 seem to be a pair. What one wants to avoid is constructing a new psalm out of bits and pieces of psalms. The responsive reading is not the place to splice together fragments of psalms.

There are a few hymnals that have relatively good psalters arranged for responsive reading. Two in my acquaintance are *The Hymnal*, published by the Presbyterian Church in 1933, and the *Trinity Hymnal*, which was published by the Orthodox Presbyterian Church in 1961. The section of responsive readings in each of these hymnals represents a different tendency. The one in the *Trinity Hymnal* includes the whole text of almost all the psalms. As I see it some of these psalms could have been edited a bit more. The "Psalter Selections" in *The Hymnal* includes the most accessible of the psalms and omits any verses of a psalm that the average worshipper might find difficult. While generally this editing is done well, sometimes it is a bit too heavy. A compromise somewhere between these two psalters would be ideal.

If a church does not have a psalter in its hymnal, one could do the responsive reading directly from the Bible. This would be a good approach if the *Revised Standard Version* or *New International Version* is next to the hymnal in the pew, since both of these translations have respected the Hebrew poetic lines.

How should we choose the psalter selection for a particular Sunday? There is much to be said for going through the more popular psalms, that is, a list of about fifty of the most appropriate, something like the list I have given above, taking each psalm in the order it is found in the canonical Book of Psalms. My practice has been, however, to use more often those psalms that my congregation will find most helpful. I have used Psalms 42–43, 46–48, 51, 64, 95–100, 103, 104, and 145–50 very often, particularly in the years when I was introducing the regular use of the psalter to the congregation. The first consideration in the choice of a psalm is how fitting the psalm is for the prayer of the congregation. The responsive reading of the psalter should give the congregation an opportunity to express its own prayers of praise and adoration. That I put above everything else. I rarely choose the psalter selections to complement the theme of the sermon.

On the other hand, during Easter season and Christmas season, I do select psalms appropriate to the feast being celebrated. Certain psalms were associated with the Feast of Passover before the time of Jesus. Apparently Jesus' thinking in regard to his own death and resurrection was profoundly shaped by his use of the Passover psalms. That he prayed particular psalms of lamentation such as Psalm 22 and Psalms 42–43 is suggested by the text of the Gospels. In all probability he and his disciples prayed the Passover Hallel, that is, Psalms 113–118, at the Last Supper. Christians have almost universally found these psalms appropriate to Holy Week and Easter.

In a similar way there are certain psalms particularly associated with Christmas. The Christmas psalmody is not, however, as firmly established, simply because the celebration of Christmas is far from being of either dominical or apostolic origin. The celebration of Christmas was not well established until the fourth Christian century. But some psalms do seem particularly appropriate to a celebration of Christmas. Most notable among these are what scholars have come to call "the royal psalms" and have identified as among the most ancient in the collection that has come down to us. They celebrate the divine election of the house of David, remember the messianic hope, and pray for the Kingdom of the anointed Son of David. Both Psalm 2 and Psalm 110 seem to have been important for Jesus as he defined his role as the long promised heir to the throne of David. But these two psalms are both difficult to understand and rather short and so do not make for good responsive readings. On the other hand Psalms 72, 89, 96, 98, and 132 have to do with many of the same themes. While Psalm 72 has long been associated with Christmas because of its references to the gifts that the kings of the East are to present to the Son of the house of David, Psalm 89 is not particularly well known as a Christmas psalm; nevertheless, it is eloquent in its celebration of the messianic hope.

Those denominations that have made heavy use of the liturgical calendar have developed elaborate selections of festal psalms. Many of them are based on rather artificial catch phrases that in one way or another associate the psalm with the particular feast. I have never been convinced that the line "God has gone up with a shout" makes Psalm 47 appropriate for the Feast of the Ascension or that

> Create in me a clean heart, O God,
>   and put a new and right spirit within me.
> Cast me not away from thy presence,
>   and take not thy holy Spirit from me.
> Restore to me the joy of thy salvation,
>   and uphold me with a willing spirit.   Psalm 51:10-12

should make Psalm 51 the right psalm for Pentecost.

While there is value in recognizing that certain psalms are appropriate for Holy Week and Easter and that certain psalms fit in with the themes of Christmas, one should not give too much time to assigning particular psalms to particular feasts or particular Sundays on the liturgical calendar. It is much more important to choose a psalm that guides the congregation in its prayers of praise and thanksgiving. The adoration of God is one of the chief reasons we come together to worship. If the responsive reading of the psalms helps us do that, that alone is sufficient. It is not necessary that some other end be served such as reinforcing the sermon or developing a theme from the liturgical calendar.

One final subject needs to be discussed in regard to the responsive reading of the Psalter, and that is the *Gloria patri*. The *Gloria patri* is one of many doxologies that have traditionally sprinkled the worship of both Church and synagogue. We will speak of these doxologies at greater length in a later chapter. That a psalm should end with a doxology seems to have been the accepted practice at an early date in the development of the Psalter. The various books into which the canonical book of Psalms is divided all end with doxologies. The first book ends with

Blessed be the LORD, the God of Israel,
    from everlasting to everlasting!
      Amen and Amen.   Psalm 41:13

We find a similar doxology after the second book:

Blessed be the LORD, the God of Israel,
    who alone does wondrous things.
Blessed be his glorious name for ever;
    may his glory fill the whole earth!
      Amen and Amen!   Psalm 72:18-19

At the end of the Psalter there is a still more elaborate doxology. In fact this final doxology takes six verses and is counted as Psalm 150. It is, nevertheless, the doxology that concludes the canonical Psalter. That a doxology should conclude a reading from the Psalter was a well-established principle when Christians first began to gather for specifically Christian services of worship. No doubt from the very earliest days Christians began to develop specifically Christian doxologies to conclude their psalm prayers. Both Basil of Caesarea and John Cassian mention use of such doxologies in the fourth century.

As time went along the Church began to find particular significance in the use of a trinitarian doxology at the conclusion of psalm readings. There have always been those who have had trouble with the idea that the Christian Church should use Jewish psalms in its worship, and for such people the *Gloria patri* makes the psalms Christian. It has sometimes been said that it baptizes the psalms. For some this reasoning may seem a bit lacking in charity. But it was only natural when Christians used the psalms in Church that they should develop trinitarian doxologies to conclude this part of the service. In fact, by the fourth century, most of the doxologies they developed were trinitarian. Unlike the actual psalms, the doxologies that concluded the psalms were not considered canonical. Though it seems to have been common practice to compose psalm paraphrases or psalm pendants such as we have in the *Odes of Solomon*, Christians wanted to maintain the praying of the canonical Psalter in their regular prayers. Psalm paraphrases had their place but they were not to replace the canonical Psalter. Christians would never have dreamed of tampering with a canonical text, but they felt perfectly free to elaborate the liturgical setting of the liturgical texts. When they elaborated the doxology they were free to elaborate it in a Christian sense.

Anthems

The word "anthem" can mean a number of things in different contexts. For most of us, when we are talking about the worship of American Protestant churches, what we mean is a piece of music sung by the choir rather than by the congregation. More technical designations could be used, but what we need to speak about here is the music sung in the worship service by specially trained and prepared musicians as opposed to music sung by the whole congregation. Most of what we want to discuss here would apply to the work of soloists as well as choirs, though that stretches the meaning of the word "anthem" a bit too much. The point we want to make is that certain kinds of psalmody are often best handled by trained musicians. There is a large repertoire of psalm settings from some of the great choral composers down through history. We have already mentioned the choral settings of Heinrich Schütz, the seventeenth-century German Protestant composer. One thinks of the psalm settings found in the oratorios of Felix Mendelssohn and George Frederick Handel. A particularly fine collection of psalm settings has been left to us by the eighteenth-century Italian composer Benedetto Marcello. The musical treasury that the psalms have inspired is inexhaustible. Any church having trained musicians will want to open up this fantastic treasury. Such things are a spiritual delight! They are a fascinating devotion for the musician and a pious pleasure for the rest of us.

As has already been suggested, shorter psalms or shorter selections from psalms, and especially arrangements of psalm texts, are treated best in worship as anthems or in settings for soloists or small groups of musicians. Psalm 93 is a short psalm for which Jacquin de Pres has composed music that can only be described as a sunburst of musical diamonds. The canonical text is quite short but the music expands it so that it is a major expression of praise. The full import of the words is flavored and cherished by the music.

At the very beginning of a service the choir might sing those beautiful lines from Psalm 43:

Oh send out thy light and thy truth;
    let them lead me,
let them bring me to thy holy hill
    and to thy dwelling!
Then I will go to the altar of God,
    to God my exceeding joy;
and I will praise thee with the lyre,
    O God, my God.

Psalm 43:3-4

These lines are a natural choral introit. Another short psalm that could be used in the same way is Psalm 122.

I was glad when they said to me,
    "Let us go to the house of the Lord!"
Our feet have been standing
    within your gates, O Jerusalem!

Jerusalem, built as a city
    which is bound firmly together,
to which the tribes go up,
    the tribes of the Lord, . . .

Pray for the peace of Jerusalem!
   "May they prosper who love you!
Peace be within your walls,
      and security within your towers!"   Psalm 122:1-4a and 6-7

The psalm is only seven verses long, yet, sung as a choral introit, it leads us to contemplate the heavenly reality of what we are doing when we come together as the people of God to pray for the establishment of the heavenly Jerusalem. The Psalms of Ascent are particularly appropriate for use as choral introits. Psalm 133 is another little gem.

Behold, how good and pleasant it is
   when brothers dwell in unity!
It is like the precious oil upon the head,
   running down upon the beard,
upon the beard of Aaron,
   running down on the collar of his robes!
It is like the dew of Hermon,
   which falls on the mountains of Zion!
For there the LORD has commanded the blessing,
   life for evermore.   Psalm 133:1-3

Here, too, we have a brief but profound poetic type for our worship. Worship is a priestly ordination that sets us apart to the service of a sacred life. Somehow in the heat and clamor of life worship is a cooling balm that refreshes our spirits. The musical setting of a choir or soloist, for that matter, can significantly unfold this short aromatic psalm. Surely such an unfolding is the essence of the ministry of choral music.

Psalm 8 is a very beautiful short psalm for which there are a number of splendid settings. Heinrich Schütz's setting expands these short lines into a solemn meditation on the mystery of creation and would be a wonderful anthem during the taking up of the collection, a time in the service when our prayers naturally turn to thanksgiving for God's gifts.

A good place for the choir to support the worship with psalmody is before one of the major prayers of the service. At such a point the choir might sing a few verses of a psalm as a choral preface to prayer. The opening verses of both Psalm 70 and Psalm 141 have been used since ancient times as admonitions to prayer and there are many choral settings to them. I have often used a particularly fine setting of the first verse of Psalm 141 as a choral preface to prayer. The English translation is a bit rearranged to fit the music, but everything is there.

O Lord, I cry to thee,
   make haste, make haste . . .
O Lord, I cry to thee,
   give ear to my supplication.
O Lord, I cry to thee,
   hear my voice when I call to thee.

All one Spring I had the choir sing this psalm verse before beginning the major prayer of the morning service. The piece must have taken several minutes as it drew even the most distracted minds into an atmosphere of calm and prayer. A wise use of this kind of musical accompaniment makes it clear that the music of the Church is infinitely more than sacred entertainment. It is a significant way of leading the congregation into prayer.

At the Scottish communion service the singing of the last few verses of the twenty-fourth Psalm has always had a reserved place.

> Lift up your heads, O gates!
> and be lifted up, O ancient doors!
> that the King of glory may come in.
> Who is the King of glory?
> The LORD, strong and mighty,
> the LORD, mighty in battle!
> Lift up your heads, O gates!
> and be lifted up, O ancient doors!
> that the King of glory may come in.
> Who is this King of glory?
> The LORD of hosts,
> he is the King of glory!   Psalm 24:7-10

Again we have a biblical type of our worship that as a choral anthem can be explored and drawn out by musical suggestion. Meditation is important in the celebration of communion, and a choral setting of a psalm like this elicits meditation. It invites the congregation to pray.

A short psalm that is appropriate for the choir to sing at the end of the service is Psalm 67:

> May God be gracious to us and bless us
> and make his face to shine upon us,
> that thy way may be known upon earth,
> thy saving power among all nations.
>
> Let the peoples praise thee, O God;
> let all the peoples praise thee!
>
> Let the nations be glad and sing for joy,
> for thou dost judge the peoples with equity
> and guide the nations upon earth.
>
> Let the peoples praise thee, O God;
> let all the peoples praise thee!
>
> The earth has yielded its increase;
> God, our God, has blessed us.
> God has blessed us;
> let all the ends of the earth fear him!

This psalm leads us to meditate on the significance of the Aaronic blessing, the classic benediction of Protestant worship.

> The LORD bless you and keep you:
> The LORD make his face to shine upon you, and be gracious to you:
> The LORD lift up his countenance upon you, and give you peace.
>
> Numbers 6:24-26

The psalm is obviously an opening up of this most ancient of sacred texts, and it opens it up in terms of a high theology of the covenant. God has blessed us that we might be a blessing to all the peoples of the earth. It leads us to pray that the God we praise might be praised by all nations: "Let the peoples praise thee, O God; let all the peoples praise thee." Nothing could be more appropriate as a doxology to follow the Benediction.

A few years ago when the "Jesus people" movement was at its height a tall and handsome young man with big brown eyes appeared at Faith Church. He was wearing a black leather jacket and motorcycle boots. After a few Sundays he introduced himself as a Jew for Jesus. He explained that he was going to be studying at Purdue for the year and asked if he could be of any help with the music. He had a guitar and he liked to sing psalms with his guitar. What a help he was! As a regular thing he would work up wonderfully meditative settings to short psalm verses as prefaces to prayer. Among those that I remember most fondly were his versions of Psalm 5.

> Give ear to my words, O LORD;
>   give heed to my groaning.
> Hearken to the sound of my cry,
>   my King and my God,
>   for to thee do I pray.
> O LORD, in the morning thou dost hear my voice;
>   in the morning I prepare a sacrifice for thee, and watch.
>
> Psalm 5:1-3

Another that I can remember was his setting of Psalm 65:1-4.

> Praise is due to thee,
>   O God, in Zion;
> and to thee shall vows be performed,
>   O thou who hearest prayer!
> To thee shall all flesh come
>   on account of sins.
> When our transgressions prevail over us,
>   thou dost forgive them.
> Blessed is he whom thou dost choose and bring near,
>   to dwell in thy courts!
> We shall be satisfied with the goodness of thy house,
>   thy holy temple!

He would often embroider the sacred text with Christian elaborations. He made it clear that the sacrifice mentioned in Psalm 5 is a type of the full, final, and perfect sacrifice of Christ that sanctifies the prayers we offer in Christ's name. He would elaborate the opening verses of Psalm 65 to make it clear that the risen body of Christ is the temple in which Christians offer their prayer. After a while I began to realize that what I was hearing was a twentieth-century Jewish cantor who had received the gospel.

Metrical Psalms

The singing of psalms as Christian hymns by the whole congregation occupied an honored place in Protestant worship until some time after the middle of the nineteenth century. This liturgical usage, so clearly biblical as it indeed is, has been exiled long enough. The practice needs to be revived, and in fact one notices that it is beginning to reappear. Back in the 1970s "Jesus people," charismatics, and avant garde evangelicals were producing very popular and singable versions of the psalms. The more standard variety of Protestants also began producing collections of metrical psalms and psalm paraphrases. One thinks especially of the versions of Fred Anderson. The magnificent hymnal that Erik Routley produced for the Reformed Church in America, *Rejoice in the Lord*, has a very large collection of psalms. When the new hymnal of the Presbyterian Church (U.S.A.) appeared in 1990 it had a generous collection of psalms. One hopes things will continue to develop in this direction.

Something needs to be said about how metrical psalms and psalm paraphrases should be used in the service of worship. While Sunday evening vespers and the daily prayer services give us more opportunity to unfold psalm prayer fully, there is a definite place in the Sunday morning service for metrical psalmody. Three ways of working metrical psalmody into the service come to mind.

First, one could make metrical psalmody a regular part of the praises and prayers that normally begin the typical American Protestant Lord's Day service. One notices that quite a number of church bulletins refer to this part of the service as the service of *praise*. There is a certain logic to this. The worship of the temple seems to have begun regularly with extensive psalmody. A good number of the psalms that have been preserved in our Psalter seem to have come from these entrance psalms that apparently began the temple service. The Psalms of Ascent — that is, Psalms 120–134, the Songs of Zion — that is, Psalms 46–48, and Psalm 24 and Psalm 84 seem to have been connected in one way or another with the entrance rites of the temple liturgy. As the synagogue service developed it was customary to begin with a whole series of psalms of praise and adoration. Psalms 93–100 were always sung at the beginning of the Sabbath services while Psalms 145–150 were thought of as the appropriate psalms for beginning a service of morning prayer.

In both temple and synagogue, then, worship normally began with a generous selection of psalms, and several passages of the New Testament suggest that the earliest Christian Church continued the practice. We have already mentioned the service reported in the fourth chapter of Acts. One might take the Christian psalms at the beginning of the Gospel of Luke as a hint in this direction as well as the report of the heavenly worship in the fourth and fifth chapters of Revelation. Even as late as the time of Gregory the Great the singing of entrance psalms was an important part of the liturgy. By the sixteenth century the singing of these entrance psalms had degenerated considerably. It was not surprising, therefore, that one of the first things Martin Luther suggested for the reform of worship was the recovery of psalm singing. Early in the Reformation Luther encouraged translating the psalms into German meter so that the common people could sing them.

Psalm singing has long been the heart of the Church's ministry of praise. There is something very natural about this. Perhaps it is that praise is sung better than said. One notices this attitude in the *Genevan Psalter* of 1542. The French title of the book is *Forme des prières et chants ecclési-astiques.* That it was intended as a comprehensive book of prayers for the worship of the Church is more than clear. In this book one finds prayers of confession and supplication and of intercession and petition to be read at the service, but there is no set prayer of praise or adoration. One wonders why there might be such an omission. Is it because the Protestants of Geneva were by nature a gloomy lot? There are those who would have us believe something of this sort. But it would seem that the answer is much more profound. In fact, Calvin makes a point of it in his introduction. Prayers of praise and adoration are most naturally sung. The psalms were the praise of the Genevan Church. In fact among the Scottish Presbyterians and English Puritans of the seventeenth century one often hears of psalm singing as "the praises." When in eighteenth-century America Jonathan Edwards or Gilbert Tennent spoke of spending time in praises, they meant that they were singing psalms. Psalmody should not be limited to praise, but surely helping us to offer up our praises is one of its chief functions.

I like to pair the metrical psalm with a responsive reading of a psalm. After the Invocation I will select a psalm of praise, such as the classic Scottish Psalter setting of Psalm 95, "O Come Let Us Sing to the Lord," then follow it with a responsive reading of a longer psalm such as Psalm 103, followed by the *Gloria patri.* By using both the straight reading of the rhythmic prose of one psalm and the singing of a metrical version of another, the full range of psalmody is brought out. The two different forms complement each other. It means, of course, that we give quite a bit of attention to psalmody in the course of a typical service. But to do so is true to the longest standing and deepest traditions of Christian prayer. Praying the psalms is at the very heart of Christian prayer. As I see it, if we are going to lead our congregations into the deeper experiences of prayer, this is where we must start.

It might be helpful at this point to list some of the metrical psalms and psalm paraphrases that are most appropriate for the beginning of the normal Sunday morning service. This list is only a beginning. It attempts to indicate both a few of the old classics and a few more contemporary versions.

Psalm 5

"Hear My Words, O Gracious Lord"	*Scottish Psalter,* 1650
"Lord, in the Morning"	Isaac Watts, 1719
"As Morning Dawns, Lord, Hear Our Cry"	Fred Anderson, 1986

Psalm 8

"Lord, Our Lord, Thy Glorious Name"	*The Psalter,* 1912
"O Lord, Our God, How Excellent"	Fred Anderson, 1986

Psalm 19

"Heaven and Earth and Sea and Air"	Joachim Neander, c. 1685
"The Heavens Declare Thy Glory, Lord"	Isaac Watts, 1719
"The Heavens Above Declare God's Praise"	Christopher Webber, 1986

Psalm 23

"The Lord's My Shepherd"	*Scottish Psalter,* 1650
"The King of Love My Shepherd Is"	Henry Baker, 1868

Psalm 24

"The Earth and All That Dwells Therein"	*The Psalter,* 1912
"Earth is Eternally the Lord's"	*The Murrayfield Psalms,* 1954
"See, All the Earth Is God's"	Arlo Duba, 1984

Psalm 27

"God Is My Strong Salvation"	James Montgomery, c. 1830

Psalm 46

"A Mighty Fortress Is Our God"	Martin Luther
"God Is Our Refuge and Our Strength"	*Scottish Psalter,* 1650
"God, Our Help and Constant Refuge"	Fred Anderson, 1986

Psalm 47

"Peoples, Gather Round"	Marie Post, 1980
"Peoples, Clap Your Hands!"	Joy Patterson, 1989

Psalm 65

"To Bless the Earth"	*The Psalter,* 1912
"Praise Is Your Right, O God, in Zion"	Stanley Wiersma, 1980

Psalm 67

"God of Mercy, God of Grace"	Henry Lyte, 1834

Psalm 72

"Hail to the Lord's Anointed"	James Montgomery, c. 1830

Psalm 84

"How Lovely Are Thy Dwellings Fair"	John Milton, c. 1630
"O God of Hosts, the Mighty Lord"	*Tate and Brady Psalter,* 1696
"Lord of the Worlds Above"	Isaac Watts, 1719
"How Lovely, Lord"	Arlo Duba, 1984

Psalm 87

"Jerusalem, the City on the Mountain"	Daniel Meeter, 1982

Psalm 90
"Our God, Our Help in Ages Past"   Isaac Watts
"Lord, You Have Been Our Dwelling Place"   Fred Anderson

Psalm 93
"God the Lord a King Remaineth"   John Keble, 1839

Psalm 95
"O Come Let Us Sing to the Lord"   Scottish Psalter, 1650
"Come Sound His Praise Abroad"   Isaac Watts
"Come, Sing with Joy to God"   Arlo Duba, 1984

Psalm 96
"O Sing a New Song"   Scottish Psalter, 1650

Psalm 98
"New Songs of Celebration"   Erik Routley

Psalm 100
"All People That on Earth Do Dwell"   Anglo-Genevan Psalter

Psalm 113
"Praise the Lord! You Servants of the Lord"   Marjorie Jillson, 1970
"Sing Praise unto the Name of God"   Fred Anderson, 1983

Psalm 117
"From All That Dwell Below the Skies"   Isaac Watts, 1719

Psalm 118
"Give Thanks unto the Lord, Jehovah"   Anonymous
"This Is the Day the Lord Hath Made"   Isaac Watts, 1719
"O Give Ye Thanks unto the Lord"   Murrayfield Psalms, 1954

Psalm 121
"Unto the Hills Around
    Do I Lift Up"   John Campbell, Duke of Argyle,
                                                        1877
"I to the Hills Will Lift Mine Eyes"   Scottish Psalter, 1650

Psalm 122
"O 'Twas a Joyful Sound to Hear"   Tate and Brady Psalter, 1696
"With Joy I Heard My Friends Exclaim"   The Psalter, 1912

Psalm 124
"Now Israel May Say"   The Psalter, 1912

Psalm 133
"How Beautiful the Sight"   James Montgomery, c. 1800
"Behold the Goodness of Our Lord"   Fred Anderson, 1986

Psalm 134
"Come, All You Servants of the Lord"   Arlo Duba, 1984

Psalm 136
"Let Us with a Gladsome Mind"   John Milton, 1624
"We Thank You Lord, for You Are Good"   John C. Dunn, 1985

Psalm 145
"O Lord, Thou Art My God and King"   *Scottish Psalter,* 1650
"My God, My King"   Isaac Watts, 1719
"O Lord, You Are My God and King"   *The Psalter,* 1912

Psalm 146
"I'll Praise My Maker"   John Wesley, c. 1750

Psalm 147
"Now Praise the Lord"   Fred Anderson, 1986

Psalm 148
"Praise Ye, Praise Ye the Lord"   *The Psalter,* 1912
"Praise Ye the Lord; Ye Heavens Adore Him"   Anonymous, 1796

Psalm 150
"Praise the Lord! His Glories Show"   H. F. Lyte, 1834
"Hallelujah! Hallelujah! In His Temple"   *The Psalter,* 1912

The proper use of psalmody in Christian worship requires a sense of balance. We have said this before, but it needs to be reemphasized. There must be a balance between the psalms of Israel and the hymns of the Church. It is a balance between promise and fulfillment; a balance between the old Israel and the new. It is a balance between remembering Solomon's Temple in ancient Jerusalem and catching sight of the heavenly Jerusalem coming down out of heaven. I like to begin the service with several psalms, and I like to conclude it with Christian hymns that marvel at God's redemptive work in Christ. If we praise God by recounting the types of Zion, then we should balance that with hymns that plainly set forth the fulfillment of these types in the gospel. If one begins a service by singing, with the *Tate and Brady Psalter,*

> O 'twas a joyful sound to hear
>   Our tribes devoutly say,
> Up Israel! to the temple haste,
>   And keep your festal day.
> At Salem's courts we must appear,
>   With our assembled powers
> In strong and beauteous order ranged,
>   Like her united towers,

then it is appropriate to end it with Wesley's

Ye servants of God,
　　your Master proclaim,
And publish abroad
　　His wonderful Name;
The Name, all-victorious,
　　of Jesus extol;
His Kingdom is glorious,
　　and rules over all.

Much of the power of psalmody is its ability to intimate, to point the finger at something not quite in view. One might say that it gets the ball rolling, which as it rolls along begins to gather up the Christian imagery. Thus it puts that imagery in its proper setting. Typology is a system of suggestive imagery. The worship of Solomon's temple heralds the heavenly worship we read about in the fourth and fifth chapters of Revelation. What a wonderful vision John shows us of that heavenly worship! And we live between the two, between the past and the future. Our worship should intimate both. The one should balance the other. It should be a two-sided inspiration.

A second way of working metrical psalmody into the service is to use it in that part of the service that directs our attention to prayers of supplication. It has often been noted that the Book of Psalms contains more prayers of lamentation than hymns of praise. It is as natural to sing our sorrows to God as it is to sing our praises. Anyone who has come to admire African-American spirituals is more than aware of this. A number of the favorites of all time in the history of psalm singing are psalms of lamentation. In the *Huguenot Psalter* the setting of Psalm 6, "Je te supply', O Sire," was known by everyone. "Aus tiefer Not," the German version of Psalm 130 written by Martin Luther, has remained a favorite of the German Church. In the Netherlands, "By the Waters of Babylon" has remained a favorite for centuries.

Crying has its rhythms and tempos every bit as much as rejoicing, and there are times when it is important to cry together — and to cry together before God. Before going to prayer the congregation might well sing that classic of the *Scottish Psalter*,

Lord, from the depths to Thee I cried:
　　My voice, Lord, do Thou hear:
Unto my supplication's voice
　　Give an attentive ear.

When it is sung slowly and in a meditative vein, this becomes a very moving lamentation. I am much more apt to use psalms of confession and lamentation as part of the service of daily prayer or at Sunday evening vespers than I am at the Lord's Day morning service. I always use this *Scottish Psalter* version of Psalm 130 to open the Maundy Thursday communion service. I would never use it to begin a Sunday morning service. Because it is the celebration of Christ's resurrection, the Sunday morning service is not the place for dwelling at great length on our sorrows. But one might well sing the first stanza of this psalm before the Prayers of Confession and Supplication even on Sunday morning.

One could easily put together a long list of metrical psalms suitable to accompany our prayers of supplication. The following list would only be a beginning.

Psalm 25
"Show Me Thy Ways"   *The Murrayfield Psalms*, 1954
"Lord to You My Soul Is Lifted"   Stanley Wiersma, 1980

Psalm 32
"How Blest Are They Whose Trespass"   *Rejoice in the Lord*, 1985

Psalm 42–43
"Like as the Hart for Water Brooks"   *Scottish Psalter*, 1650
"As Pants the Hart"   *Tate and Brady Psalter*, 1696
"Seeking Water, Seeking Shelter"   Erik Routley, 1974

Psalm 51
"God Be Merciful to Me"   *The Psalter*, 1912

Psalm 86
"To My Humble Supplication"   J. Bryan, c. 1620

Psalm 130
"Lord, from the Depths"   Martin Luther, 1524
"Lord, from the Depths"   *Scottish Psalter*, 1650
"From Out of the Depths I Cry"   *The Psalter*, 1912

Psalm 137
"By the Babylonian Rivers"   Ewald Bosh, 1964

The "penitential psalms," that is, Psalms 6, 32, 38, 51, 102, 130, and 143, have occupied a prominent place in the life of Christian devotion. It is not surprising that special attention has been given to providing suitable metrical versions of these psalms. They have been sung over and over again for centuries. When the time comes to cry before the Lord, as it regularly does in the Christian life, then it is appropriate to sing metrical versions of the psalms of lamentation, confession, and supplication.

A third and particularly treasured place for singing the metrical psalms, especially in those churches that take delight in maintaining the Reformed heritage, is at the celebration of the Lord's Supper. This will be discussed at greater length in the chapter on the communion prayers. Let it suffice here to relate a story of how this was first brought to my attention.

Back in the late 1950s I was spending the winter in Edinburgh. The boarding house in which I stayed was filled with students from the islands of Lewis and Skye. They were a high-spirited bunch, but on Sunday evening they all devoutly trooped off to St. George's West where Murdo Ewen MacDonald, the most Celtic of Scottish preachers, held forth the gospel in a melodious Highland brogue. This most conscientious of preachers would regularly invite students to his home after the evening service. The conversations we had with this dominie were always animated. I suppose it went along with the Gaelic spirit.

One time a young man from Skye asked the minister how he understood the singing of psalms in relation to singing songs "of human composure." That was the term he used. It was obvious that the young man, who wore the most beautiful tweed suit I have ever seen, felt that in a proper Scottish church service more psalms should be sung than we ordinarily sang at St. George's West. There was a good deal of soul searching, as I remember. The lads all knew in the bottoms of their hearts that psalm singing was genuine worship, but no one was about to throw out hymn singing either. I was surprised how animated the conversation was. That one should be so concerned about such a subject had never occurred to me before. Finally after a number of people had expressed their thoughts on the subject, Murdo Ewen MacDonald told us what his principles of psalm singing were. At regular services at least one hymn and at least one psalm were used. That left quite a bit of leeway, since typically a Scottish congregation will sing five selections in the course of a service. For the first selection, he told us, he invariably chose a metrical psalm. Sometimes the final selection was a psalm as well. He was particularly fond of using an obviously Christian paraphrase of a psalm at the end of the service. Nevertheless, in actual practice this usually meant that we sang more hymns than psalms. On the other hand when it came to the communion and the preparatory services before communion he never appointed anything but psalms.

Somehow that dictum has always stuck with me, like the tweeds I love to wear in winter — strong, simple, and long-lasting.

Prayers of Confession and Supplication

A full diet of Christian prayer naturally includes lamentations, confessions of sin, supplications for forgiveness, and petitions for the gifts of the Holy Spirit.

Reading through the Book of Psalms in our Bible we discover what a large portion of them are psalms of lamentation. In these prayers Israel cried before the Lord. There is considerably more to lamentation than confession of sin. Lamentations bewail before God the sorrows and sufferings that we all go through. Sometimes these psalms of lamentation are prayers of complaint. Sometimes they bewail the sins of others or complain of persecutions and hardships.

Psalms 42–43 are together one psalm and a good example of a lamentation that is not a confession of sin so much as a complaint:

> As a hart longs
> for flowing streams,
> so longs my soul
> for thee, O God.
> My soul thirsts for God,
> for the living God.
> When shall I come and behold
> the face of God?
> My tears have been my food
> day and night,
> while men say to me continually,
> "Where is your God?" Psalm 42:1-3

The psalmist complains here about persecution by the ungodly, by "deceitful and unjust men" (43:1). He recounts his pain: "Deep calls to deep at the thunder of thy cataracts; all thy waves and thy billows have gone over me" (42:7). The psalm is an expression of spiritual longing: "My soul *thirsts* for God." And yet the psalm is also an expression of hope. Three times the refrain comes back, "Hope in God; for I shall again praise him, my help and my God." We cry before God because in the end we have faith that God will deliver us. It is for this reason that prayers of confession and lamentation serve God's glory. It is for this reason that they are worship.

There are also psalms that are clear confessions of sin. The fifty-first Psalm has always been a favorite of Christians when they have felt weighed down by their sins. It expresses both our sorrow over the sins we have committed and our revulsion at sin in general.

> Have mercy on me, O God, according to thy steadfast love;
> according to thy abundant mercy blot out my transgressions.
> Wash me thoroughly from my iniquity,
> and cleanse me from my sin!
>
> For I know my transgressions,
> and my sin is ever before me.
> Against thee, thee only, have I sinned,
> and done that which is evil in thy sight,
> so that thou art justified in thy sentence
> and blameless in thy judgment.   Psalm 51:1-4

With confession of sin there is also supplication for mercy, but this prayer for mercy deals with the heart of the problem. It is prayer for the conversion of our whole being.

> Create in me a clean heart, O God,
> and put a new and right spirit within me.
> Cast me not away from thy presence,
> and take not thy holy Spirit from me.   Psalm 51:10-11

Christians have usually thought of this psalm as promising the inward presence of the Holy Spirit and the Spirit's ministry in anointing us with the Spirit's gifts so that we might not only be forgiven our sin, but *healed* of our sin as well.

The person reciting the psalm also makes a promise. To be recreated in God's image is to give one's life in the service of God.

> Then I will teach transgressors thy ways,
> and sinners will return to thee.
> Deliver me from bloodguiltiness, O God,
> thou God of my salvation,
> and my tongue will sing aloud of thy deliverance.
>   Psalm 51:13, 14

Here is a psalm that teaches us the nature of the Prayer of Confession. It is a good prayer to follow when we bring our sins before God.

Another psalm that serves as a good pattern is Psalm 130:

Out of the depths I cry to thee, O Lord!
    Lord, hear my voice!
Let thy ears be attentive
    to the voice of my supplications!

If thou, O Lord, shouldst mark iniquities,
    Lord, who could stand?
But there is forgiveness with thee,
    that thou mayest be feared.

I wait for the Lord, my soul waits,
    and in his word I hope;
my soul waits for the Lord
    more than watchmen for the morning,
    more than watchmen for the morning.

O Israel, hope in the Lord!
    For with the Lord there is steadfast love,
    and with him is plenteous redemption.
And he will redeem Israel
    from all his iniquities.

Two things stand out about this prayer. First there is the deep feeling of the lament. The words of this prayer evoke our own spiritual anguish when we know things are not right between us and God. Second there is the assurance of pardon, the rock-bottom confidence that "with the Lord there is steadfast love, and with him is plenteous redemption."

There is an important theological point involved here. These psalms make it clear that worship must include recognition of our sin. This is difficult for our age, but without it our worship lacks integrity. It is a matter of honesty. God is offended by sin, and yet he accepts sinners. As the psalm we have just quoted puts it, "If thou, O Lord, shouldst mark iniquity, Lord, who could stand? But there is forgiveness with thee that thou mayest be feared." Honesty demands that when we approach God sin be confessed. Otherwise we have an uneasy conscience about it, and, even worse, we compromise the holiness of God.

The prayers of lamentation and confession among the psalms express an important theological truth — humankind is a fallen creature and in need of redemption. As much as secular humanists would like to sweep all this under the rug, the cries of our fallen race are to be heard all about us. We need only to listen to country-western radio or to watch the television news. We are, like it or not, terribly conscious of our sin. If our worship is to be realistic, it must deal with these cries. Surely this is one of the reasons that the psalms have been used as Christian prayer so universally. They express the fact that we are creatures of need. They express our human fallibility, which is such an important aspect of the Christian doctrine of humankind. In fact, a theology that does not recognize our fallibility has lost touch with humanity as it really is.

But these psalms also point to another theological affirmation: God is holy and has created us to reflect his holiness. The holiness of God is in the end our highest hope. At the heart of the universe there is truth, justice, and peace. And that will not be compromised! It is what holiness is all about. We rejoice in the holiness of God because it will not be sullied, smeared, or confused. Holiness is a radiant light, a never-ending day whose sun will not go down.

This aspect of prayer is perhaps more private than public, yet there has usually been some sort of expression of it in public worship. We gather from a number of psalms that the Israelites said penitential prayers on entering the temple for worship. Psalm 24 asks "Who shall ascend the hill of the LORD? And who shall stand in his holy place?" and answers "He who has clean hands and a pure heart, who does not lift up his soul to what is false, and does not swear deceitfully" (vv. 3-4). Scholars have suggested that this points to some sort of penitential rite carried out as one entered the temple. Certainly the Book of Psalms itself contains a great number of prayers of lamentation, and no doubt they were used in the temple and were therefore public worship.

After the destruction of Solomon's temple and the spiritually sobering experience of the Babylonian Captivity, a very particular prayer of confession began to develop. We find a good example of this in the ninth chapter of Nehemiah. There we are told how Ezra formulated a prayer of confession for the whole people of Israel. The prayer of confession in the ninth chapter of Daniel is another example of this genre of prayer in which the sins of the whole people are confessed before God. These are not private prayers of confession but public, corporate prayers of confession. They are obviously intended for worship by the whole congregation.

Prayers for forgiveness of sin are a fundamental element in Christian prayer. One thinks immediately of the Lord's Prayer, where we find the petition "Forgive us our debts." We remember as well the parable of the tax collector and the Pharisee who went to the temple to pray. It was the prayer of that sinner, who humbly confessed his sin to God, that was accepted, not the self-affirming prayer of the Pharisee. In his Passion Jesus himself prayed the psalms of lamentation. When he offered himself up on the cross in that perfect act of worship, he presented to the Father the psalms of lamentation that Israel had prayed for a thousand years, and in those psalms were the cries of all humanity.

Interestingly enough, the services of worship of the earliest Christian Church give little indication of a prayer of confession of sin and supplication for mercy within the ordinary Lord's Day service. This genre of prayer was developed, rather, in the weekday prayer services, which were such an important part of the early Church's worship. The emphasis of the prayers for the Sunday service was on intercession. It was not until the time of Gregory the Great, in the late sixth century, that confessions and supplications became a regular part of the liturgy. The *kyrie eleison* was originally understood more as this kind of prayer. In time the *confiteor,* quite explictly a prayer of confession, was added to the Mass. At the close of the patristic age monastic prayer, which gave an important place to penitential prayer, came to have ever greater importance in shaping the prayer disciplines of the Church. During the Middle Ages, the penitential psalms occupied a place of great importance in the prayer life of the Church. For centuries, monks recited the fifty-first Psalm as a prayer of confession at the beginning of each day. In popular devotion as well, the penitential psalms played an imposing role in the prayer life of those who were outside the monastic communities.

At the time of the Reformation, the whole concept of confession changed considerably. The Reformers wrote new prayers of confession based on what they understood to be a more biblical understanding of the nature of sin and repentance. The most important of these prayers was developed for the Reformed Church of Strasbourg by its Reformer, Martin Bucer. He based this prayer on the prayer of confession in Daniel 9, working into it thoughts and expressions from some of the penitential psalms and from passages in the New Testament. This prayer then served as a pattern for the Prayer of Confession used in Geneva, for the confession written by Thomas Cranmer for the *Book of Common Prayer* of the Church of England, and for the Prayer of Confession in John Knox's *Book of Common Order*. It was this same pattern that the famous Puritan divine Richard Baxter followed when he composed his Prayer of Confession for the *Reformed Liturgy* of 1661.

At the beginning of the eighteenth century, Matthew Henry in his *Method of Prayer* very carefully worked out what should be included in a Prayer of Confession. He emphasized that such a prayer should confess both our sinful nature and our particular sins, both our sin and our sins. Henry was a great biblical expositor. He went through the whole Bible studying all the prayers of confession he could find. He obviously studied the psalms of lamentation and the confessions of Daniel and Ezra, which we have already mentioned. He also gave particular attention to Isaiah's confession, Job's meditations on the nature of sin and forgiveness, the parables of Jesus on the nature of repentance, and Paul's meditations on prevenient grace. As Henry understood it, our prayers of confession should express our humility before God. "We must acknowledge the great reason we have to lie very low before God, and to be ashamed of ourselves when we come into his presence . . ." (p. 12). We should lament our fallen nature, our constant inclination toward sin. About such things the people of God have always wept, and this weeping before God is of the essence of the Prayer of Confession. The Prayer of Confession should both lament and confess. It should confess both our trangressions and our sins of omission. But it should also confess our "impatience and murmuring under our afflictions, our inordinate dejection, and distrust of God and his providence" (p. 16). Our prayers of confession should bewail sin, recognize its deceitful nature and expose its unprofitableness. Finally our prayers of confession should give glory to God for his patience and mercy.

Isaac Watts, a leading English Congregational minister at the beginning of the eighteenth century, teaches us in a similar line. He shows that there is a strong continuity between our prayers of confession and our petitions for God's mercy. As he sees it, our prayers should include "a confession or humble representation of our wants and sorrows of every kind" (*A Guide to Prayer,* p. 20). God is more than willing to hear of our necessities and troubles. He is even willing to hear our complaints, for he loves us even in our misery. We need to pray for deliverance from evil in all its forms, both temporal and spiritual. "O Lord, take away the guilt of our sins by the atonement of Thine own Son. Subdue the power of our iniquities by

Thine own Spirit. Deliver us from the natural darkness of our own minds, from the corruption of our hearts, and perverse tendencies of our appetites and passions" (p. 21). Watts continues by saying that we should also pray for the good we want to receive, "for the pardon of all our iniquities for the sake of the great atonement, the death of our Redeemer. . . . We pray for the sanctification of our natures by His Holy Spirit, . . . we pray for the consolation of the Spirit of God, that he would work faith, and love, and every grace in our hearts" (p. 21). Watts understands that confession leads very naturally to supplication.

It has become traditional in many American congregations for the Prayer of Confession to be said in unison by the whole congregation. (It has been my own practice to use one of these prayers of confession regularly, so that the congregation will know it by heart and not have to read it from the printed page.) There are some good things about this practice of unison prayer and some bad things about it. Use of a unison prayer helps drive home the corporate nature of our prayer. Use of one of the classic prayers of confession underlines the universality of our need for repentance. Secular humanism may be offended by our crying to God in time of need, but there is something inescapably human about that cry, nevertheless. It expresses a basic human need, and to this Christians have witnessed century after century.

On the other hand the pattern of a unison Prayer of Confession followed immediately by an Assurance of Pardon can get a bit perfunctory. In my first congregation I developed the practice of adding to the unison confession a series of supplications to elaborate the general themes of confession of sin and supplication for pardon. I always thought that was a good way of doing it, but my second congregation was rather unsympathetic to the idea.

In that first congregation I also got into the habit of using the prayer of Henry van Dyke on most occasions because it is so familiar. I also felt that it was important to maintain a continuity with the best work of an older generation. Many of the prayers of Henry van Dyke and Louis F. Benson found in the *Book of Common Worship* of 1932 have already become traditional for many in our country. Those two men were pioneers of liturgical reform. Van Dyke, a professor of English literature at Princeton University, had considerable gifts as a writer. Benson was about as good a liturgical historian as America has produced. Their prayers are the product not only of good historical research but also of a great love for the Church's worship. They have already won a sort of general acceptance, and it seems to be good, therefore, to use their prayers regularly.

With many of the same considerations I began to use at communion services the Prayer of Confession found in the *Genevan Psalter*. I used the Genevan confession at the beginning of the service and the Genevan Post-Communion Thanksgiving Prayer at the end of the service, with the whole congregation saying both as general prayers. It gave a sort of symmetry to the service and reinforced the historical continuity as well.

The prayers of van Dyke, Benson, and the *Genevan Psalter* and several other prayers of confession have been included among the samples below.

One is an abridged version of Daniel's prayer of confession, to which I have added an Assurance of Pardon from the eighth chapter of Romans. There is also an abridged version of Richard Baxter's Prayer of Confession and several others to which I have added assurances of pardon.

In the course of my ministry I have found myself having to work with some very different expectations. Often one finds that any kind of unison prayer is thought of as much too formal. The first nine prayers in the following collection are designed for such a situation.

One more word needs to be said about the supplications that I have developed to follow the unison Prayer of Confession. These prayers were at the time particularly well received by my congregation, because, I think, they were the fruit of my own study, meditation, and prayer. Each prayer represents a fresh study of some biblical prayer. The synagogue had in the time of Christ drawn up a list of the heroes and heroines of prayer. Elijah was considered a particularly important model of prayer. Scripture does not tell with what words he prayed, at least not fully. But the stories of Elijah do teach us much about prayer, and the Church has followed his example in its prayer ever since. The whole story of Elijah can be regarded as a catechism on prayer. Hannah was regarded as a woman mighty in prayer. In fact the whole story of Hannah's prayer and its answer shows us much about how prayer was carried out in an ancient Israelite sanctuary. One can learn a great deal about prayer from the Book of Daniel. The highly philosophical meditations of Job were obviously understood as prayer, as were the confessions of Jeremiah. A study of these prayers can teach us much about leading in prayer.

Confession and Supplication 1 ————

(based on Psalm 6)

Holy God, Lord most gracious!

Rebuke us not in your anger,
nor chasten us in your wrath!

Holy you are, and we cannot stand in your presence.

Yet you have called us to come to you.
We feel unworthy,
for we have failed you again and again.

We feel like running away,
yet you keep calling us.

Have mercy on us, O God.
Have mercy!

Holy God, Father most gracious!

Rebuke us not in your anger,
nor chasten us in your wrath!

Heal us from our sin,
for we are troubled.

Deliver us for the sake of your steadfast love.

Our sins trouble us, O God.
We are troubled by how they have hurt others.
We are troubled by how they have hurt us.

Your ways are right! O righteous God!
and whenever we have refused to follow them
we have found out how right they are.

Have mercy on us, O God.
Have mercy!

Holy God, God and Father of our Lord Jesus Christ,
Have mercy on us for the sake of your Son,
who died to free us from our sins.

To you be honor and glory! *Amen.*

Confession and Supplication 2 ————

(based on Psalm 10)

Arise, O LORD; O God, lift up your hand.
  Forget not the afflicted.

    We call to you in our sorrow and frustration,
      Lord God, eternal, everlasting God.
    Why do you stand so far off?
    Why do you hide yourself in times of trouble?
      You are our God,
        even if we have ignored you!

Arise, O LORD; O God, we cry to you.

    It looks like evil is winning out.
    Even in our own lives sin keeps winning the battles.

      "So I find it to be a law, that when I want to do right,
        evil lies close at hand . . . making me captive to sin
          . . . wretched man that I am."   Romans 7:21-25

    Have mercy on us, O God,
      for we are sinners, captives to sin, enslaved by sin!

Arise, O LORD; O God, lift up your hand.
  Forget not the afflicted.

    Bring us into your presence
        and fill us with your Spirit,
          your Holy Spirit.
    Make us constantly aware of your presence,
        for you are not far off.
    Give us the character of those
        who are always near you.
    Give us the radiance of holiness,
        the joy of holiness,
          the peace of holiness.

In the name of Jesus, our Immanuel, we present our prayers,
    and to him, together with you, O Father,
    be all glory, now and evermore. *Amen.*

Confession and Supplication 3 ——————

(based on Psalm 22)

Our God, our God,
>   have you really forsaken us?

>>   Why are you so far away from where we need you?
        Why do you not pay attention to what seems to us
            so alarming?
        Why are you so otherworldly?

>   Day and night we have cried to you,
        and you do not seem to answer.

O God, Holy God,
>   you are holy, enthroned on the praises of Israel.

>   In you our fathers trusted;
        they trusted and you delivered them.

>   You are a trustworthy God,
        and when we have trusted in you
            we have not been disappointed.

O God, trustworthy God,
>   that is our problem!

>>   We do not always trust you.
        We are always afraid that if we follow your ways
            we will miss something.

>   Yet you are holy, and wholly trustworthy.
        It is you who brought us from our mother's womb.
        It is you who kept us safely on her breasts.

Our God, our God,
>   grant us faith — faith to trust you,
        faith to follow your ways.

>   Grant us faith in Christ,
        for it is in Him and through Him
            that we make our prayer to you.

Glory be to you, O God, our God. *Amen.*

Confession and Supplication 4 —————

(based on Psalms 42 and 43)

For you, O God, we long.
For you our souls thirst, O ever living God.

> You are our life and the source of all life.
> Oh, that we might see your face and live.
> > Our spirits are disquieted, and yet we hope in you.

Of you, O God, we have happy memories.
Our delight is in you, O wondrous, glorious God.

> We remember those times when we sensed your presence.
> We remember the joy of being in your holy temple.
> > Our hope is in you, that again we might praise you.

> O God, strengthen our hope;
> > feed us on your word, and increase our faith.

O God, our God, brilliant, splendorous God.

> Send out your light and your truth.
> > Let them lead us.
> > Let them bring us to your holy hill
> > > and to your dwelling.

> Anoint us with your Holy Spirit,
> > that we sense the truth.

> Reveal Christ in our midst,
> > that we sense his leading,
> > that we listen to his Word,
> > that we recognize his call.

> Bring us to your holy mountain,
> > to your heavenly dwelling on high,
> > to yourself.

Through Jesus Christ,
> the Way, the Truth, and the Life,
> > to whom be all glory.
Together with you, O Father, and the Holy Spirit,
> One God forever. *Amen.*

Confession and Supplication 5 ——————

(based on Psalm 51)

Have mercy on us, O God,
    according to your steadfast love;
    according to your abundant mercy.
O God, blot out our transgressions!

    We know our sin only too well.
      It is painful to us
      and offensive to you.

    We would be holy,
      but sin keeps getting in our way.

Have mercy on us, O God.
Have mercy!

    For your love is steadfast;
      your covenant is an eternal covenant.

    You are our God,
      and therefore we cry out when sin gets the better of us.
      And it does get the better of us,
        even when we do not want it that way.

Have mercy on us, O God.
Have mercy!

    Send your Holy Spirit,
      that our spirits be renewed through your Spirit.

    Send forth your Holy Spirit,
      that our lives may be recreated in the image of Christ,
      that at last we may be the men and women you always intended.

Have mercy on us, O God,
    through Jesus Christ,
    ever seated at your right hand.
And to you be all glory,
      Father, Son, and Holy Spirit,
One God, forever. *Amen.*

Confession and Supplication 6 ———

(based on Psalm 69)

O Lord God of Hosts,
  we, your people, are afflicted and in pain.

Let your salvation, O God, set us on high!

  We have come into deep waters,
    and the flood sweeps over us.
  We are weary with our crying.
    Our eyes grow dim waiting for you our God.

  Why are you always so slow?

  We wait for you to help us,
    for you are our God,
    but it seems we have been waiting a long time!

  Why are you always so slow?

O Lord God of Hosts,
  you know our folly.

  The wrongs we have done are not hidden from you.
  You seem to love us in spite of our sin.
  You are our God and we are your people!

O Lord God of Hosts,
  we are afflicted and in pain,
    and yet we are still your people.

  We have been foolish,
    and turned aside from your ways,
    and yet you are still our God.

Let your salvation, O God, set us on high!

Salvation, honor, and glory be to you,
  O Lord God of Hosts,
Father, Son and Holy Spirit,
  One God, forever. *Amen.*

Confession and Supplication 7 ————

(based on Psalm 77)

We cry aloud to you, O God,
    that you might hear us.

        The troubles of our time disturb us.
        We meditate on you, O God, and on your purposes.

        We wonder if our sins have utterly cut us off from you.
        We wonder if we have committed some sort of unforgivable sin.

            Will you spurn us forever, O God,
            and never again be favorable?

O God, you wonder worker!
    We meditate on your saving acts:
        liberation from slavery in Egypt,
        redemption from Babylon.

    You are a wonder worker!
        Clean up our lives!
        Take out the trash!
        Scrub our hearts!
        Scour our minds,
            that we might be your faithful servants.

O God, your way is holy!
    You are a holy God,
        and you have promised to make us a holy people.

        Fulfill your promises, O holy God.
        Pour out on us the purifying fire of righteousness and justice.
        Unite us to Christ,
            that we might be holy as he is holy.

For it is in Christ Jesus that we come to you,
    God and Father of our Lord Jesus Christ.

To you be glory now and ever more. *Amen.*

Confession and Supplication 8 ——————

(based on Psalm 137)

O God, our guard and guide,
    even when your people sit weeping by the waters of Babylon,
    you are still our guard and guide
        in every exile and captivity,
O everlasting God.

O God, our guard and guide,
    have mercy on us,
        for we have wandered away from your purposes.

        We had not intended to have strayed so far away,
            but we did,
        and now our seemingly innocent wandering
            has become a hopeless captivity.

O God, our guard and guide,
    have mercy on us,
        for we too easily took for granted
            your pleasant courts,
            your temple,
            the sanctuary of your presence,
        and now we hang our harps on the weeping willows
        and yearn to return to our spiritual home

O God, our guard and guide,
    have mercy on us.

        Receive us again, O God, our Father,
            for in Christ we are your sons and daughters,
            and it is in his name we pray.

For in him and through him be all glory to you, O Father,
    now and evermore. *Amen.*

Confession and Supplication 9 —————

(based on Psalm 139)

O LORD, all knowing, most wise God!
   Our Father,

      you have searched me and known me.
      You have looked into the deepest desires of my heart.
      You know my secret loyalties as well as my hesitations.
      You know my doubts and my reservations.

All knowing and still all loving Father,
   have mercy on us,

      for we have gotten confused.
      We love you and we love your ways,
         yet we have loved this world, too.

O LORD, our Father,
   have mercy on us.

      We have been wayward.
      We have fled your presence.
      We have even made our bed in Hell,
         and somehow you discovered us there, too.

All knowing and still all loving Father,
   have mercy on us.

O LORD, all knowing, most wise God.
   Our Father, have mercy on us!

      Grant to us purity of heart.
         Focus our erratic desires.
         Unite us in Christ.

      Grant that in him we may find integrity,
         that our hearts may be yours and yours alone.

To Christ, our Savior, then,
   be all praise, all honor and glory,
   together with you, O Father and the Holy Spirit.

      One God, now and evermore. *Amen.*

Confession and Supplication 10 ——————

(based on Daniel 9:4-19)

Let us confess our sin to God:

Most holy and merciful Father; we acknowledge and confess before thee our sinful nature — prone to evil and slothful in good — and all our shortcomings and offenses. Thou alone knowest how often we have sinned in wandering from thy way, in wasting thy gifts, in forgetting thy love. But thou, O Lord, have mercy on us, who are ashamed and sorry for all wherein we have displeased thee. Teach us to hate our errors, cleanse us from our secret faults, and forgive our sins for the sake of thy dear Son. And O most holy and loving Father, help us, we beseech thee, to live in thy light and walk in thy ways, according to the commandments of Jesus Christ our Lord. *Amen.*

Henry van Dyke

O Lord, great God,
    all holy, Father most gracious,
    filled with mercy and steadfast love,

        We are embarrassed to come before you,
            for we have preferred
                the ways of this world
                    to your ways,

            for we have rebelled against
                your wisdom
                    and we have gotten
                    into trouble,

            for we have rejected your
                fatherly guidance
                    and have gotten lost altogether.

    And therefore we are embarrassed.
        To you belongs righteousness, O Lord,
            and to us confusion of face.

O Lord, great God,
    all holy, filled with awe,
 Father, most gracious,
    filled with mercy and steadfast love.

        Incline your ear to our troubles.
        Hear us when we pour out our sorrows before you.

Forgive us,
    not on the ground of our own righteousness,
    but on the ground of your great mercy.
    On the ground of your great mercy
        in the gift of your Son,
            Jesus Christ.

It is in his name that we pray,
    for he is our Savior
        and the mediator of the covenant of grace. *Amen.*

Hear the Gospel of Christ:

This is the message we have heard from him and proclaim to you, that God is light and in him is no darkness at all. . . . If we walk in the light, as he is in the light, we have fellowship with one another, and the blood of Jesus his Son cleanses us from all sin. . . . If we confess our sins, he is faithful and just, and will forgive our sins and cleanse us from all unrighteousness. . . . We have an advocate with the Father, Jesus Christ the righteous; and he is the expiation for our sins, and not for ours only but also for the sins of the whole world.

I John 1:5, 7, 9; 2:1-2

O for a thousand tongues to sing
    My great Redeemer's praise.
The glories of my God and King,
    The triumphs of His grace.

Charles Wesley

Confession and Supplication 11 ————

(based on Daniel 9:4-19)

Let us confess our sin to God:

Most holy and merciful Father; we acknowledge and confess before thee our sinful nature — prone to evil and slothful in good — and all our shortcomings and offenses. Thou alone knowest how often we have sinned in wandering from thy way, in wasting thy gifts, in forgetting thy love. But thou, O Lord, have mercy on us, who are ashamed and sorry for all wherein we have displeased thee. Teach us to hate our errors, cleanse us from our secret faults, and forgive our sins for the sake of thy dear Son. And O most holy and loving Father, help us, we beseech thee, to live in thy light and walk in thy ways, according to the commandments of Jesus Christ our Lord. *Amen.*

Henry van Dyke

O Lord,
    great God,
        whom we behold in awe and wonder,
        who has kept covenant and steadfast love with your people
                from age to age.

We have sinned and done wrong
        and acted wickedly and rebelled,
            turning aside from your
                commandments and ordinances.

We have known in our hearts
        what is right,
            and yet we did wrong anyway.

We have been fascinated by evil,
        delighted with pleasing ourselves,
            satisfying our desires,
                pampering ourselves with pleasures.

O Lord,
    great God,
        have mercy on us
            according to your steadfast love.

We know you are a God
        who delights in goodness.
        Grant that we too might delight in goodness.

We know you are a God
who rejoices in peace and justice.
Grant that we might be at peace with ourselves
and each other.

O Lord,
great God,
grant that our hearts might be filled with a love of justice.
with peace beyond understanding,
with patience, with joy.

These prayers we present to you, O Father,
in the name of Jesus,
the Lamb who was slain
and yet lives forever more. *Amen.*

Hear the Gospel of Christ:

This is the message we have heard from him and proclaim to you, that God is light and in him is no darkness at all. . . . If we walk in the light, as he is in the light, we have fellowship with one another, and the blood of Jesus his Son cleanses us from all sin. . . . If we confess our sins, he is faithful and just, and will forgive our sins and cleanse us from all unrighteousness. . . . We have an advocate with the Father, Jesus Christ the righteous; and he is the expiation for our sins, and not for ours only but also for the sins of the whole world.

I John 1:5, 7, 9; 2:1-2

O for a thousand tongues to sing
My great Redeemer's praise.
The glories of my God and King,
The triumphs of His grace.

Charles Wesley

Confession and Supplication 12 ——————

(based on Daniel 9:4-19)

Let us confess our sin to God:

Most holy and merciful Father; we acknowledge and confess before thee our sinful nature — prone to evil and slothful in good — and all our shortcomings and offenses. Thou alone knowest how often we have sinned in wandering from thy way, in wasting thy gifts, in forgetting thy love. But thou, O Lord, have mercy on us, who are ashamed and sorry for all wherein we have displeased thee. Teach us to hate our errors, cleanse us from our secret faults, and forgive our sins for the sake of thy dear Son. And O most holy and loving Father, help us, we beseech thee, to live in thy light and walk in thy ways, according to the commandments of Jesus Christ our Lord. *Amen.*

Henry van Dyke

O Lord, merciful Father,
> you keep covenant and steadfast love
>> with those who love you
>>> and keep your commandments.

> We confess that
>> we have not listened to your servants
>>> the prophets.
>> We have not heeded your law
>>> nor have we rejoiced in your gospel.

> We confess that
>> things have fallen apart.
>> What your servants have warned us about
>>> has come to pass.

O Lord,
> you do keep covenant
>> even when we do not.
> Your love is steadfast
>> when ours is frail and fallible.
> You are faithful
>> even when we are faithless.

O Lord, merciful Father,
  you keep covenant and steadfast love
    with those who love you
      and keep your commandments.

We *do* want you to be our God
  and we *do* want to be your
    covenant people.

Grant us the gift of faith.

By your Holy Spirit
  work in us steadfastness
    and singleness of heart,
      that we might manifest your love
        in the keeping of your commandments
        and the living of your gospel.

O Lord, merciful Father,
  hear our prayers in the name
    of your well-beloved Son, Jesus Christ,
      the mediator of the new and eternal covenant,
    to whom be glory for ever and ever. *Amen.*

Hear the Gospel of Christ:

This is the message we have heard from him and proclaim to you,
that God is light and in him is no darkness at all. . . . If we walk in the
light, as he is in the light, we have fellowship with one another, and
the blood of Jesus his Son cleanses us from all sin. . . . If we confess
our sins, he is faithful and just, and will forgive our sins and cleanse
us from all unrighteousness. . . . We have an advocate with the Father,
Jesus Christ the righteous; and he is the expiation for our sins, and
not for ours only but also for the sins of the whole world.
                                                   I John 1:5, 7, 9; 2:1-2

O for a thousand tongues to sing
  My great Redeemer's praise.
The glories of my God and King,
  The triumphs of His grace.
                                                   Charles Wesley

Confession and Supplication 13 ——————

(based on Nehemiah 9:6-37)

Let us confess our sin to God:

> Most holy and merciful Father; we acknowledge and confess before thee our sinful nature — prone to evil and slothful in good — and all our shortcomings and offenses. Thou alone knowest how often we have sinned in wandering from thy way, in wasting thy gifts, in forgetting thy love. But thou, O Lord, have mercy on us, who are ashamed and sorry for all wherein we have displeased thee. Teach us to hate our errors, cleanse us from our secret faults, and forgive our sins for the sake of thy dear Son. And O most holy and loving Father, help us, we beseech thee, to live in thy light and walk in thy ways, according to the commandments of Jesus Christ our Lord. *Amen.*
>
> Henry van Dyke

You are the LORD and you alone!
>   You have made heaven,
>   the heaven of heavens with all their host,
>   the earth and all that is on it,
>   the seas and all that is in them,
>   and you preserve them all.

You have called us to yourself
>   and given us a covenant.
>   You have become our God
>   and made us your people,
>   and yet we have turned away from you.
>   We have rebelled against you.

You have delivered us many times
>   according to your covenant mercies.

>   You have warned us,
>   and yet we have acted presumptuously.
>   You have sent us prophets,
>   and we have turned a stubborn shoulder
>   and stiffened our necks
>   and would not obey your law.

You are the LORD and you alone.
You are our God, great and mighty.

You keep covenant and steadfast love.

We deplore our sins before you,
and before each other.
They have only gotten us into trouble.
They have only enslaved us.
They have not given us the happiness they promised.

Deliver us from our sin
and the power and attraction of sin.

Through the faithful suffering and death
of our Savior Jesus Christ,
whose intercession we plead,
and in whose name we pray. *Amen.*

Hear the Gospel of Christ:

This is the message we have heard from him and proclaim to you, that God is light and in him is no darkness at all. . . . If we walk in the light, as he is in the light, we have fellowship with one another, and the blood of Jesus his Son cleanses us from all sin. . . . If we confess our sins, he is faithful and just, and will forgive our sins and cleanse us from all unrighteousness. . . . We have an advocate with the Father, Jesus Christ the righteous; and he is the expiation for our sins, and not for ours only but also for the sins of the whole world.

I John 1:5, 7, 9; 2:1-2

O for a thousand tongues to sing
My great Redeemer's praise.
The glories of my God and King,
The triumphs of His grace.

Charles Wesley

Confession and Supplication 14 ————

(based on Isaiah 6)

Let us confess our sin to God:

Most holy and merciful Father; we acknowledge and confess before thee our sinful nature — prone to evil and slothful in good — and all our shortcomings and offenses. Thou alone knowest how often we have sinned in wandering from thy way, in wasting thy gifts, in forgetting thy love. But thou, O Lord, have mercy on us, who are ashamed and sorry for all wherein we have displeased thee. Teach us to hate our errors, cleanse us from our secret faults, and forgive our sins for the sake of thy dear Son. And O most holy and loving Father, help us, we beseech thee, to live in thy light and walk in thy ways, according to the commandments of Jesus Christ our Lord. *Amen.*

Henry van Dyke

Holy, Holy, Holy you are,
   O LORD of hosts.
The whole earth is full of your glory.

>Your holiness frightens us.
>   It fills us with awe.
>   It fills us with wonder.

>What else can we do but fall down before you
>   and confess our woe?

>We are lost.
>We are a people of unclean lips
>   and unclean thoughts.

>The light of your holiness only reveals the darkness of our sin.

Holy, Holy, Holy you are,
   O LORD of hosts.
The whole earth is full of your glory.

>Your holiness is white hot,
>   converting our sin.

>Send your seraphim to us
>   with burning coals from your altar,

>that our guilt be taken away,
>   and our sin forgiven.

Holy, Holy, Holy you are,
   O Lord of hosts.

      Your holiness is frightening,
         all consuming, fascinating.

      Sanctify us to your service.

      Make us holy,
         that we might be your people.
         that we might reflect your glory
            and serve your glory.

In the name of Jesus we pray,
   who ever stands before the altar of heaven,

      our mediator,
         who presents before your holy majesty
         our prayer and supplication,
            now and evermore. *Amen.*

Hear the Gospel of Christ:

   This is the message we have heard from him and proclaim to you,
that God is light and in him is no darkness at all. . . . If we walk in the
light, as he is in the light, we have fellowship with one another, and
the blood of Jesus his Son cleanses us from all sin. . . . If we confess
our sins, he is faithful and just, and will forgive our sins and cleanse
us from all unrighteousness. . . . We have an advocate with the Father,
Jesus Christ the righteous; and he is the expiation for our sins, and
not for ours only but also for the sins of the whole world.
                                             I John 1:5, 7, 9; 2:1-2

O for a thousand tongues to sing
   My great Redeemer's praise.
The glories of my God and King,
   The triumphs of His grace.

                                             Charles Wesley

Confession and Supplication 15 —————

(based on Job 7)

Let us confess our sin to God:

Most holy and merciful Father; we acknowledge and confess before thee our sinful nature — prone to evil and slothful in good — and all our shortcomings and offenses. Thou alone knowest how often we have sinned in wandering from thy way, in wasting thy gifts, in forgetting thy love. But thou, O Lord, have mercy on us, who are ashamed and sorry for all wherein we have displeased thee. Teach us to hate our errors, cleanse us from our secret faults, and forgive our sins for the sake of thy dear Son. And O most holy and loving Father, help us, we beseech thee, to live in thy light and walk in thy ways, according to the commandments of Jesus Christ our Lord. *Amen.*

Henry van Dyke

O LORD of hosts!
    Look on the affliction of your servants
        and remember us.

        We pour out our souls to you
            because by our own efforts we have failed.

        Nothing we have tried has worked.

        We have tried again and again
            and still we have failed.

O LORD of hosts!
    Look on the affliction of your servants
        and remember us.

        Save us from the embarrassment
            of our failure.

        Save us from envy of those
            who have so obviously succeeded.

    Grant us some signs of success,
        that we not always be ashamed.

O LORD of hosts!
    Look on the affliction of your servants
        and remember us.

You know our need.
You know our diligence,
    our anguish, our works.

You know that without your mercy
    we can do nothing.

Grant us your mercy,
    for the sake of your Son,
        Jesus Christ our Savior. *Amen.*

Hear the Gospel of Christ:

This is the message we have heard from him and proclaim to you, that God is light and in him is no darkness at all. . . . If we walk in the light, as he is in the light, we have fellowship with one another, and the blood of Jesus his Son cleanses us from all sin. . . . If we confess our sins, he is faithful and just, and will forgive our sins and cleanse us from all unrighteousness. . . . We have an advocate with the Father, Jesus Christ the righteous; and he is the expiation for our sins, and not for ours only but also for the sins of the whole world.

I John 1:5, 7, 9; 2:1-2

O for a thousand tongues to sing
    My great Redeemer's praise.
The glories of my God and King,
    The triumphs of His grace.

Charles Wesley

Confession and Supplication 16 ————

(Elijah at the Brook Cherith, I Kings 17)

Let us confess our sin to God:

Most holy and merciful Father; we acknowledge and confess before thee our sinful nature — prone to evil and slothful in good — and all our shortcomings and offenses. Thou alone knowest how often we have sinned in wandering from thy way, in wasting thy gifts, in forgetting thy love. But thou, O Lord, have mercy on us, who are ashamed and sorry for all wherein we have displeased thee. Teach us to hate our errors, cleanse us from our secret faults, and forgive our sins for the sake of thy dear Son. And O most holy and loving Father, help us, we beseech thee, to live in thy light and walk in thy ways, according to the commandments of Jesus Christ our Lord. *Amen.*

Henry van Dyke

LORD, our God!
> You are our God when things are going well.
> You are our God when things are not.

> Right now things are pretty slow.

>> The spiritual climate is hot and dry.
>> Nothing is going on,
>> and here we sit, waiting.

> Waiting on you, O LORD, our God.

LORD, our God!
> You are faithful even in our times of waiting.
> You are patient and time is in your hands.

>> But we find it so hard to be patient,
>>> and time is on our hands.
>> We try to keep busy,
>>> but we are waiting.

> Waiting on you, O LORD, our God.

LORD, our God!
> You are a fulfilling God.
> You bring our times of waiting to their end.

>> Have mercy on us, O God,
>>> faithful God.

Fulfill your promises of fulfillment,
that we might know that our waiting
was not in vain.

Help us to recognize
that Christ has come,
that he is the first and the last,
the ever present Lord.

Help us to wait in him
who has come already
and is always with us!
even Jesus Christ.
Amen and *Amen*.

Hear the Gospel of Christ:

This is the message we have heard from him and proclaim to you,
that God is light and in him is no darkness at all. . . . If we walk in the
light, as he is in the light, we have fellowship with one another, and
the blood of Jesus his Son cleanses us from all sin. . . . If we confess
our sins, he is faithful and just, and will forgive our sins and cleanse
us from all unrighteousness. . . . We have an advocate with the Father,
Jesus Christ the righteous; and he is the expiation for our sins, and
not for ours only but also for the sins of the whole world.

I John 1:5, 7, 9; 2:1-2

O for a thousand tongues to sing
My great Redeemer's praise.
The glories of my God and King,
The triumphs of His grace.

Charles Wesley

Confession and Supplication 17 ————

(Elijah prays on Mount Carmel, I Kings 18)

Most holy and merciful Father; we acknowledge and confess before thee our sinful nature — prone to evil and slothful in good — and all our shortcomings and offenses. Thou alone knowest how often we have sinned in wandering from thy way, in wasting thy gifts, in forgetting thy love. But thou, O Lord, have mercy on us, who are ashamed and sorry for all wherein we have displeased thee. Teach us to hate our errors, cleanse us from our secret faults, and forgive our sins for the sake of thy dear Son. And O most holy and loving Father, help us, we beseech thee, to live in thy light and walk in thy ways, according to the commandments of Jesus Christ our Lord. *Amen.*

Henry van Dyke

O Lord,
    God of Abraham, Isaac, and Jacob,
        be the God of your people today!

        We confess that we have
            worshipped all too many other gods.
        We have devoted ourselves to all
            too many different values.

Turn our hearts to you again!

O Lord,
    God of Abraham, Isaac, and Jacob,
        be the God of your people today!

        We confess that we have visited
            all too many sanctuaries.
        We have tried to find the sources of life
            in all too many other places.
        We thought it was pluralism,
            but it was the serving
                of one little Baal after another.

O Lord,
    God of Abraham, Isaac, and Jacob,
        be the God of your people today!

        We turn to you,
            and to you alone,
            to be our God, our only God.

Give us spiritual integrity.
Give us wholeness and holiness.

Answer us, O Lord, answer us,
     that we be in truth your people.

Answer us in the name of Christ,
     for he has promised
          to intercede for us.
     It is in him that we pray
          in the fellowship of his body.
     Together we pray
          in the communion of the Church.
All honor and power be to you,
     O Christ, forever and ever. *Amen.*

Hear the Gospel of Christ:

This is the message we have heard from him and proclaim to you, that God is light and in him is no darkness at all. . . . If we walk in the light, as he is in the light, we have fellowship with one another, and the blood of Jesus his Son cleanses us from all sin. . . . If we confess our sins, he is faithful and just, and will forgive our sins and cleanse us from all unrighteousness. . . . We have an advocate with the Father, Jesus Christ the righteous; and he is the expiation for our sins, and not for ours only but also for the sins of the whole world.

I John 1:5, 7, 9; 2:1-2

O for a thousand tongues to sing
     My great Redeemer's praise.
The glories of my God and King,
     The triumphs of His grace.

Charles Wesley

Confession and Supplication 18 —————

(Elijah on Mount Horeb, I Kings 19)

Most holy and merciful Father; we acknowledge and confess before thee our sinful nature — prone to evil and slothful in good — and all our shortcomings and offenses. Thou alone knowest how often we have sinned in wandering from thy way, in wasting thy gifts, in forgetting thy love. But thou, O Lord, have mercy on us, who are ashamed and sorry for all wherein we have displeased thee. Teach us to hate our errors, cleanse us from our secret faults, and forgive our sins for the sake of thy dear Son. And O most holy and loving Father, help us, we beseech thee, to live in thy light and walk in thy ways, according to the commandments of Jesus Christ our Lord. *Amen.*

Henry van Dyke

O Lord, God of Hosts, God of Israel,
    God of your people even today.

        We have heard the wind.
        We have heard the earthquake.
        We have heard the fire.

    Not in all of this have you spoken
        to us, but in the
            still, small voice.

O Lord, God of Hosts, God of Israel,
    God of your people even today.

        We have been lonely in your service.
        The taunts of the wicked
            have been hard to bear.
        How often we have thought,
            "I, even I, only am left."

O Lord, God of Hosts, God of Israel,
    God of your people even today.

        Speak to us again
            in that small voice,
                deep within our consciences,
      that we might know your will
            at this point in our lives.

Grant us the quiet to listen deeply
and the strength to act
courageously.

Through Jesus Christ,
our Savior,
and our Shepherd.

Through Jesus Christ,
the Word of God,
the lamp to our feet,
the light to our path,
to him be eternal praise
forever and ever. *Amen.*

Hear the Gospel of Christ:

This is the message we have heard from him and proclaim to you,
that God is light and in him is no darkness at all. . . . If we walk in the
light, as he is in the light, we have fellowship with one another, and
the blood of Jesus his Son cleanses us from all sin. . . . If we confess
our sins, he is faithful and just, and will forgive our sins and cleanse
us from all unrighteousness. . . . We have an advocate with the Father,
Jesus Christ the righteous; and he is the expiation for our sins, and
not for ours only but also for the sins of the whole world.

I John 1:5, 7, 9; 2:1-2

O for a thousand tongues to sing
My great Redeemer's praise.
The glories of my God and King,
The triumphs of His grace.

Charles Wesley

Confession and Supplication 19 ———————

(based on Esther 4:16)

    Most holy and merciful Father; we acknowledge and confess before thee our sinful nature — prone to evil and slothful in good — and all our shortcomings and offenses. Thou alone knowest how often we have sinned in wandering from thy way, in wasting thy gifts, in forgetting thy love. But thou, O Lord, have mercy on us, who are ashamed and sorry for all wherein we have displeased thee. Teach us to hate our errors, cleanse us from our secret faults, and forgive our sins for the sake of thy dear Son. And O most holy and loving Father, help us, we beseech thee, to live in thy light and walk in thy ways, according to the commandments of Jesus Christ our Lord. *Amen.*

Henry van Dyke

O Sovereign Lord,
    whose providence embraces all events,

        all that happened
            is in your hands.
        All that will happen
            is in your command.

You have brought us to this moment,
    that here we might serve you in prayer.

O Sovereign Lord,
    you are enthroned as King,
        to whom all the kings of this earth
            must bow.

        You know the ages to come.
        You know our deepest needs.
        You know what we really want.

We beseech you to hear us in your wisdom.

O Sovereign Lord,
    your justice always prevails.
    Your mercy is everlasting.
        We know your decrees are for
            our salvation.
        We know your grace overrules
            our failures.

Receive us, O Sovereign Lord,
  into the inner court of your presence.

For in Christ,
    enthroned at your right hand
  we are encouraged
    to approach you.
For in Christ
    we are assured
      of your favor.
To him be glory forever. *Amen.*

Hear the Gospel of Christ:

This is the message we have heard from him and proclaim to you, that God is light and in him is no darkness at all. . . . If we walk in the light, as he is in the light, we have fellowship with one another, and the blood of Jesus his Son cleanses us from all sin. . . . If we confess our sins, he is faithful and just, and will forgive our sins and cleanse us from all unrighteousness. . . . We have an advocate with the Father, Jesus Christ the righteous; and he is the expiation for our sins, and not for ours only but also for the sins of the whole world.

I John 1:5, 7, 9; 2:1-2

O for a thousand tongues to sing
  My great Redeemer's praise.
The glories of my God and King,
  The triumphs of His grace.

Charles Wesley

Confession and Supplication 20 ————

(based on Jeremiah 14)

Most holy and merciful Father; we acknowledge and confess before thee our sinful nature — prone to evil and slothful in good — and all our shortcomings and offenses. Thou alone knowest how often we have sinned in wandering from thy way, in wasting thy gifts, in forgetting thy love. But thou, O Lord, have mercy on us, who are ashamed and sorry for all wherein we have displeased thee. Teach us to hate our errors, cleanse us from our secret faults, and forgive our sins for the sake of thy dear Son. And O most holy and loving Father, help us, we beseech thee, to live in thy light and walk in thy ways, according to the commandments of Jesus Christ our Lord. *Amen.*

Henry van Dyke

O LORD, our hope,
  our savior in time of trouble,

    we, your people, lament;
      we cry out in pain.

    Our city is in ruins,
      the homeless wander about the streets,
      houses are broken into,
        deserted and boarded,
      our families are in shambles.

O LORD, our hope,
  our Savior in time of trouble,

    we, your people, are ashamed.
      We have trashed the beautiful land
        you have given us.

    We have devastated the forests.
    We have decimated the wild beasts.
    We have depleted the soil.
    We have polluted the rivers and lakes.

O LORD, our hope,
  our Savior in time of trouble.

    Grant to us genuine repentance.
    Turn us around,
      that the face of the earth
        might be restored.

Grant to us the spiritual gift
>of good stewardship.
Grant us a sense of discipline
>in our use of natural wealth.

O LORD, our hope,
>our Savior in time of trouble,
>>give us a sense of reverence
>>>for your works of creation.
>>Give us a sense
>>>that all things were
>>>>created in Christ.
Through Christ
>reconcile us to creation.
To him be all honor and glory. *Amen.*

Hear the Gospel of Christ:

This is the message we have heard from him and proclaim to you, that God is light and in him is no darkness at all. . . . If we walk in the light, as he is in the light, we have fellowship with one another, and the blood of Jesus his Son cleanses us from all sin. . . . If we confess our sins, he is faithful and just, and will forgive our sins and cleanse us from all unrighteousness. . . . We have an advocate with the Father, Jesus Christ the righteous; and he is the expiation for our sins, and not for ours only but also for the sins of the whole world.

I John 1:5, 7, 9; 2:1-2

O for a thousand tongues to sing
>My great Redeemer's praise.
The glories of my God and King,
>The triumphs of His grace.

Charles Wesley

Confidence and Supplication 21 ——————

(based on Jeremiah 20)

Most holy and merciful Father; we acknowledge and confess before thee our sinful nature — prone to evil and slothful in good — and all our shortcomings and offenses. Thou alone knowest how often we have sinned in wandering from thy way, in wasting thy gifts, in forgetting thy love. But thou, O Lord, have mercy on us, who are ashamed and sorry for all wherein we have displeased thee. Teach us to hate our errors, cleanse us from our secret faults, and forgive our sins for the sake of thy dear Son. And O most holy and loving Father, help us, we beseech thee, to live in thy light and walk in thy ways, according to the commandments of Jesus Christ our Lord. *Amen.*

Henry van Dyke

O Lord, our hope,
  our Savior in time of trouble,

    we come to you with our prayers,
      for again and again
        you have delivered the needy
        from the hand of evildoers.

    Yet we are confused.
      We cannot understand
        why things have happened
        as they have.

O Lord, our hope,
  our Savior in time of trouble.

    Sometimes I ask myself,
      why was I ever born?

    Why should my parents have
      rejoiced and delighted in me?

    Sometimes I ask myself
      what the purpose of my life is,
      why was I ever born?

O Lord, our hope,
  our Savior in time of trouble,

strengthen us with a sense of vocation;
    make clear to us our calling.

Give us vision and purpose.

Let us hear again the invitation
    of Christ to follow him.

Let us be true disciples,
    setting aside other engagements.

Let us know again
    the leading of Christ,
and restore us
    in his way, his truth, and his life. *Amen.*

Hear the Gospel of Christ:

This is the message we have heard from him and proclaim to you, that God is light and in him is no darkness at all. . . . If we walk in the light, as he is in the light, we have fellowship with one another, and the blood of Jesus his Son cleanses us from all sin. . . . If we confess our sins, he is faithful and just, and will forgive our sins and cleanse us from all unrighteousness. . . . We have an advocate with the Father, Jesus Christ the righteous; and he is the expiation for our sins, and not for ours only but also for the sins of the whole world.

I John 1:5, 7, 9; 2:1-2

O for a thousand tongues to sing
    My great Redeemer's praise.
The glories of my God and King,
    The triumphs of His grace.

Charles Wesley

Confession and Supplication 22 ———

(based on Job 7:1-6)

Let us confess our sin to God.

O most great, most just and gracious God; thou art of purer eyes than to behold iniquity; but thou hast promised mercy through Jesus Christ to all that repent and believe in him. We confess that we have all sinned and come short of the glory of God. We have neglected and abused thy holy worship. We have dealt unjustly and uncharitably with our neighbors. We have not sought first thy kingdom. Thou hast revealed thy wonderful love to us in Christ and offered us pardon and salvation in him; but we have turned away. We have run into temptation; and the sin that we should have hated, we have committed.

Have mercy on us, most merciful Father! In thy Son is our salvation, in thy promises our hope. Take us for thy children and give us the Spirit of thy Son, and in the end receive us into thy glory, through Jesus Christ our only Savior. *Amen.*

Richard Baxter

O God who spoke to Job from the whirlwind,
>who laid the foundations of the earth.

Have mercy on us.

O God, in our frustration we cry to you.

"Has not man a hard service upon earth,
>are not his days like the days of a hireling?
Like a slave who longs for the shadow,
>and like a hireling who looks for his wares,
so I am allotted months of emptiness,
>and nights of misery are apportioned to me.
When I lie down I say, "When shall I arise?"
>But the night is long,
>and I am full of tossing till the dawn. . . .
My days are swifter than a weaver's shuttle,
>and come to their end without hope."

Job 7:1-4, 6

O God who spoke to Job from the whirlwind,
>who mantled the earth with clouds
>>as a swaddling band.
>Have mercy on us.

O God, in our frustration we cry to you.

Our service on earth is hard.
Sometimes we delight in it.
Sometimes it is tedious.
Sometimes it is oppressive.

In our frustration we cry to you.

When we lie down
we worry, when will we have to get up.
We worry whether we can face the day.
We worry whether we will
ever be able to get up at all.

O God, our God, even in our frustration,
have mercy on us.

Our days are swifter than a weaver's shuttle,
and sometimes we wonder
if anything has been accomplished.

O God, our God, behind the wind and the storm,
restore our faith,
through the faithfulness
of your Suffering Servant,
to whom be glory now and evermore. *Amen.*

Hear the Gospel of Christ:

For God so loved the world that he gave his only Son, that whoever believes in him should not perish but have eternal life. For God sent the Son into the world, not to condemn the world, but that the world might be saved through him.

John 3:16-17

Let us sing praise to Christ!

Amazing grace — how sweet the sound
That saved a wretch like me!
I once was lost, but now am found —
Was blind, but now I see.

John Newton

Confession and Supplication 23 ——————

(based on Job 10:8-13)

Let us confess our sin to God.

O most great, most just and gracious God; thou art of purer eyes than to behold iniquity; but thou hast promised mercy through Jesus Christ to all that repent and believe in him. We confess that we have all sinned and come short of the glory of God. We have neglected and abused thy holy worship. We have dealt unjustly and uncharitably with our neighbors. We have not sought first thy kingdom. Thou hast revealed thy wonderful love to us in Christ and offered us pardon and salvation in him; but we have turned away. We have run into temptation; and the sin that we should have hated, we have committed.

Have mercy on us, most merciful Father! In thy Son is our salvation, in thy promises our hope. Take us for thy children and give us the Spirit of thy Son, and in the end receive us into thy glory, through Jesus Christ our only Savior. *Amen.*

Richard Baxter

O God who spoke to Job from the whirlwind,
    who laid the foundations of the earth,
        when the morning stars sang together,
        and all the sons of God
            shouted for joy.

    Hear our complaint,
        for we, too, cry to you
        as so many before us.

"Thy hands fashioned and made me;
    and now thou dost turn about and destroy me.
Remember that thou hast made me of clay;
    and wilt thou turn me to dust again?
Didst thou not pour me out like milk
    and curdle me like cheese?
Thou didst clothe me with skin and flesh,
    and knit me together with bones and sinews.
Thou hast granted me life and steadfast love;
    and thy care has preserved my spirit.
Yet these things thou didst hide in thy heart;
    I know that this was thy purpose."   Job 10:8-13

    Why are we so depressed?
    Why are we so frustrated?
O God, who spoke to Job from the whirlwind,

Hear our complaint:
    Sometimes we wonder if you have
        turned against us.
Are we not your creatures?
    Are we not the work of your hands?
Have you not created us for a noble purpose?
    Have you not created us for yourself?

        Why are we so depressed?
        Why are we so frustrated?

O God, who spoke to Job from the whirlwind,
    who laid the foundations of the earth,
        who shut up the sea with doors,
        who said, thus far shall you come,
            and no farther,
            and here shall your proud waves
                stop and stay.

        Grant us an end to our frustration.
        Grant us an end to our depression.
        Show us the purpose of life.

Restore us in the gospel of Christ. *Amen.*

Hear the Gospel of Christ!

For God so loved the world that he gave his only Son, that whoever
believes in him should not perish but have eternal life. For God sent
the Son into the world, not to condemn the world, but that the world
might be saved through him.   John 3:16-17

Let us sing praise to Christ!

Amazing grace — how sweet the sound
    That saved a wretch like me!
I once was lost, but now am found —
    Was blind, but now I see.
                                              John Newton

Confession and Supplication 24 —————

(based on Job 23)

Let us confess our sin to God.

O most great, most just and gracious God; thou art of purer eyes than to behold iniquity; but thou hast promised mercy through Jesus Christ to all that repent and believe in him. We confess that we have all sinned and come short of the glory of God. We have neglected and abused thy holy worship. We have dealt unjustly and uncharitably with our neighbors. We have not sought first thy kingdom. Thou hast revealed thy wonderful love to us in Christ and offered us pardon and salvation in him; but we have turned away. We have run into temptation; and the sin that we should have hated, we have committed.

Have mercy on us, most merciful Father! In thy Son is our salvation, in thy promises our hope. Take us for thy children and give us the Spirit of thy Son, and in the end receive us into thy glory, through Jesus Christ our only Savior. *Amen.*

Richard Baxter

God, wondrous, mysterious!
    O that I knew where I might find you.
    O that I might come even to your judgment seat,
        that I might lay my case before you.

Wondrous, mysterious God,
        we cry to you for justice,
        when the judges of this world
            have refused to hear us.

Wondrous, mysterious God,
        we cry to you,
        because the courts of this world
            have condemned us.

God, we cry to you,
        because we are a suspected people,
            and a rejected people.

God, wondrous, mysterious!
    We go forward, but you are not there;
        and backward, but we cannot perceive you.

On the left hand we seek you,
    but we cannot behold you.
We turn to the right,
    but we cannot see you!

Wondrous, mysterious God,
    you are hard to find.
You are so free,
    and yet so elusive.

If we could just reach out and grasp you,
    yet you are grabbed by no one.

God, wondrous, mysterious!
    We catch sight of your majesty,
        and we are terrified.
All your purposes are carried out
    and your plans for us will all be fulfilled.

You are wonderful in your sovereignty!
Your everlasting power is marvellous,
    good and great beyond our imagining.

In the name of Christ we cry out
    to you, you wondrous God. *Amen.*

Hear the Gospel of Christ!

For God so loved the world that he gave his only Son, that whoever believes in him should not perish but have eternal life. For God sent the Son into the world, not to condemn the world, but that the world might be saved through him.   John 3:16-17

Let us sing praise to Christ!

Amazing grace — how sweet the sound
    That saved a wretch like me!
I once was lost, but now am found —
    Was blind, but now I see.   John Newton

Confession and Supplication 25 ————

(based on Psalm 6)

Let us confess our sin to God.

Almighty God, who art rich in mercy to all those who call upon Thee; Hear us as we come to Thee humbly confessing our sins and transgressions, and imploring Thy mercy and forgiveness. We have broken Thy holy laws by our deeds and words, and by the sinful affections of our hearts. We confess before Thee our disobedience and ingratitude, our pride and willfulness; And all our failures and short-comings toward Thee and our fellow men. Have mercy upon us, most merciful Father; And of Thy great goodness grant that we may hereafter serve and please Thee in newness of life; Through the merit and mediation of Jesus Christ our Lord. *Amen.*

Louis F. Benson

O LORD, rebuke me not in thy anger,
    nor chasten me in thy wrath.

        You have every right to be angry!
            O holy God!
        You have every right to chasten me,
            for I have sinned,
            knowing well that I have sinned.

    I pray for mercy,
        lest your wrath overcome me.

O LORD, rebuke me not in thy anger,
    nor chasten me in thy wrath.

        My soul is sick,
            and my spirit is sagging.
        My body is in pain,
            and my flesh is weak.

    Again and again I sense my fallibility.

O LORD, I know you always hear my prayer.

        I know that you will hear my meditations.
        I know that you accept them and hear them,
            even when they are mean and angry.
        I know that you have heard
            the sound of my weeping!

O Lord, rebuke me not in thy anger,
    nor chasten me in thy wrath.
   Receive me in the name of Christ
      who still takes away the sin of the world.
    All praise be to him,
       forever and ever. *Amen.*

Hear the Gospel of Christ:

Therefore, since we are justified by faith, we have peace with God through our Lord Jesus Christ. Through him we have obtained access to this grace in which we stand, and we rejoice in our hope of sharing the glory of God. More than that, we rejoice in our sufferings, knowing that suffering produces endurance, and endurance produces character, and character produces hope, and hope does not disappoint us, because God's love has been poured into our hearts through the Holy Spirit which has been given to us.
                                         Romans 5:1-5

Let us sing praise to Christ!

Ye servants of God,
   Your Master proclaim,
And publish abroad
   His wonderful name;
The name all-victorious
   Of Jesus extol;
His kingdom is glorious,
   And rules over all.

                                      Charles Wesley

Confession and Supplication 26 ————

(based on Psalm 32)

Let us confess our sin to God.

Almighty God, who art rich in mercy to all those who call upon Thee; Hear us as we come to Thee humbly confessing our sins and transgressions, and imploring Thy mercy and forgiveness. We have broken Thy holy laws by our deeds and words, and by the sinful affections of our hearts. We confess before Thee our disobedience and ingratitude, our pride and willfulness; And all our failures and shortcomings toward Thee and our fellow men. Have mercy upon us, most merciful Father; And of Thy great goodness grant that we may hereafter serve and please Thee in newness of life; Through the merit and mediation of Jesus Christ our Lord. *Amen.*

Louis F. Benson

Thou art a hiding place for me, O LORD.
Thou dost encompass me with deliverance.

> When I am ashamed,
> I hide my face in you.
> When I have lost my way,
> I hold onto you.
> When I have failed you,
> I still know you are my God.

Thou art a hiding place for me, O LORD.
Thou preservest me from trouble.

> Things are breaking down.
> What I have tried to build up
> does not seem to be holding together.

> Sometimes I think it is my fault.
> Sometimes it is,
> sometimes it is not.
> But sometimes I know it is my fault.

Thou art a hiding place for me, O LORD.
Thou dost encompass me with deliverance.

> For some strange reason,
> you keep putting it all together.

> Blessed you are!

For some reason,
    you give me a chance to start over.

Blessed you are, O LORD!

Your mercy keeps covering over my sin.

Blessed you are, O LORD! *Amen.*

Hear the Gospel of Christ:

Therefore, since we are justified by faith, we have peace with God through our Lord Jesus Christ. Through him we have obtained access to this grace in which we stand, and we rejoice in our hope of sharing the glory of God. More than that, we rejoice in our sufferings, knowing that suffering produces endurance, and endurance produces character, and character produces hope, and hope does not disappoint us, because God's love has been poured into our hearts through the Holy Spirit which has been given to us.   Romans 5:1-5

Let us sing praise to Christ!

Ye servants of God,
    Your Master proclaim,
And publish abroad
    His wonderful name;
The name all-victorious
    Of Jesus extol;
His kingdom is glorious,
    And rules over all.   Charles Wesley

Confession and Supplication 27 ————

(based on Psalm 38)

Let us confess our sin to God.

Almighty God, who art rich in mercy to all those who call upon Thee; Hear us as we come to Thee humbly confessing our sins and transgressions, and imploring Thy mercy and forgiveness. We have broken Thy holy laws by our deeds and words, and by the sinful affections of our hearts. We confess before Thee our disobedience and ingratitude, our pride and willfulness; And all our failures and shortcomings toward Thee and our fellow men. Have mercy upon us, most merciful Father; And of Thy great goodness grant that we may hereafter serve and please Thee in newness of life; Through the merit and mediation of Jesus Christ our Lord. *Amen.*

Louis F. Benson

Do not forsake me, O LORD!
    O my God, be not far from me!

        Right now it seems you are
            so far away from me.
        Clouds have shut up the heavens,
      and you who are often so radiant,
            seem so chilly.

Do not forsake me, O LORD!
    O my God, be not far from me!

        There is no soundness in my flesh.
        There is no health in my bones.
        My iniquities have gone over my head.

Sin has sickened my life.
To you I turn for healing,
        for you are a healing God.

Do not forsake me, O LORD!
    O my God be not far from me!

        For so long I have been crying to you.
        All my longing is known to you.
            You have heard it again and again.
        But for you I wait,
            for you are my consolation.

O Lord of my salvation,
    hear me in the name of Christ!
    for in him,
        your Suffering Servant,
        you are near to
            those who suffer.
For he took upon himself
    our sin and our suffering.
All glory be to you,
    long-suffering God. *Amen.*

Hear the Gospel of Christ:

Therefore, since we are justified by faith, we have peace with God through our Lord Jesus Christ. Through him we have obtained access to this grace in which we stand, and we rejoice in our hope of sharing the glory of God. More than that, we rejoice in our sufferings, knowing that suffering produces endurance, and endurance produces character, and character produces hope, and hope does not disappoint us, because God's love has been poured into our hearts through the Holy Spirit which has been given to us.
Romans 5:1-5

Let us sing praise to Christ!

Ye servants of God,
    Your Master proclaim,
And publish abroad
    His wonderful name;
The name all-victorious
    Of Jesus extol;
His kingdom is glorious,
    And rules over all.

Charles Wesley

Confession and Supplication 28 ————

(based on Psalm 51)

Let us confess our sin to God.

Almighty God, who art rich in mercy to all those who call upon Thee; Hear us as we come to Thee humbly confessing our sins and transgressions, and imploring Thy mercy and forgiveness. We have broken Thy holy laws by our deeds and words, and by the sinful affections of our hearts. We confess before Thee our disobedience and ingratitude, our pride and willfulness; And all our failures and short-comings toward Thee and our fellow men. Have mercy upon us, most merciful Father; And of Thy great goodness grant that we may hereafter serve and please Thee in newness of life; Through the merit and mediation of Jesus Christ our Lord. *Amen.*

Louis F. Benson

Have mercy on me, O God,
    according to thy steadfast love.
Have mercy on me, O God.

    My sin has been against you,
        although others have been hurt as well.
    It is against you that I have rebelled.
    It is against you that I have been angry —
        and yet it is to you that I cry for mercy!

Have mercy on me, O God,
    according to thy steadfast love.
Have mercy on me, O God.

    Even with my best intentions
        sin seems ever to creep in.
    Even with my firmest resolve
        I keep on sinning.

    But I would be holy.
        I keep deciding for the right,
        but it just does not work out.

Have mercy on me, O God,
    according to thy steadfast love.
Have mercy on me, O God.

Wash me,
    that I be clean, fresh, and new.
Cleanse me,
    that I have integrity,
    that I do right from inside out.
Purge me,
    that I be pure with a strong purity.

O spotless Lamb of God,
    take away my sin
        by your atoning sacrifice.
In the name of Christ deliver me,
    O God of my salvation,
        and my tongue will sing aloud
            of your deliverance. *Amen.*

Hear the Gospel of Christ:

Therefore, since we are justified by faith, we have peace with God through our Lord Jesus Christ. Through him we have obtained access to this grace in which we stand, and we rejoice in our hope of sharing the glory of God. More than that, we rejoice in our sufferings, knowing that suffering produces endurance, and endurance produces character, and character produces hope, and hope does not disappoint us, because God's love has been poured into our hearts through the Holy Spirit which has been given to us.
           Romans 5:1-5

Let us sing praise to Christ!

Ye servants of God,
    Your Master proclaim,
And publish abroad
    His wonderful name;
The name all-victorious
    Of Jesus extol;
His kingdom is glorious,
    And rules over all.

           Charles Wesley

Confession and Supplication 29 ——————

(based on Psalm 102)

Let us confess our sin to God.

Almighty God, who art rich in mercy to all those who call upon Thee; Hear us as we come to Thee humbly confessing our sins and transgressions, and imploring Thy mercy and forgiveness. We have broken Thy holy laws by our deeds and words, and by the sinful affections of our hearts. We confess before Thee our disobedience and ingratitude, our pride and willfulness; And all our failures and short-comings toward Thee and our fellow men. Have mercy upon us, most merciful Father; And of Thy great goodness grant that we may hereafter serve and please Thee in newness of life; Through the merit and mediation of Jesus Christ our Lord. *Amen.*

Louis F. Benson

Hear my prayer, O LORD;
    let my cry come to thee.

    For my days pass away like smoke,
        and my bones burn like a furnace.
    My heart is smitten like grass,
        and withered.

        O God, we are in pain.
        Good times have passed us by.
        We are alone,
            and life seems useless.

Hear my prayer, O LORD;
    let my cry come to thee.

    Like dry leaves in autumn
        my life seems scattered,
            blown about,
                fragile and withered.
    I am like a lonely bird on the house top.
        Everyone else has flown away,
            and I am left alone.
    Like ashes when the fire is gone,
        like an evening shadow,
        that is nothing when night is come.

But thou, O LORD,
    art enthroned forever.

Have pity on your people,
    for the machinations of secularism
      have worn us down.
    The taunts of the humanists
      have tormented us.

You are our God,
    and you are enthroned forever.

Hear us in the name of Christ,
    your everlasting and eternal Son!
    To him be glory forever. *Amen.*

Hear the Gospel of Christ:

Therefore, since we are justified by faith, we have peace with God through our Lord Jesus Christ. Through him we have obtained access to this grace in which we stand, and we rejoice in our hope of sharing the glory of God. More than that, we rejoice in our sufferings, knowing that suffering produces endurance, and endurance produces character, and character produces hope, and hope does not disappoint us, because God's love has been poured into our hearts through the Holy Spirit which has been given to us.
                                        Romans 5:1-5

Let us sing praise to Christ!

Ye servants of God,
    Your Master proclaim,
And publish abroad
    His wonderful name;
The name all-victorious
    Of Jesus extol;
His kingdom is glorious,
    And rules over all.

                                          Charles Wesley

Confession and Supplication 30 ———————

(based on Psalm 130)

Let us confess our sin to God.

Almighty God, who art rich in mercy to all those who call upon Thee; Hear us as we come to Thee humbly confessing our sins and transgressions, and imploring Thy mercy and forgiveness. We have broken Thy holy laws by our deeds and words, and by the sinful affections of our hearts. We confess before Thee our disobedience and ingratitude, our pride and willfulness; And all our failures and short-comings toward Thee and our fellow men. Have mercy upon us, most merciful Father; And of Thy great goodness grant that we may hereafter serve and please Thee in newness of life; Through the merit and mediation of Jesus Christ our Lord. *Amen.*

Louis F. Benson

Out of the depths I cry to thee,
    O LORD!
  Lord, hear my voice!

    Wickedness like a black primeval sea
      has sucked me in,
      and I am helpless.
    I thrash about and get nowhere.
    Sin has gotten ahold of me
      and darkened my life.

Out of the depths I cry to thee,
    O LORD!
  Lord, hear my voice!

    You are a merciful God.
    You know how fallible we are.
    We fail again and again,
      and when we come back to you,
      you always receive us!

Out of the depths I cry to thee,
    O LORD!
  Lord, hear my voice!

My hope is set on you.
    It is for you that I wait.
I know you will come through.
Your grace will come like the dawn,
    like the dawn it cannot be held back.

Out of the depths I cry to thee,
    O LORD!
Lord, hear my voice!

    You will redeem your people.
    It is as sure as the sunrise in the morning.
All glory be to you, O Christ!
    O Daystar from on high! *Amen.*

Hear the Gospel of Christ:

Therefore, since we are justified by faith, we have peace with God through our Lord Jesus Christ. Through him we have obtained access to this grace in which we stand, and we rejoice in our hope of sharing the glory of God. More than that, we rejoice in our sufferings, knowing that suffering produces endurance, and endurance produces character, and character produces hope, and hope does not disappoint us, because God's love has been poured into our hearts through the Holy Spirit which has been given to us.

Romans 5:1-5

Let us sing praise to Christ!

Ye servants of God,
    Your Master proclaim,
And publish abroad
    His wonderful name;
The name all-victorious
    Of Jesus extol;
His kingdom is glorious,
    And rules over all.

Charles Wesley

Confession and Supplication 31 ───────

(based on Psalm 143)

Let us confess our sin to God.

> Almighty God, who art rich in mercy to all those who call upon Thee; Hear us as we come to Thee humbly confessing our sins and transgressions, and imploring Thy mercy and forgiveness. We have broken Thy holy laws by our deeds and words, and by the sinful affections of our hearts. We confess before Thee our disobedience and ingratitude, our pride and willfulness; And all our failures and short-comings toward Thee and our fellow men. Have mercy upon us, most merciful Father; And of Thy great goodness grant that we may hereafter serve and please Thee in newness of life; Through the merit and mediation of Jesus Christ our Lord. *Amen.*
>
> Louis F. Benson

Hear my prayer, O LORD;
    give ear to my supplications!
In thy faithfulness answer me,
    in thy righteousness!

      I am tired of enemies.
      I am tired of being chased
         from one conflict after another.
      I do not want to hear any more arguments.

Hear my prayer, O LORD;
    give ear to my supplications!
For the enemy has pursued me;
    he has crushed my life to the ground;
    he has made me sit in darkness.

      Why, O Lord, must there always
         be controversy?
      Why do we always have to be fighting,
         wrestling, struggling?

Hear my prayer, O LORD;
    give ear to my supplications!
Make haste to answer me, O LORD!
    My spirit fails!

      Show us a better way;
         your ways are all justice and righteousness.
      Teach your ways;

your ways are all peace and truth.
Teach us to do your will;
    anoint our spirits with your Spirit;
    bring us into your ways.
Let your Spirit lead us on a level path.

In the name of Christ,
    grant us your steadfast love.
All glory be to him
    ever seated at your
        right hand. *Amen.*

Hear the Gospel of Christ:

Therefore, since we are justified by faith, we have peace with God through our Lord Jesus Christ. Through him we have obtained access to this grace in which we stand, and we rejoice in our hope of sharing the glory of God. More than that, we rejoice in our sufferings, knowing that suffering produces endurance, and endurance produces character, and character produces hope, and hope does not disappoint us, because God's love has been poured into our hearts through the Holy Spirit which has been given to us.   Romans 5:1-5

Let us sing praise to Christ!

Ye servants of God,
    Your Master proclaim,
And publish abroad
    His wonderful name;
The name all-victorious
    Of Jesus extol;
His kingdom is glorious,
    And rules over all.

        Charles Wesley

The Prayer for Illumination

Long before the time of Jesus, whenever the Scriptures were read in public worship, it was thought appropriate to pray that the people would be enlightened by the reading. On that great occasion when Ezra read the Law to the people of Jerusalem, he mounted the pulpit, opened the scroll of the Law, and "blessed the LORD, the great God; and all the people answered, 'Amen, Amen'" (Nehemiah 8:6). Rabbinical scholars find in these words the first evidence of the synagogue's practice of offering a prayer of illumination before the public reading of the Scriptures. Today, in the synagogue liturgy for morning prayer, two very ancient prayers are offered before the recitation of the Shema, which for Jews is a sort of Scripture lesson which sums up all Scripture lessons. Tradition has expanded these two prayers over the centuries. They had begun to take literary form long before the time of Jesus and surely by his time much of the phraseology had become customary. These prayers, or at least their liturgical ancestor, may well have been in the mind of the author of Nehemiah when he wrote the account of Ezra's prayer.

Paul prayed for the Church,

> that the God of our Lord Jesus Christ, the Father of glory, may give you a spirit of wisdom and of revelation in the knowledge of him, having the eyes of your hearts enlightened, that you may know what is the hope to which he has called you, what are the riches of his glorious inheritance in the saints, and what is the immeasurable greatness of his power in us who believe.   Ephesians 1:17-19

It has often been suggested that words such as these in Paul's Epistles reflect the sort of prayers that he offered in the service of worship. While we would hesitate to jump to the conclusion that these lines come from a prayer for illumination prayed in the worship of the primitive Church, we do know that the earliest Christians followed many of the liturgical traditions of the synagogue. Perhaps we could even say that these lines from Ephesians hint at there being a prayer for illumination in the earliest Christian services of worship, but we would not want to press the evidence any further than that. Yet surely we would not go far astray if we let these lines inspire our prayers.

While the biblical examples for the Prayer for Illumination are suggestive, the theological reasons for offering such a prayer are compelling. God reveals himself. Revelation is an act of his grace, not a matter of our investigation or a matter of the logic of our reason. We pray for the illumination of our hearts and minds because we know that without it our reasoning and our speaking about God is in vain. Even when we read the sacred texts they mean nothing to us unless God grants us what Paul called the "spirit of revelation." The Holy Spirit who inspired the authors of these sacred texts must inspire those who read and those who preach and those who listen. Otherwise those texts will fail to move us. Revelation is from beginning to end a work of God's Spirit.

With such a strong theological mandate behind it, the Prayer for Illumination quite naturally becomes an occasion for a brief meditation on both the doctrine of the Holy Spirit and the doctrine of revelation. Both this prayer and the Communion Invocation, or *epiclesis,* as theologians have traditionally called it, give occasion for unfolding the doctrine of the Holy Spirit. We might even say that the Prayer for Illumination is an epiclesis of the reading and preaching of Scripture. Today when there is such confusion about the doctrine of revelation and the inspiration of Scripture and so much controversy over the doctrine of the Holy Spirit, it is important to give careful attention to this short prayer. It is not that our prayers should be an occasion for formulating doctrine. That should be avoided. It is rather that in prayer we meditate on these realities. We turn our thoughts to deeper truths than those that usually cross our minds. The value of doing this is shown by the use in the most diverse liturgical traditions of a Prayer for Illumination before the reading and preaching of Scripture.

In the sermons of Origen, who lived from the end of the second century to the middle of the third century, we find quite a bit of information about the Prayer for Illumination. Whatever else may be said about Origen, he was devoted to systematic expository preaching. His sermons make up the only sizeable collection of sermons that has come down to us from the first three Christian centuries. Frequently in his sermons he mentions that the reading and preaching of the Scriptures in the service of worship was prefaced by a prayer that God give to the preacher and to the congregation an understanding of what was to be preached.

While we do not have the exact text of the prayers for illumination to which Origen refers, we do have his descriptions of these prayers. The following three descriptions give us an idea of the range of ideas found in these prayers.

> We should ask God and the Holy Spirit graciously to dispel every shred of those clouds and vapors, the product of our filthy sins, which with their darkness impede our hearts' vision. Then we shall be able to understand the spirit of his Law and the marvels of it: which was what the prophet meant when he said: "Clear sight be mine, to contemplate the wonders of thy law."

> Let us keep the Scriptures in mind and meditate upon them day and night, persevering in prayer, always on the watch. Let us beg the Lord to give us real knowledge of what we read and to show us not only

how to understand it but how to put it into practice, so that we may deserve to obtain spiritual grace, enlightened by the law of the Holy Spirit, through Jesus Christ our Lord, whose power and glory will endure throughout the ages. *Amen.*

Let us ask the Lord to broaden our ideas, make them clearer, and bring them nearer to the truth, that we may understand the other things too that he has revealed to his prophets. May we study the Holy Spirit's writings under the guidance of the Spirit himself and compare one spiritual interpretation with another, so that our explanation of the texts may be worthy of God and the Holy Spirit, who inspired them. May we do this through Christ Jesus, our Lord, to whom glory and power belong and will belong through all the ages. *Amen.*

Church and Mulry, *Macmillan Book of Earliest Christian Prayers,* pp. 36-38

Serapion of Thmuis, a friend and contemporary of Athanasius, has left us a collection of prayers used in the church over which he presided as bishop in the middle of the fourth century. This sacramentary of Serapion provides the following prayer to be used before the reading of the Scripture lessons:

We beseech thee the Father of the only-begotten, the Lord of the universe, the artificer of the creatures, the maker of things that have been made; clean hands do we stretch out, and our thoughts do we unfold to thee, O Lord. We pray thee, have compassion, spare, benefit, improve, multiply (us) in virtue and faith and knowledge. Visit us, O Lord; to thee we display our own weaknesses. Be propitious and have pity on us all in common. Have pity, benefit this people. Make it gentle and soberminded and clean; and send angelic powers, in order that all this thy people may be holy and reverend. I beseech thee send thy holy Spirit into our mind and give us grace to learn the divine scriptures from (the) holy Spirit, and to interpret, cleanly and worthily, that all the lay-people present may be helped, through thy only-begotten Jesus Christ in holy Spirit, through whom to thee (is) the glory and the strength both now and to all the ages of the ages. *Amen.*

Wordsworth, *Bishop Serapion's Prayer-Book,* pp. 81-82

There is quite a bit of evidence for the use of a prayer for illumination similar to this in Egypt during the early centuries. One notices that at the heart of this prayer is the request that through the inner testimony of the Holy Spirit God's people come to an understanding of the Scriptures.

Augustine exercised his preaching ministry in North Africa as the Roman Empire was falling before the invasions of one barbarian tribe after another. He wrote a manual on preaching, *De doctrina christiana,* in which he emphasized the importance of approaching the public reading and teaching of the Scriptures with prayer. He held up the example of Queen Esther, who prayed and fasted with her maidens before going into the presence of King Ahasuerus. It is not clear from Augustine that he had any particular prayer in mind. On the other hand he may have been speaking of the prayer that in the Roman Mass eventually came to be called the collect. What Augustine may be telling us is that the original purpose of the collect was to be a prayer for illumination.

The Nestorian liturgy, which in the opinion of many retained the Semitic character of early Christian worship much more consistently than did the Greek and Latin-speaking churches of antiquity, had a very definite Prayer for Illumination:

> Thee, O Brightness of the Glory of the Father and Express Image of the person of him that begat thee, who wast revealed in the body of our manhood and didst enlighten the darkness of our knowledge by the light of thy Gospel, we confess and worship and glorify at all times, Lord of all, Father and Son and Holy Ghost, for ever. *Amen.*
>
> Glory be to the eternal mercy which sent thee unto us, O Christ the Light of the World and the life of all, for ever. *Amen.*
>
> Make us wise by thy law, enlighten the motions (of our thoughts) by thy knowledge and sanctify our souls by thy truth and grant us to be obedient to thy words and to fulfil thy commandments at all times, Lord of all, Father and Son and Holy Ghost, for ever. *Amen.*
>
> Brightman, *Liturgies Eastern and Western,*
> I, p. 258

A similar Prayer for Illumination is found in the liturgy of the Syrian Jacobites:

> Grant us, O Lord God, the knowledge of thy divine words and fill us with the understanding of thine holy Gospel and the riches of thy divine gifts and the indwelling of thine Holy Spirit and give us with joy to keep thine holy commandments and accomplish them and fulfil thy will and to be accounted worthy of the blessings and the mercies that are from thee now and at all times.   Brightman, *Liturgies,* p. 79

In time, the Prayer for Illumination dropped out of the liturgy as it was celebrated in the churches of Western Europe. Perhaps one might more correctly say that it underwent a mutation and became the calendar collect of the Roman sacramentaries and in the process lost its character as a prayer for illumination. However one wants to explain it, the Roman Mass as it was celebrated during the Middle Ages no longer had a true prayer for illumination.

At the time of the Reformation, the South German Reformers revived the Prayer for Illumination. In Zurich, Strasbourg, Geneva, and elsewhere, this prayer became a regular part of evangelical worship. Martin Bucer, the Reformer of Strasbourg, was surely among the most creative leaders in the reform of worship. We find this Prayer for Illumination in the *Strasbourg Psalter* of 1537:

> Almighty, gracious Father, forasmuch as our whole salvation depends upon our true understanding of thy holy Word, grant to all of us that our hearts, being freed from worldly affairs, may hear and apprehend

thy holy Word with all diligence and faith, that we may rightly understand thy gracious will, cherish it, and live by it with all earnestness, to thy praise and honor; through our Lord Jesus Christ. *Amen.*

Thompson, Liturgies of the Western Church, p. 170

The rubrics of the *Strasbourg Psalter* are quite explicit that the prayer was freely formulated by the minister, but also that this was the general drift of what would be contained in it.

In regard to the Prayer for Illumination, as in most other matters regarding worship, John Calvin followed Bucer's lead. The *Genevan Psalter* of 1542 directs that before the reading of the Scriptures the minister is to pray "beseeching God for the grace of His Holy Spirit, that His Word may be faithfully expounded to the honor of His name and the edification of the Church, and be received with such humility and obedience that it deserves. The form is left to the discretion of the Minister" (Thompson, pp. 198-199). For a good number of years Calvin's sermons were taken down by a stenographer. Sometimes Calvin's prayers were taken down along with the sermon. One example of Calvin's prayers for illumination is as follows:

> Most gracious GOD, our heavenly Father! in whom alone dwelleth all fulness of light and wisdom: Illuminate our minds, we beseech thee, by thine Holy Spirit, in the true understanding of thy word. Give us grace that we may receive it with reverence and humility unfeigned. May it lead us to put our whole trust in thee alone; and so to serve and honour thee, that we may glorify thy holy name, and edify our neighbours by a good example. And since it hath pleased thee to number us among thy people: O help us to pay thee the love and homage that we owe, as children to our Father, and as servants to our Lord. We ask this for the sake of our Master and Saviour. . . .

Baird, Presbyterian Liturgies, p. 37

It should be clear from this prayer that Calvin did not have the magical view of Scripture that some have ascribed to him. Once one recognizes that it is the Holy Spirit who inspires both the preaching and the hearing of Scripture, just as the Spirit inspired the prophets and the Apostles, then it becomes clear that inspiration, whatever else it may be, is an event that proves itself in the building up of the Church. One catches a certain dynamic to Calvin's doctrine of inspiration when one looks at these prayers that one does not always see in his more formal discussions of the subject. The inspiration of Scripture is for Calvin God's own empowering of his Word. God's Word is a life-giving and life-transforming power.

In a slightly different direction Ulrich Zwingli, the Reformer of German-speaking Switzerland, composed a prayer for illumination based on Psalm 119:

> Almighty, eternal and merciful God, whose Word is a lamp unto our feet and a light unto our path, open and illuminate our minds that we may purely and perfectly understand Thy Word and that our lives may

be conformed according to what we rightly understood, that in nothing we may be displeasing unto Thy Majesty, through Jesus Christ our Lord. *Amen.*   Locher, *Zwingli's Thought,* p. 28

We note in the first place the appropriateness of Zwingli's use of the psalm. Then we note that he has composed his prayer in the literary form of a collect, that from the standpoint of literary style it has all the pungent brevity of the collects of the ancient Roman sacramentaries.

The basic idea of the Prayer for Illumination is beautifully expressed in several of Charles Wesley's hymns. It is typical of Methodist worship that it is conceived in prayer and bears fruit in hymnody. One is never surprised to find the best theological insights of Methodism in the Wesleyan hymns. Here is a good example of the theology of the Prayer for Illumination in hymnic form:

> Come, Holy Ghost, our hearts inspire,
>   Let us Thine influence prove,
> Source of the old prophetic fire,
>   Fountain of light and love.
>
> Come, Holy Ghost, for moved by thee
>   The prophets wrote and spoke;
> Unlock the truth, Thyself the key,
>   Unseal the sacred Book.
>
> Expand Thy wings, celestial Dove,
>   Brood o'er our nature's night;
> On our disordered spirits move,
>   And let there now be light.
>
> God, through Himself, we then shall know,
>   If thou within us shine,
> And sound, with all Thy saints below,
>   The depths of love divine.

No one has ever put the doctrine of the sufficiency of God's self-revelation more beautifully. It is indeed God himself, in the person of his Spirit, who is the key to Scripture, and it is indeed through God himself that God is to be known.

The fundamental concern of the Prayer for Illumination is to pray that through the inner working of the Holy Spirit, the reading and preaching of the Scriptures might be heard with true understanding and might bear fruit in the enlightening and building up of the congregation. Basic to Protestant faith is Paul's affirmation that faith comes by hearing, and hearing by the Word of God (Romans 10:17), and the Prayer for Illumination is a prayer that this might come about.

This prayer protects us from a magical view of the inspiration of the Bible. It recognizes that God's Word is still God's Word. It is still in his power. The prayer recognizes that inspiration is not just something that happened when the Word of God was put down on paper long ago, but something that happens again and again, even today, when Christian preachers open the sacred book and proclaim the gospel to God's people. Joseph Parker, an English Congregational preacher back in the days of Queen Victoria, wrote this into the preface of *The People's Bible*, a seven-year series of sermons in which he covered the whole Bible from Genesis to Revelation. It is only through the work of God's Spirit that the seed is sown in our hearts and that it sprouts and takes root in our lives and grows and finally bears fruit.

Let us turn for a moment to the literary form of the Prayer for Illumination. With time, I have begun to see this prayer as a Christian *berakah*. At first I followed the general literary form, not of a Hebrew *berakah* ("blessing"), but of a Latin collect. The collect is a terse, one sentence prayer. Its beauty is its brevity. Much of its genius depends on the inflections of the Latin language. In order to do the same thing in English one's style has to become highly latinized. The classic collects of the Latin sacramentaries are masterpieces of Roman sobriety. Pope Leo the Great, Pope Gelasius I, and Pope Gregory the Great may well have composed many of these prayers. The Latin collects are surely among the most venerable antiques of the liturgy.

But as much as I love Latin I could never go along with trying to affect a highly latinized style in the prayers of the contemporary American Church. When it began to occur to me that the prayer mentioned in the eighth chapter of Nehemiah was a *berakah* and when I began to realize that the New Testament is filled with Christian *berakoth*, I decided to try my hand at composing Christian *berakoth*.

From the time of Ezra to the time of Jesus it was common to begin a prayer with a phrase something like "Blessed art thou, O Lord God, King of the universe. . . ." Jesus himself begins several prayers like this. For example, in Matthew 11:25 he prays "I thank thee, Father, Lord of heaven and earth, that thou hast hidden these things from the wise and understanding and revealed them to babes. . . ." Here "thank" is an obvious synonym for "bless." Christians quickly began to develop their own form of the *berakah*. Three prayers in the New Testament begin with "Blessed art thou, O God and Father of our Lord Jesus Christ. . . ." More and more I found myself working this phrase into the prayers that I composed. I see it as a means of claiming a very long tradition of prayer.

In a number of the prayers that follow I have taken a text from Psalm 119 to guide me in the composition of the prayer. I used this particular psalm because it is a meditation on God's gracious gift of Scripture. That project occupied me off and on for well over a year, and only a few of my attempts are included below. Some scholars have suggested that the psalm was composed as a series of doxological preludes and postludes for the reading of the Scripture lesson in the Jewish liturgy. Be that as it may, it seemed a good way of familiarizing my congregation with this unique passage of Scripture. And perhaps even more it gave me a chance to ponder this wondrous passage of Scripture again and again myself.

I have included several prayers for feast days. Here I have obviously been inspired by the collects of the Roman sacramentaries. Some will find the number of feast days rather limited and others will find them too extensive. The feasts and special days selected here reflect what it seems to me the average American Protestant Church is apt to celebrate. An elaborate festal calendar seems artificial for the typical American congregation. If a congregation actually gets around to celebrating Christmas, Easter, and Pentecost, that is really sufficient. Naturally these primary feasts entail certain auxiliary observances, such as Epiphany and Ascension. But I have never been able to get people to come out for these celebrations, so I have finally contented myself with observing them on the Sunday before or after the traditional date. Maundy Thursday Communion has always been an essential part of the Christian celebration of Passover in the churches I have served. But Good Friday was usually observed at an ecumenical service in the center of town.

Prayer for Illumination 1 ——————

(based on Nehemiah 8:6)

Blessed you are, LORD,
    Great God!
Blessed you are, eternal God
    in times past and yet today!

    You have spoken in the past
        and your people have been guided
            through all kinds of wildernesses
        and supported in all kinds of exiles and tribulations.

    Speak to us today
        in the midst of our own peculiar confusions.

    Speak to us through your Law
        and give us a sense of order and direction.

    Speak to us through your gospel.
        Transform us by your grace.
        Renew us in hope.

For yours is the future,
    even more than the past. *Amen* and *Amen.*

Prayer for Illumination 2 —————

(based on Ephesians 1:17-19)

Blessed be the LORD,
    the Great God!
Blessed be our God,
    the God of Abraham, Isaac, and Jacob,
    the God and Father of our Lord Jesus Christ!

Father of Glory!
    Give us your Holy Spirit,
        the Spirit of Wisdom,
        the Spirit of Revelation,
        the Spirit of all that is holy.

Give us the Spirit of your Son,
    that sacred power living within us!

Give us your Holy Spirit,
    that we might be your sons and daughters,
    the heirs of your Kingdom.

Through Jesus Christ, our Lord. *Amen* and *Amen.*

Prayer for Illumination 3 ———————

(based on Ephesians 1:17-19)

Blessed you are, God of our Lord Jesus Christ,
  Father of glory.
Blessed you are, eternal God,
  source of wisdom and knowledge.

  Give us a spirit of wisdom
    and of revelation in the knowledge of Christ.

  Enlighten the eyes of our hearts
    that we may know what is the hope
      to which we have been called.

  Reveal yourself to us,
    for we can only know you
      if you give yourself to be known.

Through Jesus Christ our Lord. *Amen.*

Prayer for Illumination 4 ————————

Eternal Father,
>   whose dwelling place is
>>   in the secret wellspring of heavenly light.

Send forth your light and truth,
>   that every secret fear in our hearts
>>   might be open to joy.

>   Grant to us your Holy Spirit,
>>   that we might sense the joyful secret
>>>   abiding with us.

>   Grant to us the Spirit of Truth,
>>   that we might dwell in the secret place
>>>   of the Most High
>>   and abide under the shadow of the Almighty.

Through Jesus Christ our Lord. *Amen.*

Prayer for Illumination 5 ————————

O God of the dawn,
    and God of the lightning,
    God of the full bright sun,
        and God of the colored northern lights.

Grant us your Holy Spirit,
    the Comforter that Christ has promised.

Grant that through the hearing of your Word,
    we might see the radiance
        of the transfigured Christ,

    "until the day dawns,
        and the morning star rises
            in our hearts."

Through Jesus Christ our Lord. *Amen.*

Prayer for Illumination 6 ———————

Blessed be the LORD,
    the Great God,
    the God and Father of our Lord Jesus Christ.

Blessed be the LORD,
    who created all light to be radiant,
        and all wisdom to be holy.

Bless this congregation of your people
    with your Holy Spirit,
        the Spirit of Truth,
    with the teaching of our inner hearts,
    with the inclination of our wills,
    with the drawing forth of all holy desires.

Bless us with the Word of Truth,
    that we might all sing together
        with the joy of true holiness!

Through Christ our Lord. *Amen.*

"Blessed are those who keep his testimonies,
   who seek him with their whole heart."

                                             Psalm 119:2

Let us pray.

Blessed you are, LORD, great God.

    For the testimonies of the prophets,
       we bless you.
    For the statutes of your Law,
       we bless you.
    For the gospel of Christ
          and the witness of the Apostles,
       we bless you, O glorious God.

Grant to us the Spirit of your glory
    and the brightness of your presence,
       that we might read your Word
         and understand.

Through Jesus Christ,
    our gracious Lord. *Amen.*

Prayer for Illumination 8 ─────────

"I will praise thee with an upright heart,
    when I learn thy righteous ordinances."   Psalm 119:7

Let us pray.

Blessed you are, LORD,
    Great God,
    God and Father of our Lord Jesus Christ.

Blessed you are
    for your righteous ordinances,
        for the right,
        for the good,
        for the true and holy!

Bless us with your Holy Spirit,
        your presence within us,
    the Spirit of wisdom and understanding,
    the Spirit of the knowledge of the LORD.

Bless us with an upright heart,
    that we might be right,
    that we might be good, true, and holy.

Through Jesus Christ. *Amen.*

Prayer for Illumination 9 —————

"How can a young man keep his way pure?
　　By guarding it according to thy word."　　　　　Psalm 119:9

Let us pray.

O pure bright source of light,
　　Eternal God of truth and right.

　　　By your Spirit,
　　　　dwell within us.

　　　By your Spirit,
　　　　let us dwell in you.

Pour out on us
　　the quiet purity to hear,
　　the calm purity to understand,
　　the strong purity to act,
　　　according to your most holy Word.

Through Jesus Christ our Lord. *Amen.*

"How can a young man keep his way pure?
By guarding it according to thy word."   Psalm 119:9

Let us pray.

Blessed be the LORD,
    the great God,
    the God and Father of our Lord Jesus Christ.

Blessed you are,
    O God most pure,
        pure in holy light,
        the pure source of everything right.

Purify us, O Fountain of life,
    wellspring of wisdom,
    Word of God from the beginning.

Guard us by your Word,
    the fortress of truth,
    the two-edged sword.

Through Jesus Christ. *Amen.*

Prayer for Illumination 11 ———————

"I will delight in thy statutes;
    I will not forget thy word."
                        Psalm 119:16

Let us pray.

Blessed you are,
    O LORD, great God!

O God, in whom we find our highest joy,
    our delight, and all of beauty.

Pour out again your Holy Spirit,
    that heavenly dove,
    the life-giving Spirit,
    the breath of understanding,
    that glowing tongue of holy flame,
    the soul of wisdom.

That hearing your Word
    it may not be forgotten,
        but glow within us,
    treasured in every thought,
        catching fire in every act.

Through Jesus Christ our Lord. *Amen.*

"My soul is consumed with longing
    for thy ordinances at all times."   Psalm 119:20

Let us pray.

Blessed you are, LORD,
    Great God, Everlasting Sovereign,
    God and Father of our Lord Jesus Christ.

O God whom we long to know,
O Burning Fire within our souls.

Grant to us the tongues of fire,
    the sound of rushing wind,
        your descending Holy Spirit,

        that in knowing your Word,
            we might know your presence,
        that in following your ways,
            we might live in your light.

Through Jesus Christ our Lord. *Amen.*

Prayer for Illumination 13 ——————

"Thy testimonies are my delight,
  they are my counselors."   Psalm 119:24

Let us pray.

Blessed you are, LORD,
    Great God, Eternal Majesty on High,
    God and Father of our Lord Jesus Christ!

O God, our pure delight,
    our greatest joy and holy happiness!

Pour out now your Holy Spirit,
    the inner witness,
    the Spirit of truth,
        that the covenants of the patriarchs,
        the visions of the prophets,
        and the testimonies of the Apostles
            might be for us the way of life.

Pour out now your Holy Spirit,
    that we might live in you, and you in us.

Through Jesus Christ our Lord. *Amen.*

"My soul cleaves to the dust;
    revive me according to thy word!"   Psalm 119:25

Let us pray.

Blessed you are
    Great God, our Creator,
    God and Father of our Lord Jesus Christ,

        who sent forth your Spirit
        and created Adam and Eve
            from the dust of the earth.

    Revive us, Lord, with that Creating Spirit.

    Give us the breath of life,
        and make us truly alive.

Through Jesus Christ our Lord. *Amen.*

Prayer for Illumination 15 ————————

"Make me understand the way of thy precepts,
 and I will meditate on thy wondrous works."   Psalm 119:27

Let us pray.

Lord and Creator of every wondrous light of heaven.

Grant to us that light-giving Spirit
 to understand your precepts,

that we may meditate on all your works,
 the judgments,
 the victories,
 the captivities,
 the redemptions.

And catch the reflection of your lovingkindness
 in every rising sun,
 in crystal frost and snow,
 in summer night,
 in glowing sea.

Through Jesus Christ our Lord. *Amen.*

Prayer for Illumination 16 ———

"Lead me in the path of thy commandments,
    for I delight in it."
Psalm 119:35

Let us pray.

Blessed you are, Lord,
    Great God,
    God and Father of our Lord Jesus Christ.

Your commandments are our delight,
    and your grace is our greatest joy.

    Fill us with that glad light,
        that warm flame and peaceful glow,
            Your Holy Spirit,
            the Spirit of Truth,
            the Counselor Christ has sent.

    Lead us in the path of your commandments,
        in the ancient way of your will.

Through Jesus Christ our Savior. *Amen.*

Prayer for Illumination 17 ——————

"Oh, how I love thy law!
    It is my meditation all the day."
Psalm 119:97

Let us pray.

Blessed you are, Lord,
    gracious Father,

O Lord, whose love is revealed in your Son.

O Lord, whose love is the delight of all life,
    and whose Word we love as the light of life.

Pour out your Spirit
    as we read from your prophets and Apostles,
    that in meditating on them,
        our hearts might be illumined
        and our days filled with peace.

Through Jesus Christ our Lord. *Amen.*

Prayer for Illumination 18 ————————

"Thy testimonies are my heritage for ever;
  yea, they are the joy of my heart."   Psalm 119:111

Let us pray.

Blessed you are, Lᴏʀᴅ,
  Great God,
  God and Father of our Lord Jesus Christ.

Blessed you are, Word of the Father,
  who has spoken to every generation.

  Pour out on us your blessed Spirit,
    that we, too, might know
      the heritage of the holy ones,
      the witness of the saints
        and the people of God,
      the tradition of the Apostles.

  Pour out on us that ancient presence,
    the glory from of old,
    the promise of the future,
    the seal of your coming.

Through Jesus Christ our Lord. *Amen.*

"I incline my heart to perform thy statutes,
   for ever, to the end." Psalm 119:112

Let us pray.

Blessed you are,
   O God and Father of our Lord Jesus Christ.

Great LORD, O God most High!
   Whose gracious gift of the law
      is a gift of wisdom and insight.

Pour out your Spirit,
   that he might empower our spirits,
      to order our lives by your gospel,
      to breathe the peace of Christ,
      to move in the freedom
         of the Kingdom of heaven.

Pour out your Spirit,
   that through his striving with us,
   that through his gentle voice within us,
      we might persevere to the end.

Through Jesus Christ our Lord. *Amen.*

"The unfolding of thy words gives light;
    it imparts understanding to the simple."   Psalm 119:130

Let us pray.

Blessed LORD,
    Great God, Lord of all,
    God and Father of our Lord Jesus Christ,
        whose Spirit spoke
            through the wise men of Israel.

Pour out on us that same Holy Spirit
    as we read the pages they wrote.

Unfold to us your Word,
    and give us light.

Impart to us understanding,
    simple as we are.

O Lord on high,
    grant us the wisdom that is from on high.

Through Jesus Christ our Lord. *Amen.*

Prayer for Illumination 21 —————————

"Thy righteousness is righteous forever,
    and thy law is true."   Psalm 119:142

Let us pray.

Blessed God!
    Eternal Goodness,
    Righteousness and Truth forever!

Blessed you are!
    God and Father of our Lord Jesus Christ.

    Grant to us that pure and Holy Spirit,
        that our hearts may be right,
            with your Law written on them,
        that the inspiration of our thoughts may be true,
            and all our ways truly righteous.

    Pour down your Spirit,
        that we might be lifted up into your presence,
        that we might dwell in righteousness
            and live forever,
        bathed in your truth.

Through Jesus Christ our Lord. *Amen.*

Prayer for Illumination 22 —— Christmas Eve

Ever present God,
Gracious Father,
    who from the womb of the Virgin Mary
        brought new life to all humanity.

    Grant to us your Holy Spirit,
        that hearing your Word
        we might receive it by faith,
            and thereby be born again,
                born from on high,
            and so be your sons and daughters
                for eternity.

Through Jesus Christ,
    Son of Mary, Son of God. *Amen.*

Prayer for Illumination 23 – Christmas Sunday

O God, our all-knowing Lord,
    who granted to the wise men of the East
        that most brilliant star.

Grant to us that same heavenly light,
    that we might find that Savior of the world,
    and kneeling before him,
        present what treasure we have,
            the myrrh of sacrifice,
            the gold of purity,
            the incense of praise.

Through Jesus Christ our Lord. *Amen.*

Prayer for Illumination 24 — Epiphany Sunday

God Omnipotent!
Father all loving! All forgiving!
   who at the baptism of Jesus
   revealed to those of contrite heart
      that this Jesus is truly your anointed Son.

Grant to us that same Holy Spirit
   which through the ministry
      of John the Baptist
         descended on our Savior,
  that even now,
      hearing the preaching of your Word,
      we might repent of our sins
         and begin a new life,
  that in the end
      the whole world might know
         your redemptive will.

Through Jesus Christ our Lord. *Amen.*

Prayer for Illumination 25 – Maundy Thursday

Almighty God,
Most gracious heavenly Father,
    who gave your Son to be the Passover Lamb.

    Pour out on us your Holy Spirit,
        that in reading the story of his Passion,
        we might recognize
            that Christ died for us,
        and claiming him for our Savior,
            might dedicate all that we are
                to His service.

Through Jesus Christ our Lord. *Amen.*

Prayer for Illumination 26 —————— Easter

O God, Eternal Creator,
    who on the first day of creation
        called forth light out of darkness,
    who on the first day of the age to come
        brought life from the tomb.

Grant to us your Holy Spirit,
    that the pure light of Easter morning
        might shine within our lives
        and make us children of light.

For we pray in the name of Jesus, our Lord,
    who is himself the light of the world. *Amen.*

Prayer for Illumination 27 — Ascension Sunday

O God most high!
Everlasting Lord, mighty and lifted up!

Grant to us your Holy Spirit,
    that in these words of Holy Scripture
        our hearts might be lifted up,
        and our minds set on heavenly realities,

    that contemplating the ascension of our Lord,
        we might long to be with him,
        and enter into the joy
           of eternal life.

Through Jesus Christ our Lord. *Amen.*

Almighty God,
Everlasting Lord,
    who poured out your Holy Spirit on the disciples
        gathered in the Upper Room,
    uniting the Church together as one body.

Grant to us your Holy Spirit,
    that through the hearing of your Word
    our lives might be changed,
        and the body of Christ united in holiness,
        and that showing forth
           the beauty of holiness,
           all nations might magnify your truth.

Through Jesus Christ our Lord. *Amen.*

Prayers of
Intercession

Prayers of intercession are a major focus of the public prayer of the Christian Church.

It is in prayers of intercession that we continue the ministry of intercession that Christ gave to the Church to perform in his name. One of the reasons that we come together in assemblies of worship is to pray for the coming of the Kingdom, for the progress of the Gospel, the reforming of society, and the building up of the Church. One of the distinctions between public and private prayer is that in public prayer we pray as a community for the community and for the concerns of the community.

Jesus himself taught his disciples to pray for the coming of the Kingdom. When he gave them the Lord's Prayer, this was one of the things included: "Thy Kingdom come, Thy will be done, On earth as it is in heaven." In the Upper Room, he set the example in his High Priestly Prayer. He prayed for the unity of the Church, for the sanctity of the Church, and for its continuity down through the centuries from one generation to another. On the cross, he prayed for all those who stood around him, even those who were responsible for his sufferings. He taught us to love our enemies and to pray for those who persecute us. He taught us to pray for laborers to be sent out into the harvest. On the cross itself, he began the ministry of intercession that we as his disciples are to continue.

It is not surprising that Jesus gave such a prominent place to intercessory prayer. The ministry of intercessory prayer occupied an important place in the worship of the synagogue. Even in Jesus' day the Prayer of the Eighteen Benedictions had taken on the essential form that it retains down to our own day. As the name suggests, it is a series of prayer concerns prayed through each day. The first three and last three are of a doxological nature. This is characteristic of biblical prayer: It both begins and ends with praise and thanksgiving. Furthermore, each of the Eighteen Benedictions is couched in praise and thanksgiving. That is obviously why they are called benedictions. Intercession and thanksgiving go hand in hand. In fact, the genius of this prayer is the way thanksgiving and intercession are matched. In the intercession for the judges of Israel, that is, Israel's political leaders, God is blessed as governor of human affairs. In the intercession for the restoration of Jerusalem, God is blessed as the Lord who builds up the walls of Jerusalem. This strong concern for intercessory prayer and this linking of thanksgiving and intercession in the Eighteen Benedictions has left its trace all through the New Testament and on the whole history of Christian worship.

When the Apostle Paul wrote to Timothy giving him directions for ordering the worship of the church at Ephesus, he gave him particular instructions on the ordering of public prayer:

> First of all, then, I urge that supplications, prayers, intercessions, and thanksgivings be made for all men, for kings and all who are in high positions, that we may lead a quiet and peaceable life, godly and respectful in every way. This is good, and it is acceptable in the sight of God our Savior, who desires all men to be saved and to come to the knowledge of the truth.   I Timothy 2:1-4

The Church has for centuries understood this to mean that in public worship we are to pray for those responsible for government, for preserving peace in the world, for the general welfare of society, and for spreading the gospel among all peoples. In other passages of Paul's Epistles, we find similar directions and admonitions for the Church's public prayer. He asks the Ephesians to "pray at all times," "making supplication for all the saints, and also for me, that utterance may be given me in opening my mouth boldly to proclaim the mystery of the gospel" (Eph 6:18-19). He admonishes the Colossians to pray that a door might be opened for the preaching of the Word (Col 4:3).

Christian worship puts a strong emphasis on intercessory prayer, particularly in public worship. This is evident in the New Testament and, as we have said, it is especially evident in the ministry of Jesus. As we shall see, in the ancient Church, the Church of the third and fourth centuries, as well as in the Church of the Reformation, the major prayer for the service of the Lord's Day was the Prayer of Intercession. This has strong theological foundations. First of all this practice follows naturally from the Christian doctrine of God. The Christian faith has always taught that God is open to us. God is sensitive to human need and open to our supplications, petitions, and intercessions.

Back in the days of the Enlightenment, the Deists took great pains to deny that God involved himself in our human problems. God set up the universe and left it to be governed by the laws of nature; or, at least, that is the how the Deists looked at it. In fact, they very specifically denied that God was moved by our prayer. It is no doubt one of the reasons that while Deism did much to dissipate more orthodox religious practice it never became a positive religious movement and finally dried up.

On the other hand when the Church has taught that God is responsive to human need and has encouraged people to pray, the Church has flourished in spite of Deism. It is the abiding experience of serious Christians that prayer makes a big difference in life. Deism denied the doctrine of the Trinity as well and this was quite logical on their part because that doctrine affirms that the unity of God is not monolithic but dynamic. God's unity is not closed to us but open to us. God's unity is community. The one God — Father, Son and Holy Spirit — calls us and receives us. He even gives himself for us and to us. He inspires us, comforts us, and sanctifies us. He does this not only for individuals but in the fellowship of the Church. Jesus taught this in the High Priestly Prayer where he prayed that the Church be bound together by the same love that united him to the Father. Intercessory prayer is part of the liturgical outworking of trinitarian theology. It is the inescapable logic of the central Christian teachings on the nature of God.

A second theological foundation of intercessory prayer is the doctrine of the person and work of Christ. In his ministry on earth Jesus healed the sick, restored fallen women, and blessed children. In his Passion he interceded for both his friends and his enemies. We believe that the same Jesus who was open to the needs of men, women, and children here on earth is risen and ascended into heaven. Now in eternal glory he is still open to our needs. He is, true God and true man, even now at the right hand of the Father. In his person our true humanity in all its need and dependence is brought into the presence of the Father. Our prayers, our tears, our cries of anguish are brought before the throne of grace because the Son is our brother. It is he, seated at the right hand of the Father, who is our intercessor. The intercessory prayer of the Church continues the ministry of intercession that Jesus began on earth and completes in heaven.

The third theological foundation of intercessory prayer is the doctrine of the Church. The fellowship of prayer is a manifestation of the bond of the Spirit. When we pray with each other and for each other, it is the Holy Spirit who works among us to unite us in the body of Christ. Calvin put it rather pointedly: It has pleased God to work with human beings through human beings. We are creatures of need. We need God and we need each other. It is therefore through the ministry of other people that God in his wisdom has chosen to bless us. It is in our intercession for each other that we realize what it is to be the Church.

The earliest records we have of the prayers used in Christian worship show that Christians took all these admonitions of Christ and the Apostles to heart. From Clement of Rome, Justin Martyr, and Tertullian we learn that public prayer gave considerable attention to interceding for the Church, for its unity and sanctity, for its work in spreading the gospel, for its leaders and ministers, for the civil authority, and for the preservation of peace. The Church from earliest times understood that it was important to maintain a ministry of intercession.

By the fourth century, most churches had developed a definite list of things for which the assembled Christians prayed at each service. The list differed from church to church, but it is clear that each list was an attempt to follow the directions of Jesus and the Apostles. There would always be a prayer for the Church and a prayer for the ministry; there was usually a separate prayer for the bishop, another for the presbyters, a prayer for deacons, and another prayer for widows. There were separate prayers for all kinds of people in special needs, for orphans, for prisoners, for the afflicted, the sick, and the poor. There was always a prayer for the emperor, the king, the governor, and the magistrates of the city in which the church was gathered.

Sometimes, particularly in the East, this list got rather long. The prayers of intercession found in the *Apostolic Constitutions,* which comes from Antioch in the middle of the fourth century, must contain a couple dozen separate intercessions, among them the following:

> Let us pray for the peace and happy settlement of the world and for the holy churches; that the God of the whole world may afford us his everlasting peace . . .
> Let us pray for the Holy Catholic and Apostolic Church which is spread from one end of the earth to the other; that God would preserve and keep it unshaken . . .
> Let us pray for every episcopacy which is under the whole heaven, of those that rightly divide the word of Thy truth. And let us pray for our bishop James, and his parishes; let us pray for our bishop Clement, and his parishes; let us pray for our bishop Euodius and his parishes . . .
> And let us pray for our presbyters that the Lord may deliver them from every unreasonable and wicked action, and afford them a presbyteriate in health and honor.
> Let us pray for all the deacons and ministers in Christ that the Lord may grant them an unblameable ministration.
> Let us pray for the readers, singers, virgins, widows, and orphans.
> Let us pray for those that are in marriage and in child bearing, that the Lord may have mercy on them all.
> Let us pray for the eunuchs who walk holily.
> Let us pray for those in a state of continence and piety . . .
> Let us pray for our brethren newly enlightened, that the Lord may strengthen and confirm them.
> Let us pray for our brethren exercised with sickness, that the Lord may deliver them from every sickness and every disease, and restore them sound into His holy Church . . .
> Let us pray for our enemies and those that hate us.
> Let us pray for those that persecute us for the name of the Lord, that the Lord may pacify their anger, and scatter their wrath against us.
> Let us pray for those that are without, and are wandered out of the way, that the Lord may convert them . . .
> Let us pray one for another, that the Lord may keep us and

preserve us by his grace to the end, and deliver us from the evil
one . . .   *The Ante-Nicene Fathers* VII, 485

A prayer like this obviously took quite a bit of time. In the West we find
similar prayers. They are not quite as long, perhaps, but they all have in
common this detailed list of definite categories of persons and needs that
should be mentioned before God.

In the Western Church, in the course of the Middle Ages, this prayer
of intercession dropped out of the Mass. A number of the elements of the
prayer reappeared in other places, but the Prayer of Intercession as such
was no longer a part of the regular Sunday Mass. The Reformers were
quick to restore this form of prayer. We find a long prayer of intercession
in the Liturgy of Strasbourg, in Geneva, in the *Book of Common Prayer* of
the Church of England, and in the service book drawn up by John Knox
for the Church of Scotland.

As we have said before, Martin Bucer, the Reformer of Strasbourg, was
among the most creative of the Protestant Reformers when it came to the
reform of worship. It is Bucer that we can credit with taking the lead in
restoring prayers of intercession to the regular worship of the Church. It
was he whom both John Calvin in Geneva and Thomas Cranmer in England followed in developing prayers of intercession for their respective
churches. Bucer composed several versions of this Prayer of Intercession.
In one we find the following concerns:

> Almighty God, heavenly Father, thou hast promised us through
> thy dear Son, our Lord Jesus Christ, that whatever we ask of thee in
> His name thou wilt grant unto us. Thy very Son our Lord hath taught
> us, by Himself and by His beloved apostles, to assemble in His name,
> and hath promised to be there in the midst of us, and procure and
> obtain for us at thy hand whatever we agree to ask of thee on earth . . .
>
> Wherefore we beseech Thee, O heavenly Father, for our most
> gracious rulers, thy servants: our lord Emperor and King, and all
> princes and nobles, and the magistrates of this city. Grant unto them
> thy holy and righteous sovereign Spirit, . . .
>
> That we here and everywhere may lead a quiet, peaceful life in all
> godliness and propriety, and, being delivered from the fear of our
> enemies, serve thee in all righteousness and holiness.
>
> Moreover we beseech thee, O faithful Father and Saviour, for all
> those whom thou hast established over thy faithful people as pastors
> and curates of souls, and to whom thou has entrusted the ministration
> of the holy Gospel. Grant them thy Holy Spirit . . .
>
> Merciful God and gracious Father, we beseech thee further for all
> mankind. As it is thy will to be known as a Saviour to all the world,
> draw to thy Son, our Lord Jesus, those who are still estranged from
> Him . . .
>
> And those whom thou holdest in special discipline, whom thou
> dost visit and chasten with poverty, misery, sickness, imprisonment,
> and other adversity: O Father of mercy and Lord of all consolation,

enable them to perceive thy gracious, fatherly hand, that they may turn their whole hearts to thee who alone dost chasten them, so that thou wilt comfort them as a Father and finally deliver them from all evil . . .

Thompson, *Liturgies of the Western Church,* pp. 175-176

One thing clear from Bucer's prayer is that he has quite consciously followed the lead of such New Testament admonitions to prayer as I Timothy 2:1-8; Ephesians 6:18-19; and Colossians 4:3. One notices that Bucer and the Reformers who followed his lead gradually began to discover more and more passages of Scripture to guide them in shaping their prayers.

By the time Matthew Henry and Isaac Watts wrote their manuals on leading in prayer, the list of intercessions had grown quite considerably. Henry points out that Jesus taught us to pray not only with each other but for each other. For Henry the obvious text from the second chapter of First Timothy is fundamental in shaping our prayers. "We pray as we are taught," says Henry, "for all men, believing that this is good and acceptable in the sight of God our Saviour, who will have all men to be saved, and to come unto the knowledge of the truth, and of Jesus Christ, who gave himself a ransom for all" (*Method of Prayer,* p. 48). Henry goes on to develop his prayers of intercession for the conversion of all nations with the help of the royal psalms, Psalms 2, 72, and 98 in particular, and with the help of several passages from the prophets such as Malachi 1:11, which is reflected in these words: "In every place let incense be offered to thy name, and pure offerings; and from the rising of the sun to the going down of the same, let thy name be great among the Gentiles" (p. 49). From several passages in the Pauline Epistles Henry is encouraged to pray for the conversion of the Jews. From the letters to the seven churches in the Book of Revelation he is encouraged to pray for the Eastern Churches under Muslim domination. The example of Christ in the Upper Room teaches Henry to pray for the unity of the Church, that all believing in Christ be one. This is expanded by passages from the Apostle Paul and even a passage from Jeremiah. Henry's intercessions for his own land and nation — the happy islands of Great Britain and Ireland — are laced with appropriate passages from the Psalms: "Lord, thou has dealt favourably with our land. We have heard with our ears, and our fathers have told us, what work thou didst for us in their days, and in times of old: and as we have heard, so we have seen; for we have thought of thy loving-kindness, O God, in the midst of thy temple" (p. 52; cf. Pss 85:1; 54:1; 48:8-9). From the Proverbs Henry gathers material for his intercessions for the king. Ecclesiastes 11 and 12 reminds Henry to pray for the young in their temptations and for the aged in their discouragement (pp. 56 and 57). As one studies Henry's *Method of Prayer* one is impressed by the diversity of his ministry of intercession, but even more by the constant enrichment of his ministry of prayer by his lifelong study of the Scriptures. Today his book would be hard to use directly as a manual of pastoral prayer, as it was one time, but his general principles are as valid and helpful as they ever were. The Word leads us to prayer and prayer leads us to the Word.

Charles Haddon Spurgeon was outstanding for his ministry of intercession. This English Baptist was probably the leading preacher of his day, yet his prayers were every bit as inspired as his sermons. For Spurgeon it was of the essence of intercession that it flowed from thanksgiving. One of the most important features of the prayer is the way it combines interecession with thanksgiving. The Apostle Paul makes a point of this in his admonition to Timothy. We find him expressing the same thought even more explicitly in his Epistle to the Philippians: "In everything by prayer and supplication with thanksgiving let your requests be made known to God" (Phil 4:6). This is an old principle of biblical prayer: By thanking God for having raised up faithful shepherds for his people in every generation, we pray that he will provide faithful leaders in the Church today. By blessing God as the God of all comfort, we pray for those who suffer.

Many of the prayers of intercession used in the Church have been formulated in such a way that they cover all situations. There are certain advantages in this, but I have taken a very different approach. I consider it important for the Prayer of Intercession to be very specific. Each time I lead the prayer, I think over the needs of the Church and the world, and I formulate the prayer in accordance with these needs. That is, to be sure, just what happened in the prayer that the Jerusalem church prayed after Peter and John were released from prison. It formulates the needs of the Church in a very specific time and place (Acts 4:23-31). In the same way, then, the minister of today ought to lead the congregation in prayer. When I prepare the Prayer of Intercession, I think about what I have read in the newspaper, what I have learned in calling on members of the congregation, and what I have read in *Christianity Today* or *The Christian Century*. Then I prepare my Prayer of Intercession. The Prayers of Intercession that appear later in this chapter are quite often appropriate to a particular time, and I have left them as I wrote them, simply to demonstrate that the Prayers of Intercession should concentrate on very specific problems. And these prayers have been printed with sufficiently wide margins to allow those using this book to pencil in their own specific adaptations. As I have said, it is my intention that this book be a workbook.

The literary form that I have developed for these Prayers of Intercession has been largely suggested by the classical examples provided in the history of Christian worship. I have divided up the intercessions in each prayer into five short paragraphs. First comes an intercession for the Church, then for the ministry, for all people, for the civil authority, and finally for those in the congregation with any special need or suffering any particular trial or adversity. I always maintain this order in order to teach the congregation about the nature of intercessory prayer. Because the members of the congregation know what to expect, they are better able to enter into the prayer and to add their own prayers and concerns to those expressly mentioned by the minister.

Each of the five paragraphs begins with an invocation of God's name. Often I repeat the same invocation in order to help tie the prayer together by bringing our thoughts back to the God before whom we lay our problems. One of the invocations that I am particularly fond of using is, "O God and Father of the household of faith." By coming back to this invocation again and again one emphasizes that the intercessions concern the household needs of the children of God. God is concerned with these things because he is the Father who presides over this household. Repetition is a significant part of prayer, as is evident from the prayer of Jesus in the Garden of Gethesemane, in which he repeated the same prayer over and over again. It is by this kind of repetition that we focus our minds on the power of God to help us in our need. We mention our need before God, but again and again we must return our thoughts to God's power and authority in regard to the situation that concerns us.

As I have said before, it belongs to good literary form that a prayer should have an introduction and a conclusion. Prayers are introduced by invocation. I have always liked the way Bucer introduced the intercessions of the Church of Strasbourg. After invoking God's name he recounts the promise of our Lord that when we join together and present our requests to the Father in Christ's name we can be assured that they will be heard. Prayers of Intercession have often begun with an invocation of this sort. Another approach has been to use an appropriate piece of choral music. Several times the choir director in one of my churches has suggested a choral preface to prayer that has served as a good invocation. When an appropriate choral piece is found, it will be used for three or four months before it is changed. This is done so that the musical text sets up the actual prayer or so that it becomes a doxological framework for the intercessions.

The intercessions are concluded by sealing them in the name of Jesus. The prayers that follow usually try to do this in such a way that there is some mention of the intercessory ministry of Jesus. As usual this sealing takes the form of a doxology using the usual formulas of praise and adoration, although this is often quite brief. The Prayers of Intercession are followed by the recitation of the Lord's Prayer by the congregation.

Most of these prayers have been used several times. Each time they are used they are revised. There is a different president in the White House, and there are a different governor and different senators. A new national emergency has claimed our attention. Different people are in the hospital. Very often, in the course of preparing a sermon, or even in the course of preaching it, the subject matter of the sermon suggests a concern for prayer. This is why, of course, the Prayer of Intercession should follow the sermon. John Calvin as a matter of course included in the Prayer of Intercession those concerns that logically followed from his sermon. He maintained a strong continuity between preaching and prayer. I try to do the same thing when I prepare my sermons. Often I have carefully prepared a prayer in my study and have arrived at church to discover new needs of individuals, or I have been asked to pray for some particular matter. Obviously, the prayer gets revised as it is offered.

What is important is that the minister regularly give time and thought to preparing for this ministry. Spontaneity and preparation should complement each other.

Prayer of Intercession 1 ———————

(based on I Peter 2:4-10)

O Gracious Lord God,
> you have loved us,
>> and have chosen us to be a royal priesthood,
>>> to offer to you spiritual sacrifices.
> We would serve you in a ministry of prayer
>> and intercession.

O Gracious Lord God,
> you have called us out of darkness
>> into your marvelous light.
> We bless you because you are
>> the rock of our salvation.
>>> You are solid and sure and steadfast.
> We pray for the Church, for this Church,
>> founded on the rock of Christ.
> Grant that this congregation
>> may be firmly established in Christ,
>> built up in Christ,
>> performing the work of Christ,
>> filled with the love of Christ.

Gracious Lord God,
> you have called us to be a royal priesthood
>> and a holy nation.
> We pray for the leaders of the Church,
>> for the ministers and pastors
>>> of the various churches of Trenton.
>> Particularly we remember the ministers and deacons of Shiloh
>>> Baptist Church.

O Gracious Lord God,
> you have chosen us to be a holy nation,
> God's own people,
>> a nation called out from all nations,
>> a people called out from all peoples.
> We pray for all peoples and nations.
> We pray for Afghans,
>> trying to preserve their independence.
> We pray for Ethiopians
>> struggling to maintain an ancient Christian culture.

O Gracious Lord God,
> you have chosen us to be a holy nation.

We bless you for the United States of America,
    for the expanse of our land,
    for the bounty of natural resources,
    for the traditions of honesty, justice, and hard work.
We pray for our nation,
    that as a people we might rediscover
        the beauty of holiness.
We pray for our institutions,
    our legislatures and courts,
    our businesses and industries,
    our universities and schools,
    our theaters and places of entertainment,
        that we may discover
            in the bright light of purity,
            in the radiance of holiness,
                the true light of freedom.

O Gracious Lord God,
    you have called all of us to holiness.
We bless you for the promise that we will be perfect,
    even as you, Father, are perfect.
We pray that we might fulfill our vocation,
    that we might accomplish the work you have given us to do.
We pray for those who have no work,
    for those who work but have little return,
    for those who have menial work,
        dangerous work, or burdensome work.
            Complete your work in us.

To you be all glory, Gracious Lord God,
    for we rejoice in the service
        you have called us to perform.
In Christ our great High Priest
    we pray with each other and for each other, saying,

        Our Father who art in heaven, . . .

Prayer of Intercession 2 ——————

Blessed you are, most gracious Father!
    for having prepared for us an eternal kingdom,
        a heavenly city,
        a new Jerusalem.
    As our Lord Jesus has taught us,
        we pray for the coming of that Kingdom.

Father,
    we pray for the Church,
        that she might in truth be the New Jerusalem,
            prepared as a Bride,
            adorned for her husband.
    Give to her true purity,
        that she might be without spot or wrinkle.
    Give her the grace of hope
        and the confidence of joy,
            as she awaits the coming of the Bridegroom.
    We pray for our own congregation.
        Grant that it might be a sign here on earth
            of the Church that is above.

        Blessed you are, O Father,
            for your faithfulness to the Church.

Father,
    we pray for those who lead our Church,
        for pastors,
        for elders,
        for deacons,
    Fill them with the Spirit of wisdom and understanding,
        the Spirit of counsel and might,
        the Spirit of knowledge and of fear of the Lord.

        Blessed you are, O Father,
            for your faithfulness to your servants!

Father, whose love and concern is for a world filled
    with a great variety of people,
    we pray for people in different lands,
        for Mexicans and Brazilians and Colombians,
            for Watusi, Masai, Ibu,
          and all the tribes of Africa,
        for all peoples in China,
          Malaysia, and Indonesia,

for French people and English people,
Greeks and Russians.
Grant that the gospel might be heard in all the corners of the earth.

Blessed you are, O Father,
for you have opened up your Kingdom
to all peoples!

Father,
we pray for those who lead our nation.
Anoint them with the gifts of your Spirit,
honesty, fairness, and intelligence,
love of peace and learning.

Blessed you are, O Father,
for you have specially blessed
our land!

Father and Shepherd of the flock of your people,
we pray for the members of our congregation,
for husbands and wives,
that their love for each other might be ever richer and kinder,
for children and young people,
that they might grow in every good direction,
for people who live alone,
that they might find friendship and community,
for grandparents and elderly friends,
that they might have that radiance which belongs to older years.

Blessed you are, O faithful Shepherd.

All these mercies we ask in the name of Jesus,
who ever sits at your right hand, O Father.
He it is who is our intercessor,
and it is through him
that we are taught to pray, saying,

Our Father who art in heaven, . . .

Prayer of Intercession 3 ——————————

Almighty Father, O Lord of Zion,
    whose name is great among the nations,
    we lift up our hands in the name of Jesus,
        offering up our prayers on every shore
        to you, O Father, to whom praise is ever due.

Almighty Father,
    thanks be to you,
        that you have called to yourself a people
        and established that people in the fellowship of the Church.
    We pray for our sister churches in West Lafayette,
        for Covenant Church and Federated Church,
        for St. Andrew's and Weaver Chapel,
        for the Dutch Reformed Congregation
            and the Disciples of Christ.
    Grant that we might all have a greater sense of our oneness in
        Christ.

Almighty Father,
    thanks be to you
        that Christ has ascended on high,
            leading captivity captive,
        that he has poured out on the Church all manner of gifts,
        that some might be apostles,
            some prophets,
            some evangelists,
            some pastors and teachers.
    We pray for all those whom you have sent
        to preach the gospel.
    We remember especially those who serve in ministries
        unique to our day:
            Jon Doren and his work with Lafayette Urban Ministry
            Susan Barron and her work at
                First Presbyterian Church in Gary,
            Philip Neil and his work with Inter-Varsity
                here on campus.

Almighty Father,
    thanks be to you
        for the creation of Adam and Eve
            and all the variety of their descendants.
    We pray for all peoples and nations,
        those in lands far away from us,
        those who differ from us in race and language and culture.

"Let the peoples praise Thee, O God,
   Let all the peoples praise Thee."   Psalm 67:5

Hasten the day when all peoples
   will praise you, O God,
   in a common life of peace and justice.
Let all the peoples praise you.

Almighty Father,
   thanks be to you,
      O God of peace and justice,
      God of righteousness and order.
We pray for the rulers of this world,
   for kings and emperors,
      presidents and dictators,
   both for those who have advanced the Church
      and those who have persecuted it.
We pray for President Sadat of Egypt,
   for Queen Elizabeth of England,
   for President Giscard d'Estaing of France,
   for members of the Politburo in the Soviet Union.
Grant that under their leadership,
   we might live in peace.

Almighty Father,
   thanks be to you
      for life itself,
      for health and strength.
We pray for all those who suffer,
   for those without home or clothing,
      and suffer the cold of winter
         or the drought of summer,
   for those who are oppressed with dismal or slavish work
      and those without jobs,
   for those dragged down by sickness or disability.

To you we lift up our hands, Almighty Father,
   in the name of your Son, Jesus Christ,
      who taught us to pray, saying,

            Our Father who art in heaven, . . .

Prayer of Intercession 4 ————————————

O God our Father, Eternal Lord and King,
    whose scepter rules over all the earth,
    whose sovereignty embraces all your creatures
        and all their actions.

We come before you to offer
    our prayers and supplications,
    and to continue the ministry of intercession that Christ began.

Father, we bless you for the Church,
    and for the fellowship and wisdom
        that we have found in her.
    Grant that in truth she might be
        the Bride of Christ.
    Give her faithfulness as she waits
        for the coming of her Lord.
    Particularly we pray for the Presbyterian Church.
        Keep her teaching pure,
            her ways true,
            and her witness effective.

Father, we bless you for those who proclaim the gospel of peace,
        for all that we have learned from the preaching
            and teaching of your Word.
    We ask your blessing on the ministers
        of our community.
    Grant that they be true ministers of the Word.
    Give them joy in their work, and make their labors fruitful
        for their congregation.

Father, we bless you that you have given us your Son
    to be a light to the Gentiles and glory to your people Israel.
        We pray for the lost sheep
            of the House of Israel,
                for those who have turned their back
                    on you, whether Christian or Jew.
        Grant that in the end, the hope of Israel
            be fulfilled and that all nations might
            come to the brightness of her rising.
        Grant that the Light that shines in Christ
            might be the judgment of the world.

Father, we bless you for the good and prosperous land that you
have given us.

We pray for the United States of America,
　　for the president, George Bush,
　　for the judges of the courts,
　　for our governor, Jim Florio,
　　for Senator Bradley and Senator Lautenberg,
　　for our congressman, Chris Smith.
Grant that justice might prevail in our land,
　　and equity and righteousness be upheld
　　　　by our people.

Father, we bless you for the kindnesses and mercies of ordinary life,
　　for your providential care of us and all humankind.
Give strength to those who labor for us,
　　and joy to those who work with us.
Make us willing to be of service
　　to those for whom we work.
Guide those who direct our tasks,
　　that we live in harmony.
We remember before you members of our congregation
　　　　in special need, . . .
　　neighbors and friends, . . .
　　members of our families, . . .

All these prayers and requests we present to you,
　　O Heavenly Father,
　　in the name of our Most Blessed Lord and Redeemer,
　　　　even Jesus.

Therefore we pray together his prayer, saying,

　　Our Father who art in heaven, . . .

Prayer of Intercession 5 ──────────

Heavenly Father,
    whose love for all is revealed in the life
        and ministry of your son Jesus.
    We come together, continuing his ministry of intercession
        praying for the whole household of God.

Heavenly Father,
    you have led the Church for so many centuries.
    We pray for the Church today.
        For the Church in Ethiopia, in China,
            and in Hungary,
            we ask courage in time of persecution.
        For the United Presbyterian Church,
            we ask new vision and new life.
        For our own congregation,
            we ask new commitment
                and deeper devotion.

Heavenly Father,
    in every generation you have raised up
        men and women to serve your people.
    We pray for those who lead the Church today.
    We pray for the moderator of the General Assembly,
        for the moderator of the presbytery.
        Particularly we remember Sarah North
            as she begins her new ministry in California.
    Strengthen the bond of peace and love in our presbytery,
        that it be a strong and supportive fellowship.

Heavenly Father,
    you have created an abundance of food
        for both man and beast.
    We pray for all who bring forth food
            from the earth,
        for those who tend herds of cattle,
        for those who cultivate the ground,
        for those who do their work at sea,
        and those who bake our daily bread.

Heavenly Father,
    your kingdom is above
        all nationalities and cultures;
    your authority is above every authority,
        and in your hands is our eternal destiny.

We pray for our own nation and people.
Remember our president, Mr. Bush,
    and all who work with him.
Remember our governor, Mr. Florio,
    and those who serve our state.

Heavenly Father,
    you know of every sparrow that falls;
    you see every tear we shed.
    We pray for all who suffer,
        for the young in their enthusiasm,
        for the adults in their tensions,
        for the elderly in their loneliness.
    Grant that in knowing the joy of your presence,
        they might have the confidence to continue
            their pilgrimage
            and the hope of eternal life.
    We remember those who have asked for our prayers:
        Wanda Litch,
            grieving the loss of her mother,
        Terry Farmer,
            facing an operation on Tuesday,
        Eunice Washington,
            in the Knights of Pythias Home.

Thanksgiving and honor and glory be unto you,
    O God and Father of our Lord Jesus Christ!
        For he who is our Savior
            has been obedient unto death.
        His sacrifice has been accepted
            at your heavenly altar.

Thanksgiving and laud and praise be to you
    because Jesus, risen and ascended, intercedes for us
        now and ever more.

Therefore we pray together, saying,

        Our Father who art in heaven, . . .

Prayer of Intercession 6 ────────────

O Lord and Father of the Household of Faith,
    we thank you for the gift of faith
        inspired within us by your Holy Spirit.
    We thank you for having called us to yourself,
        for consecrating us to your service,
        for having set us apart to the sacred ministry of prayer.

O Lord and Father of the Household of Faith,
    we pray for the Church
        in all her breadth and variety,
        in her pride and worldly power,
        in her simplicity and silence.
    We pray for the Church in her poverty,
        weakness, and stupidity.
    We pray for the Church in her wisdom and long experience,
        for traditional churches and folksy churches,
        for healthy churches and sick churches.
    Grant to the Church true lowliness
        and genuine humility,
            that you might fulfill your purposes
            for her.

O Lord and Father of the Household of Faith,
    we pray for those stewards to whom you have
        entrusted the affairs of your house,
            for moderators and clerks,
            for presbytery executives, synod staff,
                and board secretaries.
    Give them the Spirit of willing service
        and true humility.
    Give them a sense of spiritual devotion.
    Give them delight in those whom they serve.
    Grant that they may lead your people
        in the way of Christ,
            that thereby we might all enter the land
            of our heritage.

O Lord and Father of the Household of Faith,
    we pray for all people, especially our enemies,
        for warring people who disturb our peace,
        for selfish people who would
            take what we have,
        for ugly people who make us feel bad.

Grant that we might come to know your love for them
and be able to pray for them in truth.

O Lord and Father of the Household of Faith,
we pray for our nation,
for politicians and political scientists,
for economists and sociologists,
for statesmen and ward heelers.
Grant that they might all be led by you
as they attempt to lead us.

O Lord and Father of the Household of Faith,
we pray for those whom we know have special needs.
To all who suffer any sickness or weakness,
give health and strength.
To all who are disturbed or troubled,
give rest and understanding.
To all who are lonely and alienated,
give fellowship and love.

We pray for all those who are in any kind
of captivity or exile,
for those who cannot sing the Lord's song
in a strange land.
We particularly remember before you
the refugees from South Vietnam
who have come to our community.

All these requests we present to you,
O Father of mercy, in the name of Jesus Christ,
who even now is seated at your right hand to intercede for us.

Therefore we pray with each other
and for each other, saying,

Our Father who art in heaven, . . .

Prayer of Intercession 7 —————————

O God and Father of our Lord Jesus Christ,
    we remember that our Savior taught us
        to pray for each other.
    We remember how on the cross
        he prayed for the salvation even of those who persecuted him.
    It is following his example that we would pray.

Father of glory, whose name is blessed on every shore,
    we pray for the Church throughout the world,
        for the ancient churches of Europe
            and the Orient,
        for the young vigorous churches
            of Black Africa and East Asia,
        for the churches under the shadow
            of persecution:
                the Church of Christ in China,
                the Orthodox Church of Ethiopia,
                the Reformed Church of Hungary,
      for faint, weary, and dismal churches
        where the fervor of love has cooled.
    Grant to all the joy and power of faith.

Father of all truth and wisdom,
    in every generation you have raised up people
        to lead your Church,
            patriarchs and prophets,
            evangelists and apostles.
    We pray for those who serve your Church today,
        for the Roman Pope,
        for the Patriarch of Constantinople,
        for the leaders of the World Council of Churches,
        for deaconesses, Christian social workers, and pastoral counselors,
        for professors in seminaries, monks, abbots, and priors,
        and all others entrusted with the leadership of the Church.
    Grant to them the Spirit of Christ
        as they minister in his name.

Father of lights,
    from whom every good and perfect gift comes,
        we pray for all kinds of people,
        for farmers and factory workers,
        for artists and artisans,
        for secretaries and nurses,
            doctors and lawyers,

for businessmen and storekeepers,
teachers and students,
for mothers and fathers,
husbands and wives,
sisters and brothers.
Grant that we might receive from you
the strength to do our work
and the grace that it be useful to others.

Father of all peace and justice,
we bless you for the peace
that prevails in our land.
We bless you for the justice
with which our country is blessed.
We pray for our nation and those who lead it.
We remember before you our president,
senators, and congressmen.
We pray for those who lead our state and city,
that they might all be filled with a sense
of dedication to the welfare of our land and people.

Father of mercies and God of all consolation,
we bless you for your healing mercy.
We bless you for your loving kindness.
We pray for those who are weighed down
by sadness or tragedy.
Grant to those who despair
the hope of the gospel.
Grant to those who live in fear
confidence in your strength.
Grant to those who are bored
a sense of your glory.

All these mercies we ask in the name of our Lord Jesus,
who taught us to pray together, saying,

Our Father who art in heaven, . . .

Prayer of Intercession 8 ────────

Choral preface to prayer: "O Lord, I Cry to Thee"

O Lord, we cry to Thee,
  for the Church,
    particularly for our sister churches
      in West Lafayette:
    for Covenant Church,
    for the Church of the Good Shepherd,
    for St. Thomas Aquinas,
    for the Reformed Presbyterian Church,
    for First Methodist Church,
      and the University Church.

    Blessed you are,
      O faithful Father!
    Thanksgiving and honor and glory
      be given to you!

O Lord, we cry to Thee,
  for all who preach the gospel,
    for pastors and teachers,
    for church leaders,
    for missionaries and evangelists,
    for elders and deacons.
  Particularly this morning,
    we remember before you
      the pastors of the Yucatan Peninsula in Mexico.
    Grant to them ever deeper insight
      into your Word and will.
    Grant to them the richest rewards
      for their labors.

    Blessed you are,
      O Shepherd and Pastor of your people.
    Thanksgiving and honor and glory
      be given to you!

O Lord, we cry to Thee,
  for all the people of the earth,
  for people who do not know you,
  for people who have rejected you,
  for people who are angry at you,
  for people who mistrust you.
    Blessed you are, O Father.
      You always seek out the lost,
      bringing salvation to those who are near,

and to those who are far!
  Thanksgiving and honor and glory
    be given to you!

O Lord, we cry to Thee,
  for our own nation,
    and for those who lead our nation.
  We ask your blessing on our president
    and on officials of our state and local community.
  Grant that they might lead us in the ways
    of peace and justice.

    Blessed you are,
      O Righteous Father!
    Thanksgiving and honor and glory
      be given to you!

O Lord, we cry to Thee,
  for the poor and suffering
    of our own community.
  We remember before you
    the work of Lafayette Urban Ministry.
  We remember before you
    Jon Doren and those who work with him.
  Strengthen and guide all those who
    would serve you in this ministry.

    Blessed you are,
      O God of all comfort!
    Thanksgiving and honor and glory
      be given to you!

It is with each other and for each other
  that we pray, saying,

    Our Father who art in heaven, . . .

Prayer of Intercession 9 ────────

Gracious God,
    we bless you
        that you are a God who hears our prayers.
    We bless you
        for the promise of your Son,
            that whenever we pray to you in his name
                you hear us.
        It is therefore in the name of Christ
            that we make our intercessions.

Gracious God,
    we bless you for the Church, our mother,
        Jerusalem on high.
            For the Church on earth we pray,
                for her unity,
                for her purity,
                for her faithfulness,
                for her truthfulness.
    We pray for our own congregation as we plan a new program
        for the fall.
    We pray for those organizing the Sunday School,
        the youth work,
        the music program.
    Grant that we might be a faithful church.

Gracious God,
    we bless you for those who preach the gospel.
    We pray you, Lord of the harvest,
        that laborers might be sent out.
    Grant your blessing to those students for the ministry
        who have gone out from this congregation:
            Al Carter,
            Stan Painter,
            Jim Priest.
    Grant your blessing to those members of our congregation
        who have a special ministry with students:
            Anna Barr,
            Mary Lindsay,
            Wanda Kellogg,
            Philip Neil,
            Barry McKay,
            Nancy Lawrence,
            Ray and Beth Maldonado.

Gracious God,
    we bless you for the creation of all peoples.
    Grant to our world the spirit of peace,
        that wars, rebellions, and revolutions
        might not destroy us.
    Grant justice, O Judge of the Earth,
        that we might live in true peace.
    Particularly we remember the people of Ulster.

Gracious God,
    we bless you for our nation.
    We thank you for the good gifts
        that you have poured out on us —
      for prosperity,
      for peace and justice,
      for law and liberty.
    We bless you for our national institutions —
      our courts,
      our universities,
      our hospitals,
      our business and industry.
    We pray for our land and people,
      for the integrity of our common life.

Gracious God,
    we bless you for your guiding hand,
      for providence,
      for the healing power of your Holy Spirit,
      for the good gifts of life.
    We pray for those who specially need your presence.
      For the father of Mary Priestly,
        we ask healing.

Gracious God,
    to your Father care
      we entrust your people,
    praying as Jesus taught us,
      Our Father who art in heaven, . . .

Prayer of Intercession 10

(based on Revelation 21)

Almighty God,
    who was and is and is to come,
Holy God,
    our Alpha and our Omega,
    our beginning and our end.

We pray for the Church, the Bride of the Lamb.
We pray for her joy,
    her delight in the Lamb,
    her faithfulness to him,
    her purity and spotlessness in the world.
We pray for the Presbyterian Church
    throughout our land,
        that it be true and faithful.

Almighty God,
    our Alpha and our Omega,
    our beginning and our end,
        who brought Israel out of Egypt,
        and sent your infant Son with Mary and Joseph
            down into Egypt,
        and gave them a refuge
            in the days of King Herod.

We pray for the moderator of the General Assembly,
    Henry Buckworth.
    Support him in his ministry of encouragement
        to the Coptic Evangelical Church in Egypt.
We pray for the Patriarch of Alexandria,
    and for all those who lead the ancient
            Orthodox Church of Egypt,
        her bishops, her abbots,
        her monks and priests.

Lord God Almighty,
    who was and is and is to come,
    who has promised us a new heaven and a new earth.

We pray for our own land,
    faced with the problem of inflation.
Grant to us as a people
    a willingness to live simpler lives,
    the heart to share with other nations
        the plenty that you have given us.

Almighty God,
    who was and is and is to come,
    King of Kings and Lord of Lords,
        to whom in the end all authority belongs.

We pray for the kings of this earth,
    the leaders of China,
    the president of South Korea,
    the government of Taiwan,
    the republic of India.
Grant that rulers of these lands
    might provide justice among their people.

Lord God,
    Almighty, Everlasting, Eternal,
    who was and is and is to come,
        in whose presence every tear will be wiped away,
            death will be no more,
            and there will be no more mourning,
            nor crying, nor pain,
        for all things will have passed away.

We pray your blessing on those who mourn,
    on those who are alone,
    on those who live in hope,
    on those who wander,
    on those who are homeless.

To you we make our prayers,
    Holy, Holy, Holy God,
    who was and is and is to come,
        claiming the intercession of him
        who is at your right hand,
            Jesus Christ, the righteous,
    praying as he taught us, saying,

        Our Father, . . .

Prayer of Intercession 11 ———————

Almighty and Eternal Father,
    who revealed your Law through Moses,
    grace and truth through Jesus Christ,
we bless you for the fullness of your revelation,
    for your mighty acts of salvation,
    for the faithful record of these acts in the Bible,
    for the warnings and the promises of the prophets,
    for faithful preachers
        who have sown the seed of the Word
            in our hearts.

Almighty and Eternal Father,
we bless you for the Church,
    which you raise up in every land
    and among all peoples.
        We pray for the Methodist Church of Indiana,
            having its annual conference this week here
                in West Lafayette.
        We pray for its prosperity,
            its growth,
            its evangelistic spirit.

Almighty and Eternal Father,
we bless you for your servants and
    the stewards of your kingdom.
        For Pope John Paul,
            grant that he be a faithful follower of Christ.
        For James McCord, president of Princeton Seminary,
            grant that he be a true doctor of the Church.
        For the elders of Faith Church,
            grant that they be true shepherds of this flock.

Almighty and Eternal Father,
we bless you for the hope of salvation
    proclaimed to all peoples.
We pray for those who are near,
    and those who are far,
    for those in West Lafayette
        who have not received the gospel.
Grant them the grace to hear.
We pray for those in distant lands
    who have never even heard of Christ
        or his gospel.

Grant them the grace to know the truth,
the truth that will set them free.

Almighty and Eternal Father,
we bless you for the good land that you have given us.
We pray for our own people,
for our nation,
the United States of America.
Make us a commonwealth of peace and justice.
Reveal to us the true Law.
Make us a people faithful to your Law.

Almighty and Eternal Father,
We bless you for your fatherly comfort and mercy.
For those who suffer, we offer our prayers,
for friends and relatives who are ill,
for the elderly, who face increasing infirmity.
We particularly remember Eunice Washington at the
Knights of Pythias Home.
We remember our friends at the American Nursing Home,
Mrs. Howell,
Mrs. Stark,
Mr. Johnson.
Grant that they all have a sense of your abiding grace.

O God and Father of our Lord Jesus Christ,
We bless you for your Son our Savior,
for it is through him,
and in him,
and following him,
that we pray,

Our Father who art in heaven, . . .

Lord God, infinite, eternal, unchangeable,
O Father most gracious,
    to whom we turn in every need.
    Hear our prayer for the sake of our Lord Jesus,
        your well-beloved Son,
            our Savior and Redeemer.

Our Father in heaven,
    immortal, invisible, God only wise,
    we pray for the Church,
        the people you have called out of every land and nation.
    Grant that by the wondrous working
        of your Holy Spirit,
        the Church over this whole earth
            might be united,
            one in spirit and truth,
            one in fellowship and love.
    Particularly, we pray for
        the Church in El Salvador.
        Prosper the work so faithfully begun.
        Build up the Church by the true preaching of your Word.
        Raise up pastors and teachers
            to shepherd the flock of your people.

Our Father in heaven,
    we pray for the work of missionaries
        and evangelists.
    Grant that they proclaim the gospel in power,
        clarity, and understanding.
    Grant that their message be received
        by those to whom they are sent.
    Particularly this morning,
        we pray for young people who have gone out
        from our church:
            Mike Everts,
            Tom Newton,
            Philip Neil,
            Anna Barr,
            Mary Lindsay,
            Bill Steele,
            Stan Painter,
            Al Carter.

Our Father in heaven,
     infinite, eternal, and unchangeable,
     dwelling in highest heaven,
          beyond the reaches of our minds,
          higher than our highest thoughts.
     We pray for all peoples in all nations.
     We pray that in every land
          there might be peace and true justice.
     Grant that in our own community
          those who are troubled,
          those who suffer,
          those who are discouraged,
             might find support in time of need.
     Particularly we remember before you the work of the Lafayette
          Urban Ministry.

Our Father in heaven,
     immortal, invisible, God only wise,
          center of calm,
          source of peace.
     We pray for our nation
          and those who lead our nation.
     Particularly we remember the members of our diplomatic corps
          involved this week in disarmament talks.

Our Father in heaven,
          how patient you are with us,
          how slow you are to give us up,
          and how quickly you receive us back.
     We pray for each other,
          for those beside us in prayer.
     We pray for those whose hope has failed,
          for those whose vision has been lost,
          for those whose dreams have perished.
     Pour out on them a fresh portion of your Spirit.

It is to this end that we pray with each other
     and for each other, saying,

          Our Father who art in heaven, . . .

Prayer of Intercession 13 ————————

(based on Malachi 1:11)

O Father,
    God, Eternal and Everlasting,
    from the rising of the sun to its setting,
    your name is great among the nations.
To you, O Lord God,
    be the incense of praise,
    the pure offering of thanksgiving.

Mighty God,
Lord of your people in every land.
    We pray for the Church in Sudan,
        for the Coptic Evangelical Church in Egypt,
        for the Bethel Presbyterian Church of the Upper Nile,
        for the Orthodox Church of Abyssinia,
            that Ethiopia stretch out her hand to you.   Psalm 68:31

    Particularly we remember the work of Dr. and Mrs. Stone
        in our medical mission in the Sudan.

O Father,
    whose name is blessed on every shore,
    from the rising of the sun to its setting.
        We pray for other pastors in our community:
                John Davis and Stan Farrell,
                Ken Parks,
                Albert Hotchkins,
                Tom Hanson, Sandy Miller, Hugh Taylor.
        Strengthen them in their ministries,
            and by your Spirit give them increase.

O Lord of Hosts,
    from the rising of the sun to its setting,
        your name is great among the nations.
Lord of all the earth,
Creator of all its people,
    we pray to you for peoples who are in misery,
        for lands where there is great poverty,
        where there is war or political unrest,
        where there is oppression and tyranny.

    Particularly we remember the people of Haiti,
        Dominica, the Dominican Republic, Grenada,
        St. Vincent and the Grenadines.

Grant that the poverty of these island nations might
be relieved.

O Father,
  whose name is blessed on every shore,
O Lord of all the earth,
O Most Pure God,
  of purer eyes than to behold evil.
  We pray for our own land,
      for our president, Mr. Reagan,
      for our governor, Mr. Orr,
      for our senators, Mr. Lugar and Mr. Quayle.
  Grant that they lead our land and people
      in a life of justice and equity
      that reflects your glory.

O God,
  whose glory is from the rising of the sun
      to its setting,
O Lord of Hosts,
  we pray to you for those in our congregation
      who are in special need.
          We mention their names in the silence
              of our hearts. . . .
  Grant deliverance from suffering,
      easing of pain,
      mending of what has been broken,
          and hope for the future.

It is to you, O Father, God Eternal and Everlasting,
  that we present these prayers and supplications,
      trusting only in the merit and sacrifice of Christ,
              through whom,
              with whom,
              and in whom we pray, saying,

          Our Father who art in heaven, . . .

Prayer of Intercession 14 ————

Almighty God, Lord and Father,
    to you our prayer ever ascends.
God of all wisdom,
    in your providence the order of our lives is found.
God of grace,
    at your right hand is seated our Lord Jesus,
    through whom our prayer ever ascends.

Almighty God,
    how thankful we are for the endowment of spiritual treasures
        that you have bestowed
            on the Church,
        for the gifts of patience and long suffering.

We pray to you for the Church.
We rejoice in the reunion of the Northern and Southern
    Presbyterian churches.
Grant that with this strengthened unity
    there might be a renewal
        of purity and holiness in the Church,
        a deeper understanding of Christian truth,
        and a renewed fervor of witness.

Almighty God, Our Lord and Father,
    we pray for those who lead your Church,
        for theologians and doctors of theology,
        for teachers in seminaries
            and Bible institutes,
        for directors of Christian education.
Particularly, we remember those who teach
    in Vacation Bible School.
Grant that in the week ahead
    we might finish our course of study.
Grant that this teaching might be for our children
    a time of true growth
    in understanding and wisdom.

Almighty God, Lord of all the Earth and of all the peoples
    of the earth,
    how thankful we are for the creation of such a great variety of
        peoples over all the earth.
    We pray to you for the people of Latin America,
        and especially our friends in the Yucatan.
    We remember the people of Chelem and Chuberna Puerto,

among whom we worked last summer.
Especially we remember
Don Bernardo,
Doña Carita,
Don Agostino,
Don Joaquin,
Doña Sarita.

Almighty God, Lord of time,
Lord of the beginning and Lord of the end.
We pray to you for our country,
for our President, Mr. Reagan,
for senators and congressmen,
and all who lead our land,
that we might continue in prosperity and peace.

Almighty God, Lord and Father,
to whom our prayer ever ascends.
How thankful we are for your loving kindness
and steadfast love.
You alone know our secret longings.
You alone know our anguish and frustration.
We pray to you for those who are in need,
for those undergoing tribulation,
for those who long to see your face
and enter the fullness of your presence.

Lord and Father,
to whom our prayer ever ascends.
Thanks be to you for your eternal purposes,
for the working out of your beautiful designs.
Thanks be to you
that our chief end is to glorify you,
and enjoy you forever.
Thanks be to you for an eternal destiny.
It is as we look toward that destiny
that we pray with each other,
and for each other, saying,

Our Father who art in heaven, . . .

Prayer of Intercession 15

Gracious Almighty God,
  Eternal Lord,
    your truth is everlasting
      and your mercy endures forever.
Jesus prayed to you as a son to his father
  and taught us to pray to you as our Father,
    and so we come to you,
      confident that you hear us.

O God, our Father,
  we bless you for the Church,
    for the witness she has passed on,
    for the teaching of the Law
      and the preaching of the gospel.
  Grant to the Church today
    a true understanding of your Word,
    that she might nourish your people.
  Particularly we remember the ministry
    of Christian education
    in our own congregation,
      the work of the Sunday School,
      the work of the Bethel Bible Class.

O God, our Father,
  we bless you for those who have guided your Church
    down through the centuries,
      for prophets and apostles,
      for teachers, pastors, and evangelists
        in every age.
  We pray for the leaders of our Church today,
    for the moderator of the Presbyterian Church,
    for the archbishop of Canterbury,
    for the president of the Southern Baptist Convention,
    for the Roman Catholic pope,
    for the patriarch of Constantinople.
  Grant that through their leadership
    the Church in our day might be faithful.

O God, our Father,
  we bless you for all the peoples of the earth,
    for people who believe,
      and people who doubt,
    for people who find faith natural and easy,
      and people who find it a struggle,

for people who seem to know the truth simply,
and for those who fight against it.
Grant to all of us perseverance,
that we might press on in our pilgrimage.

O God, our Father,
we bless you for our nation,
for its vastness,
for its prosperity,
for its freedoms.
Grant to us
wisdom in the use of our wealth,
purity in the use of our freedoms,
justice in the distribution of our prosperity,
discipline in our vitality.

O God, our Father,
we bless you for our parents,
for our mothers and fathers,
who have been a priceless treasure to us,
for parents who have nurtured us
and trained us.
We pray each of us for our own parents,
remembering in the quiet of our hearts
their individual needs.
Particularly we remember before you Vince Bishop,
the father of Mary Jenson and Connie Levy,
praying for his recovery.

All these prayers and supplications we present to you
in the name of Jesus Christ our Savior.
He is our Great High Priest,
presenting our prayers
before the throne of Grace.
It is he who taught us to pray with each other
and for each other, saying,

Our Father who art in heaven, . . .

Lord God Eternal,
    your mercy and gracious love
        is toward all who revere you,
    your faithfulness never fails,
    your justice endures forever,
    your peace will be established at last.

Lord God Eternal,
    thanks be to you,
        for your steadfastness,
        for the generations your Church
            has been steadfast in this city.
    Thanks be to you
        for generation after generation
            of faithful men and women
            who have maintained your Church in this city.
    We come with our prayers for the Church,
        for our own church,
            First Presbyterian Church of Trenton,
        for our sister churches,
            Bethany,
            Prospect Street,
            Westminster,
            Lawrence Road.
        Grant that together we might carry out a faithful ministry
            to this city today.

Lord God Eternal,
    your faithfulness never fails.
    Generation after generation
        you have provided faithful pastors
            for this city.
    We pray for the pastors of this city today,
        Jerry Mayer,
        Norman Short,
        Joe Herman,
        Tim Waters.
    Bless these pastors
        with every gift of ministry,
            the gifts of compassion and zeal,
            the gifts of wisdom and learning,
            the gifts of diligence and patience,
            the gift of prayer,
      so that the Church in Trenton

might serve you for generations to come.
Lord God Eternal,
    whose justice endures forever,
        we pray for all peoples.
    We remember particularly the people
        of Central America:
            Nicaragua,
            El Salvador,
            Guatemala,
            Honduras,
            Costa Rica,
            Panama.
    Grant that justice, equity, and peace
        might be established in these lands.

Lord God Eternal,
    your mercy is toward all those who revere you,
    your peace will be established at last,
    your faithfulness never fails.
        Thanks be to you, ever gracious God!
    We pray for our own lands and people,
        for our president, Mr. Reagan,
        for our governor, Mr. Kean,
        for our civil servants of all kinds.
    Grant that they be anointed with the gifts
        of honesty, industry, fairness, and
            generosity.

Lord God Eternal,
    whose gracious love is toward all who revere you.
    We pray for members of this congregation
        in special need,
        making mention of them in the silence
            of our own hearts.
    We pray for ourselves.
        You know our needs,
            and we lay them before you,
            for you are our God.

To you, Lord God Eternal,
    our God for ever and ever,
        be all praise and honor.
And to your Son, all power and glory,
    for we pray in his name and as he taught us, saying,

        Our Father who art in heaven, . . .

Prayer of Intercession 17 ————————

(based on Christ's prayer on the cross)

Eternal God,
    you so loved the world
        that you gave your only Son
        and offered him up on the cross.
For the gift of your Son, we thank you.
    We offer up our prayers in his name.
    We continue the ministry of intercession
        which he began on the cross.

Eternal God,
    you so loved the world
        that the whole world might know
            of the outpouring of your love.
We pray for the Church,
    that the Church might be faithful,
        a true witness of your suffering love
            in a world of such suffering,
            in a city of such suffering.
We pray for this church,
    that we might be faithful
        in the service of love.
We remember before you the Trenton Academy,
    and the principal.
Grant that this ministry be filled
    with your love and your truth.

Eternal God,
    you so loved the world
        that you offered up your only Son.
We pray to you in Christ's name
    and in his service.
We pray to you for our minister,
    Neill Williams.
    Particularly we pray for him this week as he
        travels to San Salvador.
    Grant that he might be ministered to.
    Grant that his faith be strengthened.
    Grant that he be inspired by the deep faith
        of Christians enduring such suffering.
Thanks be to you, compassionate God!

Eternal God,
    you so loved the world
        that you opened yourself up to suffering.
    We pray for all peoples,
        particularly the peoples of Central America,
            the Nicaraguans,
            the Costa Ricans,
            the Hondurans,
        that in those lands peace and justice might be established.

Eternal God,
    you so loved the world.
        You even love the lost people of our own city,
            the street people of Trenton.
        You died for the thief on the cross,
            and so we pray for criminals,
                for inmates at Trenton State Prison.
        We pray for those who maintain a prison ministry.
    Thanks be to you, compassionate God!

Eternal God, God of all Comfort,
    you so loved the world
        that you gave your Son
        that he might pass through suffering,
        that he might be the firstborn
            from the dead,
        that he is even now seated
            at your right hand.
    Thanks be to you, compassionate God!
        We remember those suffering in our own congregation —
            Maude Alberts,
            Marianne Root,
            Janet Stokes.

Eternal God,
    we offer up our prayers
        in the name of Christ,
        through the intercession of Christ,
        in the fellowship of the body of Christ.

        Our Father who art in heaven, . . .

Prayer of Intercession 18 ——————

Father Eternal,
God Almighty,
    you have brought forth from the root of Jesse
        a shoot,
      Jesus our Savior.
    Your Spirit rests on him.
    He is your anointed one, the promised Messiah,
      and in him you are well pleased.
    We come to you in his service,
      to offer our prayers of intercession
      for the coming of his kingdom.

Father Eternal,
    you have anointed Jesus
      to be both Lord and Christ.
    We pray for the Church of Christ,
      that she might be faithful to her Lord,
      bearing witness to his reign
        in every land and among every people.
    We pray for the Church in Korea,
      for the Church in Taiwan,
      for the Church in Hong Kong.
        Blessed you are, Eternal Father,
        Savior of the Church in every land!

Father Eternal,
    you have anointed Jesus
      to be our Lord and Shepherd.
    We pray for those whom you have anointed with Christ's Spirit
      to be for us prophets and apostles.
    Grant that they may faithfully proclaim
      the gospel of your coming.
    We pray for young ministers beginning their ministry,
      and for elderly ministers who have retired from active service.
    Grant that their work might bear its fruit
      in its season.
        Blessed you are, Eternal Father,
        strength of your servants!

Father Eternal,
    you have anointed Jesus
      to be Lord of all the earth.
    We pray for all the peoples of the earth,
      that there be peace on earth,

good will toward all humankind.
Particularly we remember the Near East,
    the land of the shepherds and the wise men,
    the land of Israel, Syria, and Egypt,
    the tensions between Jews and Arab Christians and Muslims.
Grant that they might kneel
    before the Prince of Peace.
        Blessed you are, Eternal Father,
        source of never-failing peace!

Father Eternal,
    you have anointed Jesus
        King of Kings and Lord of Lords.
We pray for the kings and rulers of the world
    that they might be wise,
    recognizing the Lord
    to whom they must bow in the world to come.
Grant to our president
    and the political leaders of our nation
        a consciousness of the true nature of their power and authority.
        Blessed you are, Eternal Father,
        you are in the end the final authority!

Father Eternal,
    you have anointed Jesus
        a counselor and comforter of your people.
We pray for those among us that suffer,
    for those who are lonely,
    for those without home or family,
    for broken families,
    for those in financial need.
Grant to each the fullness of life
    for which you have created them.
        Blessed you are, Eternal Father,
        Father of the fatherless!

Praise, honor and glory be to you, Father Eternal,
    and to the eternal Son in whom we pray, saying,

        Our Father who art in heaven, . . .

Prayer of Intercession 19 ——————

(based on Psalm 80)

Give ear, O Shepherd of Israel,
>who leadeth Joseph like a flock.
Thou who art enthroned upon the cherubim shine forth.
Give ear, O Good Shepherd,
>stir up thy might
>>and come to save us!

O Shepherd of Israel,
>we pray for the Church wherever she is gathered.
We pray for the Church in China,
>>that she might have the strength to endure,
>>that she have the courage
>>>to maintain her witness,
>>that she might be comforted
>>>in her tribulation,
>>and that in the end we might all rejoice
>>>in her victory.
We pray for the Church here in Trenton,
>>that she might present a faithful
>>>witness in the center of this ruined city, devastated
>>>>by the sins of our day.
Restore us, O Lord God of hosts!
>Let thy face shine, that we may be saved!

O Shepherd of Israel,
>we pray for those whom you have called
>>to shepherd your flock in our day.
We pray for our pastor, Neill Williams,
>>for his assistant, Hugh Driver.
We pray for the elders,
>>that all together they might lead your people
>>>in soundness of doctrine,
>>>in vitality of example,
>>>in purity of life,
>>>in genuineness of love,
>>>in fervor of commitment.
Restore us, O Lord God of hosts!

O Shepherd of Israel,
>enthroned on the cherubim,
>we pray for all peoples.
>>Particularly we pray for street people,

those who spend the night in our cemetery.
We pray for those who are enslaved by drugs,
by alcohol,
by prostitution and fornication.
Restore us, O Lord God of hosts!

O Shepherd of Israel,
give ear to the cries of the city of Trenton.
Stir up thy might and come to save us,
"Thou dost make us the scorn of our neighbors."
We pray for the civil authority,
for our mayor, Mr. Holland,
for our governor, Mr. Kean,
and for our newly elected president, Mr. Bush.
Restore us, O Lord God of hosts!

Give ear, O Shepherd of Israel,
judge of the earth,
whose reign is for the healing
of the nations,
the salvation of the world.
We pray for those who are suffering,
Daniel, John, Raymond, and Terry.
We pray for those in nursing homes,
Mrs. Farley,
Miss Wrightly.
Restore us, O Lord God of hosts!

Praise, honor, and blessing
ever be to you, O God, our God,
and to the eternal Son our Savior.
Hear our prayer in his name,
for in him we pray as he taught us, saying,

Our Father who art in heaven, . . .

Prayer of Intercession 20 ———

Father Above,
    whose glorious dwelling is in the heavens,
    even when the light of heaven is hidden by dark clouds.
    Ever to you, Father Above, is our praise,
        honor, and thanksgiving.
      From your hand comes every blessing.
    Therefore, before your heavenly temple
      we offer our prayers of intercession.

Father Above,
    giver of every good and perfect gift.
We pray for the Church,
    wherever she is gathered this Lord's Day.
    Particularly we pray for our own congregation.
    Grant that her witness may be sure,
      her teaching apt,
      her fellowship open,
      and her doctrine sound.

Father Above,
    in your service is our highest joy.
We pray for the ministry.
    We ask your presence with the preachers of our land
      as they open to us your Word.
    Ever deepen their understanding of the Scripture,
      and their ability to rightly divide the word of truth.
    We remember as well those who lead
      the service of praise,
        the organist,
        the choir and its director.
    Fill them with your Spirit,
      that there be melody in their hearts
        as well as on their tongues.

Father Above,
    we pray for all peoples.
You are a God over all.
    The heavens are telling your glory,
      and your Word is heard to the end of the world.

    Grant that the gospel of the risen Christ
      may be proclaimed this day
      to every people in every tongue.

Grant that in this community,
    those who have no peace,
    those who are alienated,
    those who are alone,
        might find reconciliation,
        through the faithful witness
            of your people and the fellowship
            of your house.

Father Above,
    we pray for our nation.
King above all gods.
    You have been our strength,
        our rock,
        our fortress.
    You have been the God of our forefathers,
        and still in you we trust.
    Grant that our nation might be ever faithful
        to you, Great God our King.

Father Above,
    God of all comfort.
We pray for those who suffer,
    for those who endure poverty,
    for those burdened by debt,
    for the crippled,
        the sick,
        the troubled and tormented.
    Particularly we remember. . . .
        Grant the easing of their pain.
        Give them healing and grant them peace.

Our prayers we present in the name of Jesus,
    our Great High Priest,
        who has entered into the heavenly sanctuary
            to present our prayers before you.
    It is therefore that we pray as he taught us, saying,

    Our Father who art in heaven, . . .

Communion Prayers

The Lord's Supper should be a feast of praise and thanksgiving. It is here above all that the minister should give attention to leading the congregation in prayer. Here particularly the minister wants to avoid a perfunctory celebration — the sort of celebration that simply gets out the book and reads it from beginning to end.

When Jesus celebrated the Passover with his disciples in the Upper Room, he undoubtedly followed the usual pattern of the Passover Seder. There was first, before the meal actually began, a short blessing over the first cup; this cup served as a sort of aperitif (Luke 22:17). It was followed by the singing of the first two or three of the six Hallel Psalms. Even in the time of Jesus the Hallel Psalms, that is, Psalms 113–118, had long been a traditional part of the Passover Seder. Only then was the meal actually begun. The bread was broken and with this there was a short blessing. At the end of the meal, there was a long prayer over another cup of wine. This cup was called the cup of blessing (I Cor 10:16). After the meal, the remainder of the Hallel Psalms were sung as the conclusion of the service (Mark 14:26).

The Passover Seder, then, included three prayers and the singing of the Passover Psalms. We know the wording of these prayers fairly well, but we also know that in those days a man of recognized spiritual authority, such as Jesus, was supposed to elaborate the traditional themes and wording of the Seder prayers. When we read in the Gospels that Jesus gave thanks over the bread at the beginning of the meal, he may have given thanks at considerably greater length than what was at that time becoming the traditional benediction over bread. Then when he gave thanks over the cup of blessing, he may have given thanks not only for the mighty works of redemption through the history of Israel but also for what God was even then doing in him for the redemption of the world. One thing is sure: Jesus told the disciples that from that time on, they were to celebrate the meal not only in memory of the redemption from Egypt, but in memory of him and God's redemptive work in him (I Cor 11:25).

That is exactly what we find in the communion prayers of the earliest Christians. The *Didache* provides us with not just a single eucharistic prayer but a full set of communion prayers. There is a prayer over the first cup, a prayer over the bread, and finally a prayer over the cup of blessing. There is even a fairly strong indication that the Hallel Psalms were sung at the service. All the prayers are prayers of thanksgiving for our redemption in

Christ. They particularly emphasize the Christian hope and expectation of Christ's coming again finally to establish the kingdom.

The prayers of the *Didache* fit very well into the pattern of prayers of the Passover Seder. There is no reason to doubt that these prayers are in fact typical early Christian prayers for the sacrament of communion. Those who have tried to explain them as prayers for a nonsacramental agape feast, it seems to me, are a bit too eager to insist on certain doctrinal theories that the earliest Christians simply did not have. The earliest Christians did not understand these prayers as some sort of formula for transforming bread and wine into the body and blood of Christ, nor were these prayers the means of presenting some sort of sacrifice to God. The text speaks for itself:

> And concerning the Eucharist, hold Eucharist thus: First concerning the Cup, "We give thanks to thee our Father, for the Holy Vine of David thy child, which, thou didst make known to us through Jesus thy child; to thee be glory for ever."
>
> *Didache* 9:1-2

The text could hardly make it more clear that it is the sacrament of the eucharist that is under discussion. The prayer, or benediction over the bread, runs as follows:

> We give thee thanks, our Father, for the life and knowledge that thou didst make known to us through Jesus thy child. To thee be glory for ever. As this broken bread was scattered upon the mountains, but was brought together, and became one, so let thy Church be gathered together from the ends of the earth into thy kingdom, for thine is the glory and the power through Jesus Christ for ever.
>
> *Didache* 9:3-4

One notices here the form of the Hebrew *berakah* or blessing. The Christian tetragrammaton, "Our Father" (ABBA), has replaced the Jewish tetragrammaton, "Lord" (YHWH). One notices that the prayer is concluded by a doxology that seals the prayer in the name of Jesus. All this shows how closely related these prayers are to the worship of the New Testament Church. What we find most interesting, however, is the theme of this prayer. It prays for the gathering together of the Church in this act of sharing together the bread. One finds the same theme in I Corinthians 10:16-17. This should surely be one of the primary themes of the communion prayers.

The major prayer of the communion service reported in the *Didache* is the prayer over the cup of blessing:

> We give thanks to thee, O Holy Father, for thy Holy Name which thou didst make to tabernacle in our hearts, and for the knowledge and faith and immortality which thou didst make known to us through Jesus thy Child. To thee be glory for ever. Thou, Lord Almighty, didst create all things for thy name's sake, and didst give food and drink to men for their enjoyment, that they might give thanks to thee, but us

hast thou blest with spiritual food and drink and eternal light through thy Child. Above all we give thanks to thee for that thou art mighty. To thee be glory forever. Remember, Lord, thy Church to deliver it from all evil and to make it perfect in thy love, and gather it together in its holiness from the four winds to thy kingdom which thou has prepared for it. For thine is the power and glory forever. Let grace come and let this world pass away. Hosanna to the God of David. If any man be holy, let him come! if any man be not, let him repent: Maranatha, Amen.   *Didache* 10:2-6

While this prayer is clearly a prayer of thanksgiving for God's works of creation and redemption in Christ, the subject is presented in a way that is not familiar to us. Jesus is called "thy Child," and this implies that Jesus is both the messianic Son of God referred to in the psalms and the Suffering Servant referred to in Isaiah. When the prayer gives thanks that we have received "spiritual food and drink and eternal light through thy Child," we are hearing an understanding of God's saving work in Christ very close to the Wisdom theology in the sixth chapter of the Gospel of John. The allusion to the Hallel Psalms, "Hosanna to the God of David," likewise implies a doctrine of the incarnation and even a doctrine of the resurrection of Christ.

These prayers are extremely terse in comparison to the prayers of later generations, but then that is the style of the whole document. The people who produced the *Didache* were not lavish in their use of pen and paper, but when they began to pray in an actual service of worship they may have been considerably more lavish in their use of words. The *Didache* hints at this when it suggests that the prophets were free to pray as they were given inspiration (10:7).

In the second century, it became more and more the practice to make one great prayer over both the bread and the wine. This prayer, as it is reported by Justin Martyr in the middle of the second century, was a thanksgiving for God's works of creation and redemption. Justin tells us that the one who presided was expected to formulate this eucharistic hymn of praise in his own words. This tradition continued for some time. The heart of the prayer was a recounting of the whole history of redemption.

Basil of Caesarea has left us a particularly eloquent Eucharistic Prayer from the fourth century in which he blesses God at length for creation, for the calling of Israel, for his sending of his Son to redeem the world, for Christ's incarnation, for his sacrifice on the cross, and for his resurrection from the grave. There has been quite a bit of speculation as to whether this prayer was actually composed by St. Basil. There seem to be several compelling reasons for accepting his authorship. It may well be, however, that Basil was in the practice of formulating the prayer afresh each time he celebrated the sacrament and that the text we have represents only one version, which at one time or another was taken down by a stenographer. Basil preached extemporaneously and he may have prayed extemporaneously too, especially when it was a matter of offering the festive thanksgiving that traditionally began the Eucharistic Prayer. In the *Apostolic Constitutions* we find a very similar prayer.

As time went on, other elements crept into this Eucharistic Prayer. Beginning with Hippolytus, early in the third century, the prayer began to become a prayer of consecration, by which the bread and wine were transformed into the body and blood of Christ, and then offered up as a sacrifice to God. More and more the prayer became fixed, and by the time of Gregory the Great at the end of the sixth century, the celebrant was to say the prayer exactly as it had by that time been formulated. All the way through the Middle Ages, this Eucharistic Prayer remained the canon of the Roman Mass.

With the Reformation, things changed. Luther was very critical of the canon of the Roman Mass because it made of the Lord's Supper a sacrifice. The other Reformers were very much in agreement with Luther in this matter, and they tried to recover the eucharistic nature of the communion prayers. In the Reformed Church of Strasbourg, there were two communion prayers, a Communion Invocation at the beginning asking that God grant the grace promised in the sacrament, and a Prayer of Dedication at the end after the bread and wine had been shared. The Reformers generally gave particular attention to recovering the communion psalmody. Not only the Hallel Psalms but also a number of other psalms were used.

It was John Knox who, noting that the Scriptures are quite clear that Jesus took the bread and the wine and then gave thanks, developed a prayer of thanksgiving to be said at the breaking of the bread and the pouring of the wine. This prayer was a thanksgiving for God's works of creation and redemption. It was truly a Eucharistic Prayer because it gave thanks at length for God's gracious acts of redemption in Christ.

O Father of Mercy, and God of all consolation! Seeing all creatures do acknowledge and confess thee as Governor and Lord: It becometh us, the workmanship of thine own hands, at all times to reverence and magnify thy godly Majesty. First, for that thou hast created us in thine own image and similitude: But chiefly in that thou has delivered us from that everlasting death and damnation, into the which Satan drew mankind by the means of sin, from the bondage whereof neither man nor angel was able to make us free.

We praise thee, O Lord! that thou, rich in mercy, and infinite in goodness, hast provided our redemption to stand in thine only and well-beloved Son, whom of very love thou didst give to be made man like unto us in all things, sin excepted, in his body to receive the punishment of our transgression, by his death to make satisfaction to thy justice, and through his resurrection to destroy him that was the author of death; and so to bring again life to the world, from which the whole offspring of Adam most justly was exiled.

O Lord! we acknowledge that no creature is able to comprehend the length and breadth, the depth and height of that thy most excellent love, which moved thee to show mercy where none was deserved, to promise and give life where death had gotten the victory, to receive us in thy grace when we could do nothing but rebel against thy justice.

O Lord! the blind dullness of our corrupt nature will not suffer us sufficiently to weigh these thy most ample benefits; yet, nevertheless, at the commandment of Jesus Christ our Lord, we present ourselves at this His table, which he hath left to be used in remembrance of his death, until his coming again: to declare and witness before the world, that by him alone we have received liberty and life; that by him alone thou dost acknowledge us thy children and heirs; that by him alone we have entrance to the throne of thy grace; that by him alone we are possessed in our spiritual kingdom to eat and drink at his table, with whom we have our conversation presently in heaven, and by whom our bodies shall be raised up again from the dust, and shall be placed with him in that endless joy, which thou, O Father of Mercy! hast prepared for thine elect before the foundation of the world was laid.

And these most inestimable benefits we acknowledge and confess to have received of thy free mercy and grace, by thine only beloved Son Jesus Christ: for the which, therefore, we thy congregation, moved by thine Holy Spirit, render all thanks, praise, and glory, for ever and ever. Amen.

After the bread and wine had been shared there was a concluding Prayer of Dedication.

Most merciful Father, we render to thee all praise, thanks, and glory, for that it hath pleased thee, of thy great mercies, to grant unto us, miserable sinners, so excellent a gift and treasure, as to receive us into the fellowship and company of thy dear Son Jesus Christ our Lord, whom thou hast delivered to death for us, and hast given him unto us as a necessary food and nourishment unto everlasting life. And now, we beseech thee also, O heavenly Father, to grant us this request, that thou never suffer us to become so unkind as to forget so worthy benefits; but rather imprint and fasten them sure in our hearts, that we may grow and increase daily more and more in true faith, which continually is exercised in all manner of good works; and so much the rather, O Lord, confirm us in these perilous days and rages of Satan, that we may constantly stand and continue in the confession of the same, to the advancement of thy glory, who art God over all things, blessed for ever. So be it. Amen.

Baird, *Presbyterian Liturgies,* pp. 124-127

Like several of the other Reformers, Knox gave attention to the use of appropriate psalms at the communion service. The Scottish custom of beginning the communion service with Psalm 23 and ending it with Psalm 103 may well go back to John Knox.

The Puritans developed the Communion Invocation along the lines of a prayer that asked that the Holy Spirit be given, that the congregation be united together in the body of Christ, and that those who partook of the sacrament be sanctified and nourished for eternal life. The Puritan Communion Invocations are surprisingly similar, in this respect, to the prayers of the *Didache.* Richard Baxter is one of the best witnesses to how the Puritans actually shaped their prayers. The Communion Invocation that he wrote for *The Reformed Liturgy* of 1661 is a particularly fine example:

Most Holy Spirit, proceeding from the Father and the Son: by whom Christ was conceived; by whom the prophets and apostles were inspired, and the ministers of Christ are qualified and called: that dwellest and workest in all the members of Christ, whom thou sanctifiest to the image and for the service of their Head, and comfortest them that they may shew forth his praise: illuminate us, that by faith we may see him that is here represented to us. Soften our hearts, and humble us for our sins. Sanctify and quicken us, that we may relish the spiritual food, and feed on it to our nourishment and growth in grace. Shed abroad the love of God upon our hearts, and draw them out in love to him. Fill us with thankfulness and holy joy, and with love to one another. Comfort us by witnessing that we are the children of God. Confirm us for new obedience. Be the earnest of our inheritance, and seal us up to everlasting life. Amen.

In many ways, the Puritans developed this prayer in similar directions to the way the Eastern Orthodox Churches had developed their epiclesis.

As I read the tradition, I find three communion prayers: first, the Communion Invocation at the beginning of the celebration of the sacrament; second, the Eucharistic Prayer over the bread and wine; and third, a Post-Communion Thanksgiving at the end of the service that gives thanks for the grace received in the sacrament and as a consequence promises the dedication of ourselves to God's service. I will say considerably more about the ordering of the service as a whole in the last chapter of this book, but here I should stress that in arranging the communion service one has to be sensitive to the spiritual intensity of the congregation.

My first congregation in Pennsylvania had inherited that high regard for the sacrament typical of Old School Presbyterianism. Preparatory services were observed and everyone expected the service to run a half an hour longer on a communion Sunday. Attendance was noticeably higher if the Lord's Supper was to be celebrated. The elders and the deacons all knew their appointed tasks. Bread had been specially baked and the Lord's Table had been spread with fresh linen and set with carefully polished silver. My second congregation was quite different. The minister was allowed no more than the shortest "communion meditation" lest the service run over. One expected the whole thing to be read out of a book, but with large chunks left out. I will never forget the first communion service I celebrated there. When I arrived at the church nothing had been prepared. Someone had to run home for bread and wine. The silver was noticeably tarnished and the linen had not been pressed in a long time. As a matter of course I took an hour and a half to celebrate the service. Quite mistakenly, I assumed that that was what they expected me to do. When it was over everyone was stunned. They could not believe the impropriety of the minister in taking so much time, but then the solemnity of it all had impressed them. I think it began to dawn on them that there must be more to the Lord's Supper than they had realized.

Let me suggest two orders, the first shorter, the second longer, and let me encourage the minister to use what seems to fit the congregation's spiritual intensity. One way to do this is to use the shorter order most of the time but then the longer order at certain stated times such as Christmas and Easter. First the shorter service:

Prelude

Doxology

INVOCATION

HYMN OF PRAISE   *(metrical psalm or paraphrase)*

PRAYER OF CONFESSION

Assurance of Pardon

Doxology

Prayer for Illumination

SCRIPTURE LESSON

SERMON

HYMN   *(metrical setting of one of the communion psalms, such as Psalm 23 or 24, sung while the minister and elders gather around the Lord's Table and uncover it)*

INVITATION

APOSTLES' CREED

EUCHARISTIC PRAYER
for creation
for the gift of a Savior
for his sacrifice
for his resurrection
for the gift of the Holy Spirit

THE GIVING OF THE BREAD AND WINE
(An anthem may be sung while the elements are being served.)

PRAYER OF DEDICATION

HYMN   *(metrical setting of one of the communion psalms, such as Psalm 103 or 138, sung while the table is being covered and the minister and elders return to their places.)*

COLLECTION   *(A short anthem or single stanza of a hymn could be sung during the collection.)*

BENEDICTION

Doxology

Postlude

While much has been cut out of this service there has been an attempt to avoid a feeling of being hurried. The Reformed communion service should encourage meditation. One of the pitfalls of the medieval teaching that the sacrament is an *opus operandum,* that is, an act that is of value simply by its being performed correctly, is that it encourages hurried and perfunctory celebrations. The order of service suggested here is intended to progress slowly and allow much time for psalmody, hymnody, music, and even silence. This is done to invite the faithful to meditate on the sacred sign unfolded among them. The first part of the service has been shortened considerably. There is no responsive reading of the Psalter, but the generous use of communion psalms compensates for this. There is no hymn to go with the sermon and only one Scripture lesson is included, but as I see it, it is very important not to truncate the sermon when communion is celebrated. Except on Christmas Eve and Maundy Thursday, when much longer Scripture lessons are read, I always preach a full sermon at communion. The Prayers of Intercession have also been left out. This is to be regretted, but on most Sundays the intercessions are prominently featured. The Communion Invocation has been completely left out. Over the years it has become one of my guiding principles that not everything has to be done every Sunday. An *opus operandum* approach to worship might worry about whether a service that leaves some important part of the rite out could still be considered valid. We do not have to worry about that sort of thing.

This order of service assumes that the members of the congregation are served the bread and the wine seated in their pews. This has long been the practice in Congregational, Presbyterian, and Baptist churches. I think it is a good practice, and because it has great symbolic advantages it should be maintained in those churches where it is the tradition. Methodists will, of course, look at it a bit differently. As Reformed as John Wesley was in so many matters, here is one place where he went in another direction. Among Reformed churches there is some variation in this matter. Members of French Reformed Churches usually receive the sacrament while standing in a circle around the table, while in Dutch Reformed Churches special tables are sometimes set up so that the people can come forward and sit around them. The important thing is to preserve the visual appearance of sharing in a meal.

A Reformed church should be constructed in such a way that the whole congregation is seated around the Lord's Table. An altar has no place in a Reformed church. In the German Rhineland, in Switzerland, and in the Netherlands one of the first things the Reformers did was to remove the altars from the churches and replace them with tables. The Puritans made a big point of this early in the English Reformation, and it is a point we should continue to uphold. Again, Methodists have their own traditions, but for most American Protestants the tradition is that we *sit* at the Lord's Table. Reformed Churches, historically, have tried to emphasize that the essential action of the Lord's Supper is the sharing of a meal, and therefore we serve one another rather than file up to some sort of altar to receive the bread and wine at the hands of the clergy. This order of service also assumes the older practice of each person serving his or her neighbor rather than passing out the elements and then holding them until a signal is given and everyone partakes at the same moment. This newer way of doing it somehow loses the sense that we all serve one another.

Something needs to be said about what with a bit of hesitation I have called the Invitation. For many years I simply read an abridged version of Calvin's Communion Exhortation. This classic text begins with the Words of Institution, warns the unrepentant not to approach the sacred table, and encourages the faithful to receive the body and blood of Christ offered for their salvation. Sometimes this part of the service has been called "the fencing of the table." I have always suspected the term of being a bit malicious, but it seems to have stuck. As time went on and I had come to know the text almost by memory I realized that the intention of these words was to encourage the faithful to receive Christ in partaking of the covenant meal. In my study of Calvin's eucharistic doctrine it became more and more clear that for Calvin the Lord's Supper had both a strong covenantal dimension and a strong evangelistic dimension. Church historians are beginning to tell us that it was from the Scottish communion seasons that the American revivals evolved. This is patent in the communion sermons of Gilbert Tennent and Samuel Davies. In fact, in reading Calvin's communion sermons I found just this, and very clearly. One went to the Lord's Table to make the covenant vows of faith. More and more I began to formulate the Communion Invitation myself. I tried to do it in such a way that the faithful would be encouraged to come to the Lord's Table to receive Christ. At least once or twice a year I still read my abridged version of Calvin's Communion Exhortation. But again I invoke my principle that not everything has to be done every Sunday.

When the Lord's Supper can be celebrated without having to worry too much about the ticking of the clock, the order of service might go much as any other Lord's Day service up through the sermon. The communion service proper would then begin with the singing of one of the communion psalms following the sermon:

HYMN   *(A metrical setting of one of the communion psalms, such as Psalm 23, 24, 113, or 133, or one of the creation psalms. During the singing of the psalm the minister and elders should gather around the table.)*

COMMUNION INVOCATION

INVITATION   *(If new members are to be received, it should be at this point. The covenant vows conclude with the Creed.)*

APOSTLES' CREED

ANTHEM   *(setting forth God's works of creation)*

EUCHARISTIC PRAYER
    for creation
    for the election of Israel
    for the incarnation
    for Christ's sacrifice
    for his resurrection
    for the sending of the Holy Spirit

The Lord's Prayer

THE GIVING OF THE BREAD AND WINE

ANTHEM   *(setting forth God's works of redemption in Christ)*

PRAYER OF DEDICATION

HYMN   *(A metrical setting of one of the communion psalms, such as
103, 116, 117, or 138. The table is covered, and the elders and
the minister return to their places.)*

The service concludes, then, with the collection and the Benediction as on
any other Lord's Day. One notices here that much time has been given to
a full development of the Eucharistic Prayer, to the communion psalmody,
and to a hymnic rejoicing in God's mighty acts of creation and redemption
through a generous use of choral anthems.

Let us look more closely at each of these prayers and what should be
included in them.

The Communion Invocation

In shaping the Communion Invocation, I have been influenced by several
models. First, I have taken the High Priestly Prayer of Jesus in the seventeenth chapter of the Gospel of John as a model. In this prayer, there is a
strong emphasis on the unity, sanctity, and continuity of the Church. What
we are really dealing with is a series of intercessions. It is not so much that
the Communion Invocation has replaced the Prayers of Intercession as it
is that when Communion is celebrated the intercessions are seen in a
special light. When the intercessions are made before communion, they
become prayers for the gathering of all God's people about his table.

This is just what we find in the *Didache,* which is the second model
that I have used. We have seen that the prayer of the *Didache* asks that the
Church be brought together into one body as the grains of wheat scattered
on the hillsides have been brought together into one loaf of bread.

Third, I have taken the themes of the Eastern Orthodox epiclesis, which
emphasize the work of the Holy Spirit in producing the benefits of the
sacrament in our lives. Particularly in regard to the theme of epiclesis, I
have followed the line of thought suggested by the *Westminster Directory
for Worship* and Richard Baxter's *Reformed Liturgy.* It seems to me that this
emphasis on the Holy Spirit is most appropriate for the celebration of
communion. (In the shorter service I have taken the theme of epiclesis
and worked it into the Eucharistic Prayer, giving thanks at length for the
pouring out of the Holy Spirit on the day of Pentecost. My main reason
for doing this has been a concern for brevity. My preference is to have a
separate Communion Invocation.)

It has been my practice to offer the Communion Invocation at the
point in the service where the elders, having come forward during the
singing of one of the traditional communion psalms, have gathered around
the table and uncovered the bread and wine. The Communion Invocation

thus becomes a prayer, as I have said, for the gathering of God's people around the table. Quite logically, then, it is here that an Invitation is given to make or renew the covenant vows of faith. New members are received, and we all affirm our faith in the Apostles' Creed. After that, I like to have the choir sing an anthem. This anthem should lead us into the Eucharistic Prayer, which celebrates the mighty acts of creation and redemption. An arrangement such as this encourages us to give full attention both to the themes of the Communion Invocation and to the themes of the Eucharistic Prayer.

As for the theological significance of the Invocation, it seems to me that the rich theological insights of Eastern Orthodoxy on the subject of the eucharistic epiclesis have strongly influenced the Reformed Church ever since the sixteenth century and still today have much to teach us. Even if complete agreement with the Eastern Orthodox churches in all points of eucharistic theology is not possible, we find much of their thought quite edifying. Even if we prefer to think that the miracle of the sacrament is a miracle of grace receiving us into the household of the Father and sanctifying us for his service — rather than some sort of transformation of bread and wine into the body of Christ — we do believe that in the celebration of the sacrament we enter into the presence of God. We believe that in the celebration of the sacrament we enter the heavenly presence of God in a unique way, and we believe that way has been opened up by the breaking of Christ's body and the pouring out of his blood. It is indeed in him and through him and with him that we enter into that presence both now and in the last day. The theological point behind the Communion Invocation is that we do this not of our own power but by the sanctifying power of the Holy Spirit working in our hearts and uniting us together in the body of Christ. It is the Holy Spirit who gathers the Church, unites the Church, and builds up the Church. Worship is the work of the Holy Spirit in the body of Christ to the glory of the Father. The Communion Invocation, then, prays that the Holy Spirit be poured out among us to that end.

There is another theological point to be made here. It is through the Holy Spirit that the ascended Christ, who is seated at the right hand of the Father, is present to Christians. Jesus promised the disciples that although he was going to the Father to prepare a place for them he would send them his Spirit to be their comforter. He promised them that he would be with them to the end of the world and indeed, through the Holy Spirit, he is. It is, therefore, that we pray for the pouring out of the Holy Spirit in order that Christ sup with us and we with him (Rev. 3:20). The Communion Invocation asks that the Father pour out on us his Holy Spirit so that we may be united to Christ and sanctified by his presence.

The Eucharistic Prayer

I have followed several models in the Eucharistic Prayer also. In the first place, I have given primary attention to the fact that when Jesus took the bread and then the wine, he gave thanks. I have noticed that in the Passover Seder the traditional blessings over the first cup and over the bread are thanksgivings for God's creation of bread and wine. Often I have begun the Eucharistic Prayer with these two blessings as they are found today in the Jewish Passover Seder. I find it to be a positive affirmation of the Jewish liturgical heritage. The prayer over the cup of blessing in the Passover Seder is a considerably longer prayer that blesses God for his redemptive acts for Israel. This historical prayer has always been in the back of my mind in remembering that Jesus himself told his disciples that from that time on, whenever they celebrated the Supper, they were to celebrate it in memory of him. The recounting of God's mighty acts of redemption should culminate in recounting God's sending of the Son, the offering of him as a sacrifice, and the raising up of him in the resurrection.

The second model that has influenced me is the psalms and prayers of the Old Testament, which recount the mighty acts of God in a hymnic way. A number of theologians of our century, such as Gerhard von Rad, have pointed out the importance of recounting the mighty acts of God to the biblical theology of worship. It is in reciting the history of salvation that we claim our place in the covenant community and bless to our own use all the benefits that God through history has poured out on his people. In giving thanks for God's deliverance of Israel from Egypt, we take our place in that triumphant procession out of the land of Egypt, through the sea, and into the Promised Land. Psalms 78, 105, and 136 and the prayer from the liturgy of the Feast of Tabernacles, which begins with "A wandering Aramean was my father . . ." (Deut 26:5-10), are all examples of the hymnic recounting of the history of salvation. In the Christian celebration of communion it is appropriate to remember the mighty acts of redemption toward Israel, because they are types of God's mighty act of redemption in Christ. When Christians give thanks to God for the history of salvation, then the incarnation, the passion, and the resurrection become the primary themes of this prayer. When such a prayer is at the center of the celebration of communion, then the service indeed proclaims Christ's death and resurrection until he comes (I Cor 11:26).

It is as we thank God for his mighty acts of creation and redemption that covenant theology comes most clearly into play. From the standpoint of biblical theology, and particularly the biblical theology of worship, *remembrance* and *thanksgiving* are profound ideas.

As we read in the Ten Commandments, taking both versions together, the Sabbath was to be observed by remembering that God made "heaven and earth, the sea, and all that is in them" (Exod 20:11) and that "you were a servant in the land of Egypt, and the LORD your God brought you out thence with a mighty hand and an outstretched arm" (Deut 5:15). The Sabbath of the old covenant was sanctified by remembering the mighty acts of God that had brought the children of Israel into existence, delivered them from slavery, and brought them into the Promised Land. Recounting that story in the reading and preaching of Scripture and in prayers and hymns of praise was at the heart of Israel's worship. These *mirabilia Dei* had established Israel as the covenant people. As the people remembered these mighty acts in the observance of worship each Sabbath, the covenant was renewed and Israel was confirmed in the covenant relationship.

So now the Church of the new covenant sanctifies the Christian Sabbath by remembering the mighty acts of God in Christ by which we have been saved from our sins and established before him. When we worship, we do it as Christ directed us, "in remembrance of me" (I Cor 11:24). Whenever the Church prays the Eucharistic Prayer, it affirms that God is not only a creating God, but an electing, redeeming, and covenant-giving God. The Eucharistic Prayer with its hymnic recital of holy history is a profound theological affirmation that "God was in Christ reconciling the world to himself" (II Cor 5:19). This prayer affirms that our relation to God has a history, a long history, a meaningful history. Our history is not inconsequential to God. He himself in the person of his Son has entered into it and given it a hope and a purpose. That God acts in history is fundamental to our theology; that we rejoice in these mighty acts is fundamental to our worship.

The second thing we need to say about the theology that lies behind the Eucharistic Prayer is also fundamental to covenant theology. It has to do with the biblical understanding of thanksgiving. The Eucharistic Prayer is in its simplest sense the prayer of thanksgiving said over a meal — a table blessing. Paul expressed a very basic theological insight when he told us that the good things of life are to be received with thanksgiving because when we give thanks for them they are consecrated for our use (I Tim 4:4-5). It is not by recitation of a formula that bread and wine are consecrated but by the giving of thanks for them. This consecration or blessing, which is such an important theme in biblical theology, is nothing less than a recognition that the good things of life come to us from the hand of God and by our giving thanks for them they are freed for our use, or, perhaps better, they are blessed to our use or set aside for our enjoyment.

Now let us go a step further. When we celebrate the Lord's Supper we are giving thanks for more than simple bread and wine. The bread and wine are signs in the full biblical sense of the word. They are signs of God's mighty acts of creation and redemption. When we give thanks for these signs of the mighty acts of salvation, then they are blessed to our spiritual use: They are appropriated for our salvation. How we pray this prayer has everything to do with our theology of consecration. How is it that we are consecrated or made holy? How is it that we are redeemed? How is it that we are justified and sanctified? How is it that we enter into salvation? It is in God's mighty acts of redemption in Christ that our salvation was accomplished. Therefore, when we give thanks for the broken bread and the poured out wine, we recount at length the history of salvation culminating in Christ's incarnation, his sacrifice on the cross, his resurrection and ascension into heaven, his pouring out of his Spirit, and his coming again. What we are really giving thanks for is the history of our salvation. Giving thanks for it makes it ours!

Several of the Eucharistic Prayers of the ancient Church have inspired me, particularly the prayers of St. Basil and the prayers of the *Apostolic Constitutions*. I find their hymnic recounting of the works of creation and redemption particularly beautiful. The thanksgivings for the works of creation and redemption in both prayers are long and detailed. It is this part that inspires me. On the other hand, I try to avoid making the Eucharistic Prayer into a canon in the sense of a precise doctrinal formulation. One should try, rather, to make it a hymn of praise and thanksgiving. When these classic prayers begin to recite formulas of consecration and oblation, they introduce elements that do not belong in the celebration of the Lord's

Supper according to the historic Protestant position, which I think is quite correct. I carefully leave the Words of Institution out of the Eucharistic Prayer, reciting them after the prayer is over, so that there is no possibility of mistaking it for a prayer of consecration intended to change the bread and wine into the body and blood of Christ. I carefully avoid saying in the prayer anything that sounds like the offering up of any kind of sacrifice, whether of Christ's body and blood or even of praise and thanksgiving. I particularly avoid the sort of ambiguous formulations that the framers of the *Book of Common Prayer* insisted on. Ambiguity has rarely promoted the unity of the Church. All this can be avoided by sticking to a simple and straightforward recounting of the works of creation and redemption. This, I insist, is the biblical pattern.

Another prayer that I have taken as a model is the Eucharistic Prayer of John Knox, which is indeed a thanksgiving for creation and redemption. While it eloquently celebrates our redemption in Christ, it dwells rather onesidedly on Christ's atoning death. I feel it needs to be supplemented by an equal emphasis on Christ's resurrection and ascension and the out-pouring of the Holy Spirit. Each time I formulate the Eucharistic Prayer, I try to celebrate the creation, God's redemption of Israel, the sending of the Savior, the atoning sacrifice of Christ on the cross, his victory over death, his ascension, and the pouring out of the Holy Spirit. At Christmas and on Maundy Thursday, Easter, and Pentecost, I have celebrated the appropriate themes of the feast, but always mentioning the cardinal events of the history of redemption. At other times, I may elaborate different aspects of God's grace to the Patriarchs, his promises to David, or his revelation to the prophets. Or I might elaborate the themes of Jesus' ministry of teaching and healing, the ministry of the Apostles, or the Christian hope. I try to do this in such a way that the history of salvation is recounted in each prayer.

The Prayer of Dedication

In the Prayer of Dedication, which comes at the end of the meal, my primary biblical model has been the votive thanksgiving psalms, especially two of the Hallel Psalms, Psalm 116 and Psalm 118. These psalms recognize that God has granted his grace and favor to us in very specific acts of mercy and that in recognition of our debt to him we pledge him our lifelong service. There is an important theological point here, and again it is covenantal theology. Here is where the doctrine of prevenient grace needs to be made very clear. It is because we have received God's gift of himself that we in return are able to give ourselves to him. By putting this theme here at the end of the service, after the bread and wine have been received, we make clear a strong theology of grace. We love God because he first loved us. In the Eucharistic Prayer we celebrate God's gracious gift of himself, and in the post-communion dedication prayer we give ourselves in return.

If there was anything that all the Reformers, Luther, Bucer, Zwingli, and Calvin, agreed on, it was that the doctrine of the eucharistic sacrifice seriously compromised the doctrine of grace. In the Roman Mass the offertory and then the prayers of oblation in the canon had come before the giving and receiving of the bread and wine. It was because of their strong theology of grace that the Reformers discontinued the offertory and removed the prayers of oblation from the canon. Then they substituted a Prayer of Dedication after the communion. In this prayer they made a point of offering themselves to God in a life of service and devotion. They asked that the new covenant be written on the tablets of their hearts so that their lives might produce the works of righteousness and the fruit of the Spirit appropriate to the children of God. They prayed that, having received the grace of God in Christ, they might live the rest of their lives to the glory of God and the service of their neighbors.

For the Prayer of Dedication I have usually used Calvin's prayer, and I have had the congregation pray it as a unison prayer. Calvin's prayer is a thanksgiving for the grace promised to us in the sacrament and a dedication of ourselves to God's service for the rest of our lives. In more recent years I have tried my hand at formulating the prayer myself, but I have always gone back to using Calvin's prayer. One reason I have done so is that I find great value in using a classical prayer such as this prayer as a means of helping the Church to sense the continuity of the tradition. Besides, by that time my congregation had come to know the prayer fairly well. About this prayer, I would want to say the same things as I have said about the Prayer of Confession. I find it helpful when using a unison prayer always, or almost always, to use the same prayer so that the congregation comes to know it by heart and does not need to read it from the printed page.

Communion Psalmody

The Gospels of Matthew and Mark are quite specific that the service in the Upper Room ended with the singing of a hymn (Matt 26:30; Mark 14:26). Anyone reading this account who was familiar with the Passover Seder would know this hymn consisted of the Hallel Psalms. At the time of the Protestant Reformation this was fairly common information. The Reformers were fond of singing these psalms at communion, and there were other psalms that they sang as well. Psalms 103 and 138 are known to have been used at a very early date in their churches. The communion psalmody was an essential part of their communion service. One gets a completely distorted impression of the Reformed eucharistic liturgy unless one is aware of the psalm texts that were sung during the service.

Three psalms have a solid place in the Reformed tradition for use as the elders gather around the table: Psalm 23; Psalm 24:7-10; and Psalm 133. Not only in Reformed tradition, but in patristic tradition as well, Psalms 23 and 24 have been closely associated with the celebration of the Lord's Supper. That Psalm 23 should be chosen comes naturally enough from the text itself: "Thou preparest a table before me" and, a bit further on, "My cup overflows." In the Eastern Churches, Psalm 24 was associated in ancient times with the Great Entrance when the bread and wine were brought to the table. In Scotland also Psalm 24 was sung when the elders brought in the communion vessels. There is a very elaborate typology behind this: The psalm is supposed to have been sung when the ark of the covenant was brought into the temple. One might see in the ark of the covenant a type of the sacrament. But aside from the typology, which we can take or leave, the psalm expresses in its literary figures a sense of tremendous exaltation. This psalm has many settings. For a particularly grand occasion one might use the arrangement for choir and congregation to the tune St. Georges West, which is found in the *Scottish Psalter* of 1929. For Christmas Eve the paraphrase of Georg Weissel is appropriate. I am told that the use of Psalm 133 is particularly beloved among Reformed Presbyterians.

For the anthem sung by the choir just before the Eucharistic Prayer I like to have a setting of a psalm that celebrates creation, such as Psalm 8; Psalm 19:1-6; Psalm 29; Psalm 93; Psalm 104; Psalm 136:1-9; Psalm 147; or Psalm 148. When I had a first-rate choir that loved to tackle the classics we heard some beautiful things from Haydn's *Creation*, Jacquin des Pres's setting of Psalm 93, or Heinrich Schütz's setting of Psalm 8. On the other hand one summer some of the young people in the church organized a gospel quartet that specialized in bits of old Americana. They gave us some psalm settings of Justin Morgan, the famous Vermont horse breeder and Congregational deacon. A soloist, to be sure, can provide one of these classic psalms just as easily and just as effectively.

Included by long tradition in the Psalter are the biblical canticles. Only after years of developing the use of psalmody have I done much with the canticles, and even then I have focused on their use at Sunday vespers. There have been a few exceptions. At the Christmas Eve service I have used three of the canticles from the nativity narrative of the Gospel of Luke: the *Gloria in excelsis* (Luke 2:14) as the anthem just before the Eucharistic Prayer, the *Magnificat* (1:46-55) for the anthem sung during the distribution of the bread and wine, and the *Nunc dimittis* (2:29-32) after the Benediction at the very end of the service. On Maundy Thursday I like to use Isaiah 53, the Song of the Suffering Servant. In my first church I had an especially fine choir director — in fact my ministry has been blessed by wonderful choir directors. This particular director found a setting of Isaiah 53 that was perfect. It was angular and avant garde contemporary music, as I remember it, but alas, the memory is too distant for me to remember the name of the composer.

For the psalm sung at the close of the service there are several strong traditions. Psalm 138 was intended as a votive thanksgiving psalm in the temple and is therefore particularly appropriate. Calvin used it often, imitating the usage of the Reformed Church of Strasbourg, which used Martin Luther's version. Psalm 103 is also a votive thanksgiving psalm. Its usage in Scotland seems to go back to John Knox. From a theological standpoint I find Isaac Watts's version of Psalm 116:12-19 the perfect post-communion psalm.

Another liturgical tradition in which I find great meaning is the use of Passover Psalms in celebrating Easter. I developed this only very slowly, but I finally got to the place where on Maundy Thursday and Easter we used all six psalms. At the beginning of the Maundy Thursday service we used Psalms 113–115 as a responsive reading. At the close we sang Psalm 116. Then as the first hymn on Easter Sunday morning we sang Psalm 117 in that joyous version of Isaac Watts, "From All That Dwell below the Skies." Finally as the elders gathered around the table we sang Psalm 118. I searched a long time for a good setting of this psalm. I finally found one in the *Trinity Hymnal* set to the *Genevan Psalter* tune *Rendez à Dieu*.

When celebrating Christmas, Maundy Thursday, Easter, and Pentecost I have often replaced psalmody with hymnody, particularly at Pentecost, where the most traditional proper psalms did not seem quite right. Psalm 29 does seem to have been connected with the feast of Pentecost even in pre-Christian Jewish tradition. Besides, it seems to have a sort of poetic appropriateness. Beyond that I do not find much in the way of Pentecost psalmody. On the other hand the medieval hymn *"Veni creator spiritus"* is such a classic! It ought to be used regularly in worship. I feel the same with Charles Wesley's "Come Holy Ghost, Our Hearts Inspire."

Then there are a few things I have done since my earliest years in the ministry that have just clicked and I have seen no reason for changing them. At my first Maundy Thursday communion service I chose the Tate and Brady paraphrase of the Words of Institution, "'Twas on the Night When Doomed to Know," to sing as the elders gathered around the Lord's Table. During the distribution of the bread and wine I like to have the choir sing Martin Luther's "Christ Jesus Lay in Death's Dark Bands." That hymn is perfect for Maundy Thursday because while it confesses the resurrection it does so with the sobriety of Maundy Thursday.

On Easter I always close the service with Charles Wesley's "Christ the Lord Is Risen Today," using the tune known as Easter Hymn. The first year I was in Indiana several students who had organized a brass quartet accompanied the hymn in a way that gave sparkle to the whole service. We did it again the next year and the year after; before long it was tradition. Somehow trumpets and Easter just seem to go together. Even more than that I cannot ever remember Easter Sunday morning being concluded with any other hymn. It must be a solid American Protestant tradition.

Communion Service 1 ——————————

The Lord's my shepherd, I'll not want;
    He makes me down to lie
In pastures green; He leadeth me
    the quiet waters by.

My soul he doth restore again;
    And me to walk doth make
Within the paths of righteousness,
    E'en for his own Name's sake.

Yea, though I walk in death's dark vale,
    Yet will I fear none ill;
For Thou art with me; and Thy rod
    And staff me comfort still.

My table Thou hast furnished
    In presence of my foes;
My head Thou dost with oil anoint,
    And my cup overflows.

Goodness and mercy all my life
    Shall surely follow me;
And in God's house forevermore
    My dwelling place shall be.   *Scottish Psalter,* 1650

Invocation

Father Most High,
    Lord and God of all creation,
        who sent forth your Spirit on the waters,
        brooding upon the deep,
            that ordered life might come forth.
    Grant to us that same creating Spirit,
        that we might enter into the new creation.
        We cry out to you about
            the moral confusion of our country,
            the corruption in civil government,
            perversion in the entertainment industry,
            apathy in the Church.
    Pour out your Holy Spirit,
        that our human society might be renewed and restored.

Father Most High,
    who sent forth your Holy Spirit upon the Virgin Mary
        that she might conceive and bring forth a son,
            who is Christ the Lord.

Grant to this congregation
    the pouring out of your Spirit,
        that we might be born from above
            into the new life of the Kingdom,
        that we may be born again,
            renewed in strength,
            sanctified in body and soul.

Father Most High,
    God and Father of our Lord Jesus Christ,
        who on the day of Pentecost
            poured forth your Holy Spirit,
            bringing together
            Greeks, Romans, Arabians, and Jews.
    We pray for the pouring forth of your Spirit
        on the people of the earth,
            the Church of Jerusalem in our own day,
            the Orthodox churches of Syria and Egypt,
            the Church of modern Rome.
    Grant that we might be joined together at your table.

Blessing, and honour, and glory, and power
    be unto him that sitteth upon the throne,
        and unto the Lamb for ever and ever. *Amen.*

Invitation

Apostles' Creed

I believe in God the Father Almighty, Maker of heaven and earth:
And in Jesus Christ his only son, our Lord; who was conceived by
the Holy Ghost, born of the Virgin Mary, suffered under Pontius Pilate,
was crucified, dead, and buried; he descended into hell; the third day
he rose again from the dead; he ascended into heaven, and sitteth on
the right hand of God the Father Almighty; from thence he shall come
to judge the quick and the dead.
I believe in the Holy Ghost, the holy catholic Church; the communion of saints; the forgiveness of sins; the resurrection of the body;
and the life everlasting. Amen.

Anthem   (Heinrich Schütz's setting of Psalm 8)

Blessed art thou, O Lord God,
    King of the Universe,
        who bringeth forth bread from the earth.
Blessed art thou, O Lord God,
    King of the Universe,
        who bringeth forth wine from the vine.

O Father,
God Eternal and Everlasting,
Invisible, Immutable, Immortal Lord,
Creator of all,
    we bless you
        for the stars of the sky, so vast in number,
        for the heat of the day
            and the cool of the evening,
        for the clouds filled with rain
            and the hills covered with grass,
        for snow and hail and frost,
        for all the wonders of the sea.
    O God, Creator of all,
        we thank you!

O Sovereign God,
    who so generously provided
        for all your creatures,
        filling our land with the finest wheat,
            with corn and beans,
        leading us as a shepherd
            through all the paths of life,
        for the blessing of home and family,
        for the prospering of our work.
    O God, for your kindly works of providence,
        we thank you!

O God of Abraham, Isaac, and Jacob,
    we bless you for the Word
        declared to your people of old,
        for the law of Moses
            and the sermons of the prophets,
            their insights and their promises,
            the vision of a coming king
                and an eternal kingdom.
    O God, for the election of Israel,
        we thank you!

O God and Father of our Lord Jesus Christ,
    we bless you,
        that in the birth of your Son,
            the promises have been fulfilled,
            the star of Jacob has risen,
            the Rose of Sharon has blossomed,
            the Son of David has begun to reign.
    O God, for the coming of the promised Messiah,
        we thank you!

O God, whose ways are past finding out,
    we bless you,
        that you so loved the world
            that you gave your only begotten Son,
            offering him up as a sacrifice
                for our redemption.
    O God our Redeemer,
        we thank you!

Blessed you are Glorious God.
    Christ is risen, risen indeed!
        Our captain of salvation is victorious
            over the forces of evil.
    Death hath no more dominion.
    Christ is risen, ascended into heaven,
        and seated at your right hand, O Father.

Blessed art thou,
    O God and Father of our Lord Jesus Christ,
        who has blessed us in Christ
            with every spiritual blessing,
        who has poured out on us the Holy Spirit,
            filled us with the gifts of the Spirit,
                love, joy, and peace,
            and has moved us in that same Spirit
                to prayer with each other
                and for each other.

Therefore, we pray together as our Lord has taught us, saying,

Our Father, who art in heaven, hallowed be thy name. Thy Kingdom come. Thy will be done on earth, as it is in heaven. Give us this day our daily bread. And forgive us our debts, as we forgive our debtors. And lead us not into temptation, but deliver us from evil: For thine is the kingdom, and the power, and the glory, for ever. Amen.

Giving of the Bread and Wine

For I have received of the Lord that which also I delivered unto you, That the Lord Jesus the same night in which he was betrayed took bread:

(Here the minister should take up the loaf of bread.)

And when he had given thanks, he broke it,

(Let the minister break the loaf and hand it to the elders, who then help the minister break it into small pieces. It is appropriate that only one loaf of bread be used and that it be broken in the course of the service [cf. I Cor 10:16-17])

and said, Take, eat: this is my body, which is broken for you: this do in remembrance of me.

(The bread should be held out to the congregation in a gesture indicating that the bread is for them to eat.)

After the same manner also he took the cup, when they had supped, saying, This cup is the new covenant in my blood . . . shed for many for the remission of sins.

(With this let the minister pour the cup.)

This do, as often as you drink it,
in remembrance of me.
All of you drink of it.

(With this the cup should be held out to the congregation in a gesture of offering it to them to take and drink.)

Anthem: The Song of Simeon (Luke 2:29-32)

Now let thy servant, Lord!
    At last depart in peace;
According to thy word,
    My waiting soul release:
For thou my longing eyes hast spared
To see thy saving grace declared.

To see thy saving grace,
    that soon dispersed abroad,
The nations shall embrace
    And find their help in God:
A light to lighten every land,
The glory of thy chosen band.

Clement Marot, 1542,
translated by C. W. Baird

Prayer of Dedication

Heavenly Father! we give thee immortal praise and thanks, that upon us thou hast conferred so great a benefit, as to bring us into the communion of thy Son Jesus Christ our Lord; whom having delivered up to death for us, thou hast given for our food and nourishment unto eternal life. Now, also, grant us grace, that we may never be unmindful of these things; but rather carrying them about engraven upon our hearts, may advance and grow in that faith that is effectual unto every good work. Thus, may the rest of our lives be ordered and followed out to thy glory and the edification of our neighbours: Through Jesus Christ our Lord; Who with thee, O Father! and the Holy Ghost, liveth and reigneth in the unity of the Godhead, world without end. *Amen.*

Genevan Psalter of 1542,
Baird, *Presbyterian Liturgies,* p. 58

Psalm 103

O thou my soul, bless God the Lord;
    And all that in me is
Be stirred up His holy Name
    To magnify and bless.

Bless, O my soul, the Lord thy God,
    And not forgetful be
Of all His gracious benefits
    He hath bestowed on thee:

All thine iniquities who doth
    Most graciously forgive;
Who thy diseases all and pains
    Doth heal, and thee relieve:

Who doth redeem thy life, that thou
    To death mayst not go down;
Who thee with lovingkindness doth
    And tender mercies crown:

Who with abundance of good things
    Doth satisfy thy mouth;
so that, even as the eagle's age,
    Renewed is thy youth.

Scottish Psalter, 1650

Communion Service 2 ——————

Psalm 24:7-10

Ye gates, lift up your heads on high;
    ye doors that last for aye
Be lifted up, that so the King
    of glory enter may.
But who of glory is the King?
    The mighty Lord is this;
Ev'n that same Lord, that great in might
    and strong in battle is.
Ye gates, lift up your heads; ye doors,
    doors that do last for aye,
Be lifted up, that so the King
    of glory enter may.
But who is he that is the King
    of Glory? who is this?
The Lord of hosts, and none but he,
    the King of glory is.

Scottish Psalter, 1929

Invocation

Holy Father,
    whose glory is revealed in your Son,
        to whom you have given power
        to give eternal life to all
            whom you have given him.
Send forth your Holy Spirit,
    through the whole of this world,
        that good seed be sown,
        that each branch bear fruit,
        that the harvest be bountiful.
We pray for the work of our missionaries,
        the Shipleys in Taiwan,
        the Whites in Colombia,
        the Paulsons in the Yucatan,
        Elizabeth Early in Korea.

Holy Father,
    we join in the prayer of Jesus
        that the Church be one even as you, O Father,
            are one with your Son, Jesus, our Savior.
    Send forth your Holy Spirit,
        that the Church be united in love
            and true Christian fellowship.

    We pray for the union
        of the Presbyterian Church in the North
        and the Presbyterian Church in the South.

Holy Father,
    we join in the prayer of Jesus
        for those who would receive the
        witness of the Apostles in faith
        down through the years,
            generation after generation.
    Send forth your Holy Spirit,
        on the ministry of Inter-Varsity and Campus Crusade
            here at Purdue University,
                that this generation might receive the gospel.

Blessing, and honour, and glory, and power
    be unto him that sitteth upon the throne,
        and unto the Lamb for ever and ever. *Amen.*

Invitation

Apostles' Creed

I believe in God the Father Almighty, Maker of heaven and earth:
And in Jesus Christ his only son, our Lord; who was conceived by
the Holy Ghost, born of the Virgin Mary, suffered under Pontius Pilate,
was crucified, dead, and buried; he descended into hell; the third day
he rose again from the dead; he ascended into heaven, and sitteth on
the right hand of God the Father Almighty; from thence he shall come
to judge the quick and the dead.

I believe in the Holy Ghost, the holy catholic Church; the communion of saints; the forgiveness of sins; the resurrection of the body;
and the life everlasting. Amen.

Anthem Psalm 93, setting by Jacquin du Pres

Lord God, King of the universe,
> we are thankful
>> for the creation of heaven and earth,
>> for the light of the sky,
>> for the stars of the night,
>>> the snow of winter,
>>> and the light that returns in the spring.

Lord God of Israel,
> we are thankful
>> for the creation of our first parents
>>> in the Garden of Eden,
>> for your supporting them
>>> when they failed you,
>> for the first proclamation of the gospel
>>> that evil cannot prevail,
>> for the redemption promised to Abraham and Sarah,
>> for the hope of a Messiah proclaimed
>>> by Isaiah, Jeremiah, Micah, and Zechariah,
>> for the gift of the Law,
>>> and the challenge of a holy life.

God and Father of our Lord Jesus Christ,
> we are thankful
>> that the promise given by the prophets
>>> has been kept.
>> In Bethlehem, a prince of the house of David
>>> has been born,
>>> who is Christ the Lord.
>> Mary, the new Eve, in deep humility
>>> brought forth the new Adam.

Eternal Lord and God,
> we are thankful
>> that out of obedience to the Father,
>> that out of love for us,
>>> Jesus took on himself
>>>> the curse so long borne by Adam and Eve,
>>> and having died under that curse,
>>>> brought its power to an end.

Almighty Father,
>> we are thankful
>>> that death has not had the last word.
>>>> The veil of the temple
>>>>> was rent in two.
>>>> The immovable stone was rolled away.
>>>>> Christ is risen!

Gracious God,
>> we are thankful
>>> that Christ, having risen from the dead,
>>>> the head of the serpent has been crushed,
>>>> the power of Satan has been overcome.
>>> Christ has become the firstborn from the dead,
>>>> the firstborn of a new creation.
>>>>> Christ is risen!
>>>>> He is risen indeed!

>> We are free
>>> to live the life of the children of God,
>>> to exercise the gifts of love, joy, and peace,
>>> to share our bread and wine,
>>>> one with another.
>> The gates of heaven are open before us,
>>> and we are free to enter without fear.

O God,
>> we bless you
>>> that by the power of your Holy Spirit
>>>> we, too, have been begotten from on high,
>>>> born again of imperishable seed.
>>> We are now your children by faith,
>>>> heirs and joint heirs with Christ.

Therefore, we pray together as our Lord has taught us,
> saying,

Our Father, who art in heaven, hallowed be thy name. Thy Kingdom come. Thy will be done on earth, as it is in heaven. Give us this day our daily bread. And forgive us our debts, as we forgive our debtors. And lead us not into temptation, but deliver us from evil: For thine is the kingdom, and the power, and the glory, for ever. Amen.

Giving of the Bread and Wine

For I have received of the Lord that which also I delivered unto you,
That the Lord Jesus the same night in which he was betrayed took
bread:

(Here the minister should take up the loaf of bread.)

And when he had given thanks, he broke it,

*(Let the minister break the loaf and hand it to the elders, who then help the
minister break it into small pieces. It is appropriate that only one loaf of bread be
used and that it be broken in the course of the service [cf. I Cor 10:16-17])*

and said, Take, eat: this is my body, which is broken for you: this do
in remembrance of me.

*(The bread should be held out to the congregation in a gesture indicating that the
bread is for them to eat.)*

After the same manner also he took the cup, when they had supped,
saying, This cup is the new covenant in my blood . . . shed for many
for the remission of sins.

(With this let the minister pour the cup.)

This do, as often as you drink it, in remembrance of me.
All of you drink of it.

*(With this the cup should be held out to the congregation in a gesture of offering it
to them to take and drink.)*

Anthem Psalm 34:8 (version of Ralph Vaughn Williams)

O taste and see
    how gracious the LORD is:
blest is the man
    that trusteth in him!

Prayer of Dedication

Heavenly Father! we give thee immortal praise and thanks, that upon us thou hast conferred so great a benefit, as to bring us into the communion of thy Son Jesus Christ our Lord; whom having delivered up to death for us, thou hast given for our food and nourishment unto eternal life. Now, also, grant us grace, that we may never be unmindful of these things; but rather carrying them about engraven upon our hearts, may advance and grow in that faith that is effectual unto every good work. Thus, may the rest of our lives be ordered and followed out to thy glory and the edification of our neighbours: Through Jesus Christ our Lord; Who with thee, O Father! and the Holy Ghost, liveth and reigneth in the unity of the Godhead, world without end. Amen.

Genevan Psalter, 1542
Baird, *Presbyterian Liturgies,* p. 58

Psalm 117

From all that dwell below the skies
Let the Creator's praise arise:
    Alleluia! Alleluia!
Let the Redeemer's name be sung
Through every land, in every tongue.
    Alleluia! Alleluia!
    Alleluia! Alleluia! Alleluia!

In every land begin the song,
To every land the strains belong:
    Alleluia! Alleluia!
In cheerful sound all voices raise
And fill the world with joyful praise.
    Alleluia! Alleluia!
    Alleluia! Alleluia! Alleluia!

Eternal are Thy mercies, Lord;
Eternal truth attends Thy word:
    Alleluia! Alleluia!
Thy praise shall sound from shore to shore,
Till suns shall rise and set no more.
    Alleluia! Alleluia!
    Alleluia! Alleluia! Alleluia!   Isaac Watts, 1719

Communion Service 3 ————————

Psalm 113   This version © Fred R. Anderson 1989, from *Singing Psalms of Joy and Praise* (Westminster/John Knox Press)

Sing praise unto the name of God.
　　Come, servants, now and offer laud.
Blest is Your name, O living Lord.
　　From this time forth and evermore,
O'er all the world from shore to shore,
　　O may Your name be long adored.
You, Lord, are ruler of all lands;
　　The works of states are in Your hands.
There is no other like You, God;
　　Your power is great, Your love is broad.
All people live within Your power.
　　Sing praise in this and every hour.

You help the needy in distress,
　　And give them life that conquers death,
The great and small for You are one.
　　You grant the homeless sheltered space,
And empty people feel Your grace,
　　That in all times Your will is done.
I'll praise the Lord with all my breath,
　　And trust my Maker unto death.
Praise to the one who brings us life,
　　And holds us safe in every strife.
For God has conquered and is King;
　　Eternal One, to You we sing.

Invocation

Holy Father,
　　Almighty God, Everlasting Lord,
　　　　whose glory pervades the whole universe.
Holy Father, glorified by your Son,
　　we, too, would glorify you,
　　　　your sons and daughters by faith.

Send forth your Holy Spirit,
　　that we might keep your Word,
　　　　that your law be within us,
　　　　that it be written on the
　　　　　　tablets of our hearts.

Holy Father, glorified by your Son,
    we would have his joy fulfilled in us.
    Send forth your Holy Spirit,
        that we may be sanctified in truth,
            for your Word is truth,
        and filled with your Spirit
        be sent into the world
            to witness to your Word,
            and to live your Word.

We remember before you those who
    have gone out from this church in missions
        of truth and mercy.

Holy Father, glorified by your Son,
    we, too, would have that love
        which unites you to your Son.

Send forth your Holy Spirit,
    that we may be united together
        in the new and eternal covenant.

Blessing, and honour, and glory, and power
    be unto him that sitteth upon the throne,
        and unto the Lamb for ever and ever. *Amen.*

Invitation

Apostles' Creed

I believe in God the Father Almighty, Maker of heaven and earth:
And in Jesus Christ his only son, our Lord; who was conceived by
the Holy Ghost, born of the Virgin Mary, suffered under Pontius Pilate,
was crucified, dead, and buried; he descended into hell; the third day
he rose again from the dead; he ascended into heaven, and sitteth on
the right hand of God the Father Almighty; from thence he shall come
to judge the quick and the dead.

I believe in the Holy Ghost, the holy catholic Church; the communion of saints; the forgiveness of sins; the resurrection of the body;
and the life everlasting. Amen.

Anthem Psalm 136 (setting by Heinrich Schütz, 1619)

Blessed you are,
O God and Father of our Lord Jesus Christ!
You have brought
bread from the earth!
Blessed you are,
O God and Father of our Lord Jesus Christ!
You have brought
wine from the vine!

Lord God our Creator,
we are thankful
for the creation of heaven and earth,
for the light of the sky,
for the grains of the field,
for the sea and forests
and all the creatures with which they are filled.

We bless you for our own creation,
for Adam and Eve,
made good and in your image,
for the whole race of humankind,
spread about the face of the earth.

Lord God of Israel,
we are thankful,
for the covenant made with Abraham,
for forming a people for yourself,
as Sarah rejoiced in old age,
for revealing your Law to Moses on Sinai,
providing a sanctuary and a way of life,
for sending the prophets
to warn us of sin
and point us to the future,
for sending the sages of Israel
to unroll the Scriptures
and show us their wisdom.

God and Father of our Lord Jesus Christ,
we are thankful
that the provisions of the Law
have been fulfilled in Christ,
who was conceived of your Spirit,
born of the Virgin Mary,
that in his life all righteousness was fulfilled —
the blind were healed,
the lepers were cleansed,
the hungry were fed,
that in his sacrifice,

the Law of sacrifice was fulfilled,
and that our Savior passed beyond the veil
into the Holy of Holies.
Even now he is our great High Priest!
He intercedes for us before the throne of grace,
having sprinkled his own blood
upon the mercy seat.

Even now he is the Lamb of God,
having borne away the sin of the world.

Gracious God,
we are thankful
that Christ is risen from the dead.
For this, above all, we thank you.
Christ is risen!
He is risen, indeed!
His sacrifice has been accepted on high!
He is risen, ascended,
and received into heaven.

Ever faithful God,
we are thankful
that through the pouring out of your Spirit,
that Holy Spirit,
that guiding Spirit,
the Spirit of Wisdom and Counsel,
your Law has been written on the tablets
of our hearts,
and we have been made partakers
of the new and eternal covenant.

Therefore, we pray together as our Lord has taught us,
saying,

Our Father, who art in heaven, hallowed be thy name. Thy Kingdom
come. Thy will be done on earth, as it is in heaven. Give us this day
our daily bread. And forgive us our debts, as we forgive our debtors.
And lead us not into temptation, but deliver us from evil: For thine is
the kingdom, and the power, and the glory, for ever. Amen.

Giving of the Bread and Wine

For I have received of the Lord that which also I delivered unto you,
That the Lord Jesus the same night in which he was betrayed took
bread:

(Here the minister should take up the loaf of bread.)

And when he had given thanks, he broke it,

*(Let the minister break the loaf and hand it to the elders, who then help the
minister break it into small pieces. It is appropriate that only one loaf of bread be
used and that it be broken in the course of the service [cf. I Cor 10:16-17])*

and said, Take, eat: this is my body, which is broken for you: this do
in remembrance of me.

*(The bread should be held out to the congregation in a gesture indicating that the
bread is for them to eat.)*

After the same manner also he took the cup, when they had supped,
saying, This cup is the new covenant in my blood . . . shed for many
for the remission of sins.

(With this let the minister pour the cup.)

This do, as often as you drink it, in remembrance of me.
All of you drink of it.

*(With this the cup should be held out to the congregation in a gesture of offering it
to them to take and drink.)*

Anthem Revelation 3:20

Behold, I stand at the door and knock;
if any one hears my voice and opens the door,
I will come in to him and eat with him,
and he with me.

Prayer of Dedication

Heavenly Father! we give thee immortal praise and thanks, that upon us thou hast conferred so great a benefit, as to bring us into the communion of thy Son Jesus Christ our Lord; whom having delivered up to death for us, thou hast given for our food and nourishment unto eternal life. Now, also, grant us grace, that we may never be unmindful of these things; but rather carrying them about engraven upon our hearts, may advance and grow in that faith that is effectual unto every good work. Thus, may the rest of our lives be ordered and followed out to thy glory and the edification of our neighbours: Through Jesus Christ our Lord; Who with thee, O Father! and the Holy Ghost, liveth and reigneth in the unity of the Godhead, world without end. Amen.

Genevan Psalter, 1542
Baird, *Presbyterian Liturgies,* p. 58

Psalm 116:12-19

What shall I render to my God
    For all his kindness shown?
My feet shall visit thine abode,
    My songs address thy throne.

How much is mercy thy delight,
    Thou everblessed God!
How dear thy servants in thy sight!
    How precious is their blood!

How happy all thy servants are!
    How great thy grace to me!
My life, which thou hast made thy care,
    Lord, I devote to thee.

Now I am thine, for ever thine,
    Nor shall my purpose move;
Thy hand hath loosed my bonds of pain,
    And bound me with thy love.

Here in thy courts I leave my vow,
    And thy rich grace record;
Witness, ye saints who hear me now,
    If I forsake the Lord.

Isaac Watts, 1719

Communion Service 4 ————————

Psalm 133   This version © Fred R. Anderson, 1986, in *Singing Psalms of Joy and Praise* (Westminster/John Knox Press)

Behold the goodness of our Lord,
How blest it is to be
A company of God's beloved,
In holy unity.

Like precious oil upon the head,
A healing for our strife,
It flows throughout our common bond,
Refreshing all of life.

As dew on Zion's mountaintop
Brings freshness to its door,
our Lord commands this in our midst
And brings life evermore.

Invocation

Blessed you are,
    O God and Father of our Lord Jesus Christ,
        whose Spirit brooded on the face of the deep,
        whose Spirit brought forth a Savior
            from the womb of Mary,
        whose Spirit never ceases to beget
            sons and daughters for your kingdom.

Send forth your Spirit
    on the Church today,
        that children of God might be born
            from every nation on earth.

We pray for the Church in Ethiopia,
    at this time of persecution and famine.
We pray for the Church in China;
    give her strength to endure.

Send forth your Spirit,
    that we may be your sons and daughters in truth.
        Sanctify us in body and soul,
            that we may be a holy people,
                set apart for your service.

Blessed you are,
O God and Father of our Lord Jesus Christ
who at Christ's baptism anointed him
with the Holy Spirit,
providing the gifts
of wisdom and understanding,
of counsel and might,
of knowledge and of the fear of the Lord.

Fill us with the gifts of your Spirit,
that we might carry out
the mission our Savior has given us.

We pray for the missions in which we are engaged,
Americana Nursing Home,
Lafayette Urban Ministry,
Navigators,
the Church in the Yucatan.

Anoint us with the Spirit of Christ
and prepare us for the consummation of his
glorious kingdom.

Blessing, and honour, and glory, and power
be unto him that sitteth upon the throne,
and unto the Lamb for ever and ever. *Amen.*

Invitation

Apostles' Creed

I believe in God the Father Almighty, Maker of heaven and earth: And in Jesus Christ his only son, our Lord; who was conceived by the Holy Ghost, born of the Virgin Mary, suffered under Pontius Pilate, was crucified, dead, and buried; he descended into hell; the third day he rose again from the dead; he ascended into heaven, and sitteth on the right hand of God the Father Almighty; from thence he shall come to judge the quick and the dead.

I believe in the Holy Ghost, the holy catholic Church; the communion of saints; the forgiveness of sins; the resurrection of the body; and the life everlasting. Amen.

Anthem Psalm 19:1-6

Eucharistic Prayer

Lord God, King of the Universe,
    we are thankful
        for the heavens, the work of thy fingers,
            the moon and the stars, which thou hast ordained.

Lord and Creator of all flesh,
    we thank you
        for the creation of the human race
        for Adam and Eve and all their descendants
            on every continent of the earth,
            and in every age past and yet to come,
                in all our variety,
                in all our ability,
                in all our fallibility.

Lord God,
    we are thankful
        that in spite of human disobedience
            and rebellion,
        you nevertheless provided a way
            of reconciliation,
                sending Christ, the image of your glory.
        So that he might be our Savior
            he humbled himself,
                becoming obedient,
                taking the form of a servant.

God and Father of our Lord Jesus Christ,
    we are thankful
        for the gift of a Savior,
            that he took on our flesh,
            that we might receive his Spirit,
            that the creation foreshadowed in Adam
                is fulfilled in Christ.

Father, your ways are past finding out.
    We are thankful
        that your love for us is revealed
        in the giving up of your Son to death.
            It is your well-beloved Son
                whom we behold as the Lamb of God
                who takes away the sin of the world.

Gracious Father,
　we are thankful.
　　Christ is risen.
　　Your servant has been highly exalted.
　　The sacrifice has been received on high.
　　The Lamb that was slain lives for evermore.

　　　For this above all we praise you.
　　　Death is swallowed up in victory.

　　Christ is risen!
　　All glory be to you, O Father.
　　He is risen,
　　　ascended into heaven,
　　　　and seated at the right hand of eternal glory.

Almighty Father,
　we are thankful!
　　Your Holy Spirit has been poured out on us,
　　　the Comforter whom Christ promised.
　　Your Spirit is even now
　　　renewing us in the image of Christ,
　　　preparing us for the day of his coming.

Rejoicing in that glorious day,
　we pray as our Savior has taught us,

Our Father, who art in heaven, hallowed be thy name. Thy
Kingdom come. Thy will be done on earth, as it is in heaven. Give
us this day our daily bread. And forgive us our debts, as we forgive
our debtors. And lead us not into temptation, but deliver us from
evil: For thine is the kingdom, and the power, and the glory, for
ever. Amen.

Giving of the Bread and Wine

For I have received of the Lord that which also I delivered unto you,
That the Lord Jesus the same night in which he was betrayed took
bread:

(Here the minister should take up the loaf of bread.)

And when he had given thanks, he broke it,

*(Let the minister break the loaf and hand it to the elders, who then help the
minister break it into small pieces. It is appropriate that only one loaf of bread be
used and that it be broken in the course of the service [cf. I Cor 10:16-17])*

and said, Take, eat: this is my body, which is broken for you: this do
in remembrance of me.

*(The bread should be held out to the congregation in a gesture indicating that the
bread is for them to eat.)*

After the same manner also he took the cup, when they had supped,
saying, This cup is the new covenant in my blood . . . shed for many
for the remission of sins.

(With this let the minister pour the cup.)

This do, as often as you drink it, in remembrance of me.
All of you drink of it.

*(With this the cup should be held out to the congregation in a gesture of offering it
to them to take and drink.)*

Anthem John 11:25-26

I am the resurrection and the life;
he who believes in me, though he die,
yet shall he live,
and whoever lives and believes in me shall never die.

Prayer of Dedication

Heavenly Father! we give thee immortal praise and thanks, that upon us thou hast conferred so great a benefit, as to bring us into the communion of thy Son Jesus Christ our Lord; whom having delivered up to death for us, thou hast given for our food and nourishment unto eternal life. Now, also, grant us grace, that we may never be unmindful of these things; but rather carrying them about engraven upon our hearts, may advance and grow in that faith that is effectual unto every good work. Thus, may the rest of our lives be ordered and followed out to thy glory and the edification of our neighbours: Through Jesus Christ our Lord; Who with thee, O Father! and the Holy Ghost, liveth and reigneth in the unity of the Godhead, world without end. Amen.

Genevan Psalter, 1542
Baird, *Presbyterian Liturgies,* p. 58

Psalm 138   From Christopher L. Webber, *A New Metrical Psalter* (New York: Church Hymnal Corporation, 1986). Used by permission. All rights reserved.

I will give thanks with my whole heart,
    Before the gods my praise express;
I will bow down before your throne
    And praise Your love and faithfulness.

Above all things, O Lord, my God,
    You glorified Your name and Word;
I called and then You answered me
    And gave me increased strength, O Lord.

All kings on earth who hear Your words,
    O Lord, will give You thanks and praise
And tell how great Your glory is,
    And they will sing of all Your ways.

The Lord is high, yet scorns the proud,
    Protects the lowly on their path;
Although I walk in trouble, Lord,
    You keep me safe from my foe's wrath.

Lord, Your right hand shall save my life
    And make Your purpose for me sure;
Do not forsake what You have made;
    Your love forever will endure.

Communion Service 5: ———— Christmas Eve

Psalm 24

Lift up your heads, ye mighty gates,
Behold, the King of glory waits;
The King of kings is drawing near;
The Saviour of the world is here!

Fling wide the portals of your heart;
Make it a temple, set apart
From earthly use for Heaven's employ,
Adorned with prayer, and love, and joy.

Redeemer, come! I open wide
My heart to Thee; here, Lord, abide.
Let me Thy inner presence feel;
Thy grace and love in me reveal.   Georg Weissel, 1642

Invocation

O Father,
        you have brought us into your house,
        seated us at your table,
        and spread this feast before us.

    Grant to us your Holy Spirit,
        that all of us here
            might be filled with love toward each other.

O Father,
        you have sought us out
        from every highway and hinterland.

    Grant to us your Holy Spirit,
        that through the preaching of the gospel,
        people from all corners of the earth be gathered
            around this table,
                wise men from the East,
                shepherds from Israel and Jordan,
                farmers from the Midwest,
                our friends at Priscilla Girls' School in Mexico,
                truck drivers from Tennessee.
    Join us together as your family.

O Father,
    you have loved us
        that we might love one another.

    Grant to us your Holy Spirit,
        that all Christians might be one
            in the body of Christ,
        that no division of clan or creed
            break the fellowship of this table.

Blessing, and honour, and glory, and power
    be unto him that sitteth upon the throne,
        and unto the Lamb for ever and ever. *Amen.*

Invitation

Apostles' Creed

I believe in God the Father Almighty, Maker of heaven and earth:
And in Jesus Christ his only son, our Lord; who was conceived by
the Holy Ghost, born of the Virgin Mary, suffered under Pontius Pilate,
was crucified, dead, and buried; he descended into hell; the third day
he rose again from the dead; he ascended into heaven, and sitteth on
the right hand of God the Father Almighty; from thence he shall come
to judge the quick and the dead.

I believe in the Holy Ghost, the holy catholic Church; the communion of saints; the forgiveness of sins; the resurrection of the body;
and the life everlasting. Amen.

Anthem Canticle from Luke 2:14

Glory to God in the highest,
    and on earth peace,
    good will among men.

Father,
> we are thankful
>> for your creation,
>> for the sun,
>> for the daytime and the light of heaven,
>> for snow and frost and winter nights,
>> for warm hearths,
>> for family, relatives, and friends.

Father,
> we are thankful
>> for the old covenant, given to Moses on Mt. Sinai,
>>> the tablets written on stone,
>>> the establishing of a moral order of life.

We bless you for justice and righteousness
> wherever it is found.

Father,
> we are thankful
>> for the promise of the prophets
>>> that a Prince of Peace should come,
>>>> one who would establish at last
>>>> your peace in our hearts,
>>> that a Day Star should shine forth
>>>> and overcome all darkness in this world.

Father,
> we are thankful
>> for the quiet faith of Mary,
>>> who believed the promise that was given her,
>> for the humble faith of the shepherds
>>> who were obedient to the vision
>>>> that had been given them,
>> for the searching faith of the wise men,
>>> who sought and found the wisdom of heaven.

Father,
  we are thankful
    that in Christ
      all these promises have been fulfilled:
        A Prince has been born
          from the house of David,
        the Root of Jesse has sent forth
          a righteous branch,

    that this Messiah,
      anointed by your Spirit,
        made himself a sacrifice for us,
        and having perfected this priestly service
          is now seated at your right hand
          in eternal glory.

Father,
  we are thankful
    for the new covenant,
      whereby your Holy Spirit
        has written your Law
          on the tablets of our hearts.
      whereby the Spirit of Christ
        has filled our spirits with your love
        and united us together in one body.

It is that same Spirit who cries out to you:
      Abba, Father!
  Therefore we pray together, saying,

Our Father, who art in heaven, hallowed be thy name. Thy
Kingdom come. Thy will be done on earth, as it is in heaven. Give
us this day our daily bread. And forgive us our debts, as we forgive
our debtors. And lead us not into temptation, but deliver us from
evil: For thine is the kingdom, and the power, and the glory, for
ever. *Amen.*

Giving of the Bread and Wine

For I have received of the Lord that which also I delivered unto you, That the Lord Jesus the same night in which he was betrayed took bread:

(Here the minister should take up the loaf of bread.)

And when he had given thanks, he broke it,

(Let the minister break the loaf and hand it to the elders, who then help the minister break it into small pieces. It is appropriate that only one loaf of bread be used and that it be broken in the course of the service [cf. I Cor 10:16-17])

and said, Take, eat: this is my body, which is broken for you: this do in remembrance of me.

(The bread should be held out to the congregation in a gesture indicating that the bread is for them to eat.)

After the same manner also he took the cup, when they had supped, saying, This cup is the new covenant in my blood . . . shed for many for the remission of sins.

(With this let the minister pour the cup.)

This do, as often as you drink it, in remembrance of me.
All of you drink of it.

(With this the cup should be held out to the congregation in a gesture of offering it to them to take and drink.)

Anthem Canticle from Luke 1:46-55

My soul magnifies the Lord,
    and my spirit rejoices in God my Savior,
for he has regarded the low estate of his handmaiden.
For behold, henceforth all generations will call me blessed;
for he who is mighty has done great things for me,
    and holy is his name.
And his mercy is on those who fear him
    from generation to generation.
He has shown strength with his arm,
he has put down the mighty from their thrones,

and exalted those of low degree;
he has filled the hungry with good things,
    and the rich he has sent empty away.
He has helped his servant Israel,
    in remembrance of his mercy,
as he spoke to our fathers,
    to Abraham and to his posterity for ever.

Prayer of Dedication

Heavenly Father! we give thee immortal praise and thanks, that upon us thou hast conferred so great a benefit, as to bring us into the communion of thy Son Jesus Christ our Lord; whom having delivered up to death for us, thou hast given for our food and nourishment unto eternal life. Now, also, grant us grace, that we may never be unmindful of these things; but rather carrying them about engraven upon our hearts, may advance and grow in that faith that is effectual unto every good work. Thus, may the rest of our lives be ordered and followed out to thy glory and the edification of our neighbours: Through Jesus Christ our Lord; Who with thee, O Father! and the Holy Ghost, liveth and reigneth in the unity of the Godhead, world without end. Amen.

Genevan Psalter, 1542
Baird, *Presbyterian Liturgies*, p. 58

Psalm 98

Joy to the world! the Lord is come:
    Let earth receive her King:
Let every heart prepare Him room,
    And heaven and nature sing.

Joy to the earth! the Saviour reigns:
    Let men their songs employ;
While fields and floods, rocks, hills, and plains,
    Repeat the sounding joy.

No more let sins and sorrows grow,
    Nor thorns infest the ground;
He comes to make His blessings flow
    Far as the curse is found.

He rules the world with truth and grace,
    And makes the nations prove
The glories of His righteousness,
    And wonders of His love.

Isaac Watts, 1719

Communion Service 6: —— Maundy Thursday

Hymn (paraphrase of I Cor 11:23: "Twas on that Night . . .")

Invocation

(Remembering that during his passion Jesus gave particular attention to the ministry of intercession, we would do well to give special attention to intercessions on Maundy Thursday.)

O God, Our Father,
 who has accepted Christ as the spotless Lamb,
 the lamb who has taken away the sin of the world.

   We pray for the Church,
    the Bride of the Lamb.
   From the scandal of her compromises
    with the world, purify her.
   In spite of the sin of her division,
    unite her.
   In the shame of her apathy,
    vivify her;
     fill her again with your Spirit.

O God, Our Father,
 you who have given your only Son
  to be the suffering servant,
  to bear the sins of many.
 We pray for the ministry,
  for pastors and teachers,
  elders and deacons.
    Heal them from every form of sin
     or inclination toward sin.
 We pray for apostles who have denied you,
  ministers who have failed you,
  teachers who have misunderstood your Word.
    Fill them again with your Spirit.

O God, Our Father,
 who loved us while we were yet sinners,
  and gave for us your most precious Son.
 We pray for the world
  in the midst of its oppression and perversion,
  in the midst of its anger and pride and selfishness.
 Take away the sin of the world,
  and take away our sin; fill us with your Spirit,
    that the face of the world might be renewed,
    and that we may be the humanity you intended.

O God, Our Father,
>   we pray for our nation.
>>   Purge out the leaven of sin from the land.
>>   Remove scandal and dishonesty from our government.
>>   Remove degeneracy from our intellectual life.

O God, Our Father,
>   who has accepted Christ as the spotless Lamb
>   that bore away the sin of your people.
>   We pray for our congregation,
>>   for all of us who, like sheep, have strayed,
>>>   and have taken our own way,
>>   for those suffering from the sins of others,
>>   for those suffering from their own sin,
>>   for all of us who are angry with you,
>>   for all who are ashamed to enter your presence.
>   Grant us your peace,
>>   bring us home,
>>   and seat us at your table.

Blessing, and honour, and glory, and power
>   be unto him that sitteth upon the throne,
>>   and unto the Lamb for ever and ever.

Invitation

Apostles' Creed

>   I believe in God the Father Almighty, Maker of heaven and earth:
>   And in Jesus Christ his only son, our Lord; who was conceived by the Holy Ghost, born of the Virgin Mary, suffered under Pontius Pilate, was crucified, dead, and buried; he descended into hell; the third day he rose again from the dead; he ascended into heaven, and sitteth on the right hand of God the Father Almighty; from thence he shall come to judge the quick and the dead.
>   I believe in the Holy Ghost, the holy catholic Church; the communion of saints; the forgiveness of sins; the resurrection of the body; and the life everlasting. *Amen.*

Anthem Isaiah 53:3-7

He was despised and rejected by men;
>   a man of sorrows, and acquainted with grief; . . .
Surely he has borne our griefs
>   and carried our sorrows; . . .
Upon him was the chastisement that made us whole,
>   and with his stripes we are healed.
All we like sheep have gone astray;
>   we have turned every one to his own way;
and the LORD has laid on him

the iniquity of us all.
He was oppressed, and he was afflicted,
   yet he opened not his mouth;
like a lamb that is led to the slaughter,
   and like a sheep that before its shearers is dumb,
   so he opened not his mouth.

Eucharistic Prayer

Blessed art thou, O Lord God,
      King of the Universe,
   who brings wine from the vine.
Blessed art thou, O Lord God,
      King of the Universe,
   who brings bread from the earth.

Lord God, King of the Universe,
   we are thankful for the creation of heaven and earth.
      You formed the great lights,
         the one to rule the day,
         the other to rule the night.

We bless you
      for the glory of sunrise and sunset,
      for the sky at night,
         its ordered constellations,
      for the planets in their orbits,
      for the paschal moon,
         and the coming of spring.

Lord God of Israel,
   we are thankful
      for revealing your name to Moses,
      for sending him to bring the children of Israel
         out of Egypt,
      for providing a way through the Red Sea,
      for the Song of Miriam:
         Sing to the LORD,
            for he has triumphed gloriously;
         the horse and his rider
            he has thrown into the sea.

We bless you
      for leading the children of Israel
         through the wilderness
         and over the Jordan into the Promised Land.

Lord God of the prophets,
　　we are thankful,
　　　　for having kept your hand on your people,
　　　　　　even when we sinned against you,
　　　　for having sent prophets
　　　　　　to preach repentance,
　　　　for the message of Hosea,
　　　　　　that you will not give us up,
　　　　　　that once again you will bring us out of Egypt,
　　　　for the message of Isaiah,
　　　　　　that you would send us a Savior,
　　　　　　　　a suffering servant,
　　　　　　　　a Passover lamb.

Blessed art thou, O God and Father of our Lord Jesus Christ,
　　that Christ our Passover has been sacrificed:
　　　　"Surely he has borne our griefs
　　　　　　and carried our sorrows . . .
　　　　He was wounded for our transgressions.
　　　　He was bruised for our iniquities.
　　　　Upon him was the chastisement that made us whole."

Blessed art thou, O God and Father of our Lord Jesus Christ,
　　your faithful servant,
　　your only begotten Son,
　　　　"despised and rejected by men,"

　　has been highly exalted,
　　　　raised on the third day,
　　　　ascended into heaven.
　　Many are astounded, for "we esteemed him not."

Blessed art thou, O God and Father of our Lord Jesus Christ.
　　Christ has led captivity captive.
　　The Lamb that was slain lives for evermore.
　　　　"He bore the sin of many
　　　　and made intercession for the transgressors."
　　Seated at your right hand
　　　　he intercedes for us.

Therefore we pray
　　through him,
　　　　with him,
　　　　　　and in him,

Our Father, who art in heaven, hallowed be thy name. Thy Kingdom
come. Thy will be done on earth, as it is in heaven. Give us this day
our daily bread. And forgive us our debts, as we forgive our debtors.
And lead us not into temptation, but deliver us from evil: For thine is
the kingdom, and the power, and the glory, for ever. *Amen.*

Giving of the Bread and Wine

For I have received of the Lord that which also I delivered unto you, That the Lord Jesus the same night in which he was betrayed took bread:

(Here the minister should take up the loaf of bread.)

And when he had given thanks, he broke it,

(Let the minister break the loaf and hand it to the elders, who then help the minister break it into small pieces. It is appropriate that only one loaf of bread be used and that it be broken in the course of the service [cf. I Cor 10:16-17])

and said, Take, eat: this is my body, which is broken for you: this do in remembrance of me.

(The bread should be held out to the congregation in a gesture indicating that the bread is for them to eat.)

After the same manner also he took the cup, when they had supped, saying, This cup is the new covenant in my blood . . . shed for many for the remission of sins.

(With this let the minister pour the cup.)

This do, as often as you drink it, in remembrance of me.
All of you drink of it.

(With this the cup should be held out to the congregation in a gesture of offering it to them to take and drink.)

Anthem

Christ Jesus lay in death's strong bands,
    for our offenses given;
but now at God's right hand he stands
    and brings us life from heaven;
wherefore let us joyful be,
    and sing to God right thankfully
loud songs of Alleluia! Alleluia!

It was a strange and dreadful strife
    when life and death contended;
the victory remained with life:
    the reign of death was ended.
Holy Scripture plainly saith
    that death is swallowed up by death;
its sting is lost forever. Alleluia!

So let us keep the festival
    whereto our Lord invites us.
Christ is himself the joy of all,
    the Sun that warms and lights us.
By his grace he doth impart
    eternal sunshine to the heart;
the night of sin is ended. Alleluia!   Martin Luther, 1524

Prayer of Dedication

Heavenly Father! we give thee immortal praise and thanks, that upon us thou hast conferred so great a benefit, as to bring us into the communion of thy Son Jesus Christ our Lord; whom having delivered up to death for us, thou hast given for our food and nourishment unto eternal life. Now, also, grant us grace, that we may never be unmindful of these things; but rather carrying them about engraven upon our hearts, may advance and grow in that faith that is effectual unto every good work. Thus, may the rest of our lives be ordered and followed out to thy glory and the edification of our neighbours: Through Jesus Christ our Lord; Who with thee, O Father! and the Holy Ghost, liveth and reigneth in the unity of the Godhead, world without end. Amen.

Genevan Psalter, 1542
Baird, *Presbyterian Liturgies*, p. 58

Psalm 116:12-19

What shall I render to my God
    For all his kindness shown?
My feet shall visit thine abode,
    My songs address thy throne.

How much is mercy thy delight,
    Thou everblessed God!
How dear thy servants in thy sight!
    How precious is their blood!

How happy all thy servants are!
    How great thy grace to me!
My life, which thou hast made thy care,
    Lord, I devote to thee.

Now I am thine, for ever thine,
    Nor shall my purpose move;
Thy hand hath loosed my bonds of pain,
    And bound me with thy love.

Here in thy courts I leave my vow,
    and thy rich grace record;
Witness, ye saints who hear me now,
    If I forsake the Lord.   Isaac Watts

Communion Service 7 ———————— Easter

Psalm 118

> Give thanks unto the Lord, Jehovah,
>   For he is good, O praise his Name!
> Let Israel say: The Lord be praised,
>   His mercy ever is the same.
> Let Aaron's house now praise Jehovah;
>   The Lord is good, O praise his Name;
> Let all that fear the Lord extol him,
>   His mercy ever is the same. . . .
>
> I shall not die, but live, declaring
>   The works of God, who tried me sore,
> And chastened me; but in his mercy
>   Not unto death hath giv'n me o'er.
> The gates of righeousness set open,
>   The gate of God! I'll enter in
> To praise thee, Lord, who pray'r hast answered,
>   and savedst me from all my sin.
>
> The stone — O Lord, it is thy doing —
>   The stone, the builders did despise,
> Is made the headstone of the corner,
>   And it is marv'lous in our eyes.
> This is the day, of days most glorious,
>   The Lord hath made; we'll joy and sing:
> Send now prosperity, we pray thee;
>   and O our God, salvation bring!

Anonymous

Invocation

> Holy Father,
>   you have sent your Son to gather us about this table.
>   Send forth now your Holy Spirit,
>   that as this grain was scattered on the hillsides,
>   was harvested, and was made into one loaf of bread,
>   so gather us together from all parts of the world
>   to be one Church.

Holy Father,
    whom we have known in your Son.
        The world has not known you,
           but we have known you,
           because your word is truth.
    Send forth your Holy Spirit,
        that we may be united in the truth,
        that the Church may be one
           in its preaching, teaching, and witness.

Holy Father,
    we have believed because of the Word
        that was preached to us.
    We have not yet seen,
        and yet we have believed.
    Send forth your Holy Spirit,
        that our eyes may be opened,
        and that Christ may be known to us
        in the breaking of bread.

Blessing, and honour, and glory, and power
    be unto him that sitteth upon the throne,
        and unto the Lamb for ever and ever. *Amen.*

Invitation

Apostles' Creed

I believe in God the Father Almighty, Maker of heaven and earth:
And in Jesus Christ his only son, our Lord; who was conceived by
the Holy Ghost, born of the Virgin Mary, suffered under Pontius Pilate,
was crucified, dead, and buried; he descended into hell; the third day
he rose again from the dead; he ascended into heaven, and sitteth on
the right hand of God the Father Almighty; from thence he shall come
to judge the quick and the dead.

I believe in the Holy Ghost, the holy catholic Church; the communion of saints; the forgiveness of sins; the resurrection of the body;
and the life everlasting. Amen.

Anthem Canticle from Revelation 5:12-13

Blessing and honor and glory and power,
Ringeth the earth with His glory and fame;
Give ye to Him who our battle hath won,
Whose are the Kingdom, the crown, and the throne. . . .

Horatius Bonar, 1866

Eucharistic Prayer

Blessed art thou, O God and Father of our Lord Jesus Christ,
    Creator of heaven and earth.

We bless you for the dawn,
    the fresh light of day,
    the end of the night.
This is the day that the Lord has made.
We shall rejoice and are glad in it!

Lord God, our Creator,
    we bless you for Adam and Eve
        and all the race of humanity,
            that has gone before us,
        for mother and father, husband and wife,
        for colleagues and companions.

Lord God of Israel,
    we are thankful
        for the tradition of godliness
            known from most ancient times,
        for patriarchs and prophets,
            judges and kings,
        and for the promises, covenants,
            and blessings granted to them.

God and Father of our Lord Jesus Christ,
    we are thankful
        for the gift of a Savior,
        for his ministry of preaching and healing.
        He opened the eyes of the blind.
        He healed the fevered.
        He calmed those who were tormented,
            and gave peace to the anguished.

Almighty God, whose ways are past finding out,
    we are thankful
        that your love for us is revealed
            in the giving up of your Son,
        that Christ took this bitter cup of suffering,
        that in suffering death he conquered death.

Gracious Father,
  we are thankful.
    Christ is risen.
    Your suffering Servant has been highly exalted.
  For this above all we thank you,
    that the powers of death
    he has trampled underfoot.
  Christ has burst the gates of hell,
    and led us forth to eternal light.
  He lives, that we might live,
    the firstborn from the dead,
    the firstfruits of them that slept.

Blessed art thou, O God and Father of our Lord Jesus Christ,
  you who have anointed us with the Spirit of Christ,
    joining us together in one body
      with him and with each other,
    dwelling in our hearts,
    and uniting us to Christ
      until the day of his coming.

Gracious Father,
  we are thankful
    for the promise of your coming again,
    for the final establishment of your Kingdom,
    for the wiping away of all tears,
    for the victory of your people,
    for the vision of a heavenly Jerusalem
      and the promise of eternal life.

Rejoicing in that glorious day,
  we pray as our Savior has taught us, saying,

Our Father, who art in heaven, hallowed be thy name. Thy
Kingdom come. Thy will be done on earth, as it is in heaven. Give
us this day our daily bread. And forgive us our debts, as we forgive
our debtors. And lead us not into temptation, but deliver us from
evil: For thine is the kingdom, and the power, and the glory, for
ever. *Amen.*

Giving of the Bread and Wine

For I have received of the Lord that which also I delivered unto you,
That the Lord Jesus the same night in which he was betrayed took
bread:

(Here the minister should take up the loaf of bread.)

And when he had given thanks, he broke it,

*(Let the minister break the loaf and hand it to the elders, who then help the
minister break it into small pieces. It is appropriate that only one loaf of bread be
used and that it be broken in the course of the service [cf. I Cor 10:16-17])*

and said, Take, eat: this is my body, which is broken for you: this do
in remembrance of me.

*(The bread should be held out to the congregation in a gesture indicating that the
bread is for them to eat.)*

After the same manner also he took the cup, when they had supped,
saying, This cup is the new covenant in my blood . . . shed for many
for the remission of sins.

(With this let the minister pour the cup.)

This do, as often as you drink it, in remembrance of me.
All of you drink of it.

*(With this the cup should be held out to the congregation in a gesture of offering it
to them to take and drink.)*

Anthem Canticle from Revelation 19:6-8: the "Hallelujah" chorus by G. F. Handel

Hallelujah: for the Lord God omnipotent reigneth.

. . . The kingdom of this world is become the kingdom of our Lord,
and of his Christ; and he shall reign for ever and ever.

. . . King of Kings, and Lord of Lords.

. . . Hallelujah!

Prayer of Dedication

Heavenly Father! we give thee immortal praise and thanks, that upon us thou hast conferred so great a benefit, as to bring us into the communion of thy Son Jesus Christ our Lord; whom having delivered up to death for us, thou hast given for our food and nourishment unto eternal life. Now, also, grant us grace, that we may never be unmindful of these things; but rather carrying them about engraven upon our hearts, may advance and grow in that faith that is effectual unto every good work. Thus, may the rest of our lives be ordered and followed out to thy glory and the edification of our neighbours: Through Jesus Christ our Lord; Who with thee, O Father! and the Holy Ghost, liveth and reigneth in the unity of the Godhead, world without end. Amen.

Genevan Psalter, 1542

Baird, *Presbyterian Liturgies,* p. 58

Hymn

"Christ the Lord is risen today," Alleluia!
Sons of men and angels say: Alleluia!
Raise your joys and triumphs high; Alleluia!
Sing, ye heavens, and earth, reply; Alleluia!

Vain the stone, the watch, the seal; Alleluia!
Christ has burst the gates of hell: Alleluia!
Death in vain forbids His rise: Alleluia!
Christ hath opened Paradise. Alleluia!

Lives again our glorious King; Alleluia!
Where, O death, is now thy sting? Alleluia!
Once He died, our souls to save; Alleluia!
Where thy victory, O grave? Alleluia!

Soar we now where Christ has led, Alleluia!
Following our exalted Head; Alleluia!
Made like Him, like Him we rise; Alleluia!
Ours the cross, the grave, the skies. Alleluia!

Hail, the Lord of earth and heaven! Alleluia!
Praise to Thee by both be given; Alleluia!
Thee we greet triumphant now; Alleluia!
Hail, the Resurrection Thou! Alleluia!

Charles Wesley, 1739

Communion Service 8 ——————— Pentecost

Psalm 29   This version by Michael Perry, © 1973 Hope Publishing Co.,
Carol Stream, Illinois. All rights reserved. Used by permission.

The God of heaven thunders,
    Whose voice in cadent echoes
Resounds above the water,
    And all the world sings,
"Glory, glory, glory!"

The desert writhes in tempest,
    Wind whips the trees to fury,
The lightning splits the forest
    and flame diffuses
Glory, glory, glory!

The mighty God eternal
    Is to the throne ascended,
And we who are God's people,
    Within these walls cry,
"Glory, glory, glory!"

Invocation

Holy Father,
    who sent forth your Spirit
        on the day of Pentecost,
    pour out your love on us,
        as you did on those who were gathered
            in the Upper Room,
        uniting in one Church a people from every nation
            on the face of the earth.

Holy Father,
    send forth your Holy Spirit on us as a purifying fire,
        that we may be united in holiness,
        that we may be purified as the sons of Levi,
            a priesthood to offer up
                spiritual sacrifices on every shore,
            serving you together in prayer,
                in the bond of love,
                and in works of mercy.

Holy Father,
    pour out on us today your Holy Spirit.
    Send down to us the glowing coals
        from your heavenly altar,
        that our lips might be cleansed
            to proclaim Christ's death until he comes.

We pray for ourselves,
   that we be purified, sanctified,
   and at last glorified in your presence.

Blessing, and honour, and glory, and power
   be unto him that sitteth upon the throne,
   and unto the Lamb for ever and ever. *Amen.*

Invitation

Apostles' Creed

I believe in God the Father Almighty, Maker of heaven and earth:
And in Jesus Christ his only son, our Lord; who was conceived by
the Holy Ghost, born of the Virgin Mary, suffered under Pontius Pilate,
was crucified, dead, and buried; he descended into hell; the third day
he rose again from the dead; he ascended into heaven, and sitteth on
the right hand of God the Father Almighty; from thence he shall come
to judge the quick and the dead.
I believe in the Holy Ghost, the holy catholic Church; the communion of saints; the forgiveness of sins; the resurrection of the body;
and the life everlasting. *Amen.*

Anthem

Come, O Creator Spirit, come,
   and make within our hearts thy home;
to us thy grace celestial give,
   who of thy breathing move and live.

O comforter, that name is thine,
   of God most high the gift divine:
the well of life, the fire of love,
   our souls' anointing from above.

Thou dost appear in sev'nfold dower,
   the sign of God's almighty power,
the Father's promise, making rich
   with saving truth our earthly speech.

Our senses with thy light inflame;
   our hearts to heav'nly love reclaim;
our bodies' poor infirmity
   with strength perpetual fortify.

Our mortal foe afar repel;
   grant us henceforth in peace to dwell;
and so to us, with thee for guide,
   no ill shall come, no harm betide.

May we by thee the Father learn,
    and know the Son, and thee discern,
who art of both, and thus adore
    in perfect faith forevermore.   Medieval Latin

Eucharistic Prayer

Blessed you are, Lord God,
    King of the Universe.
Blessed you are, ruler of all being,
    God from the beginning
    and God in the end.

You are lord of creation,
    sending your Spirit to brood upon the deep,
    and giving to Adam the breath of life.

We bless you for the human spirit,
    for the intelligence you have granted to us
        and to all humankind,
    for the energy of our bodies,
        the strength of our arms,
    for the determination of our wills,
        the power of our imagination.

We bless you that even in our fallen state
    we have a thirst for you.
    We cry out for you.
        Our spirits crave the anointing of your Spirit.

Blessed you are, Lord God of Israel,
    calling the patriarchs,
        and speaking through the prophets,
    enlightening their visions,
        kindling their hope,
           teaching them wisdom.
    Praise be to you,
        O Shepherd of the flock of Jacob.

How blessed you are, Eternal Lord!
    for the gift of a Savior,
        conceived of the Spirit,
        born of the Virgin.
    We bless you for his baptism,
        for the descent of the dove,
            the anointing of the Spirit,
        for his divine empowering,
        for his illumination by the Spirit of Truth.
    We bless you for his ministry of mighty works
        and tender mercies.
    We praise you
        for his obedient suffering,
            his sacrifice on the cross,
            his rest in the tomb,
        for his glorious resurrection
            and ascension into heaven.
    How thankful we are, Great God.
    To you be eternal praise.

Blessed you are, O Father,
    that on the day of Pentecost,
        Christ poured out the fire of his Spirit
            on his disciples,
            and made them one body,
    that in this last day,
        your Spirit is being poured out
            on all flesh,
            making us a holy people,
            and a royal priesthood.

It is in the unity of that same Spirit
    that we pray, saying,

Our Father, who art in heaven, hallowed be thy name. Thy Kingdom
come. Thy will be done on earth, as it is in heaven. Give us this day
our daily bread. And forgive us our debts, as we forgive our debtors.
And lead us not into temptation, but deliver us from evil: For thine is
the kingdom, and the power, and the glory, for ever. *Amen.*

Giving of the Bread and Wine

For I have received of the Lord that which also I delivered unto you, That the Lord Jesus the same night in which he was betrayed took bread:

(Here the minister should take up the loaf of bread.)

And when he had given thanks, he broke it,

(Let the minister break the loaf and hand it to the elders, who then help the minister break it into small pieces. It is appropriate that only one loaf of bread be used and that it be broken in the course of the service [cf. I Cor 10:16-17])

and said, Take, eat: this is my body, which is broken for you: this do in remembrance of me.

(The bread should be held out to the congregation in a gesture indicating that the bread is for them to eat.)

After the same manner also he took the cup, when they had supped, saying, This cup is the new covenant in my blood . . . shed for many for the remission of sins.

(With this let the minister pour the cup.)

This do, as often as you drink it, in remembrance of me.
All of you drink of it.

(With this the cup should be held out to the congregation in a gesture of offering it to them to take and drink.)

Anthem

Come, Holy Ghost, our hearts inspire,
let us thine influence prove,
source of the old prophetic fire,
fountain of life and love.

Come, Holy Ghost (for moved by thee
the prophets wrote and spoke),
unlock the truth, thyself the key,
unseal the sacred book.

Expand thy wings, Celestial Dove,
brood o'er our nature's night;
on our disordered spirits move,
and let there now be light.

God, through himself, we then shall know,
if thou within us shine,
and sound, with all thy saints below,
the depths of love divine.

Charles Wesley, 1740

Prayer of Dedication

Heavenly Father! we give thee immortal praise and thanks, that upon us thou hast conferred so great a benefit, as to bring us into the communion of thy Son Jesus Christ our Lord; whom having delivered up to death for us, thou hast given for our food and nourishment unto eternal life. Now, also, grant us grace, that we may never be unmindful of these things; but rather carrying them about engraven upon our hearts, may advance and grow in that faith that is effectual unto every good work. Thus, may the rest of our lives be ordered and followed out to thy glory and the edification of our neighbours: Through Jesus Christ our Lord; Who with thee, O Father! and the Holy Ghost, liveth and reigneth in the unity of the Godhead, world without end. Amen.

Genevan Psalter, 1542

Baird, *Presbyterian Liturgies,* p. 58

Psalm 72

Jesus shall reign where'er the sun
Does his successive journeys run;
His Kingdom stretch from shore to shore,
Till moons shall wax and wane no more.

For him shall endless prayer be made,
And praises throng to crown His head;
his name, like sweet perfume, shall rise
With every morning sacrifice.

People and realms of every tongue
Dwell on His love with sweetest song;
And infant voices shall proclaim
Their early blessings on His Name.

Blessings abound wher'er He reigns;
The prisoner leaps to loose his chains,
The weary find eternal rest,
And all the sons of want are blest.

Let every creature rise and bring
Peculiar honors to our King;
Angels descend with songs again,
And earth repeat the loud Amen!

Isaac Watts, 1719

Prayers of Thanksgiving

There is a logical distinction that puts praise at the beginning of the worship service and thanksgiving at the end. To be sure, "praise" and "thanksgiving" are nearly synonyms, and often we find the two words used together synonymously in Scripture, as in Psalm 100:4, "Enter his gates with thanksgiving, and his courts with praise!" But there is a distinction: Praise comes out of the experience of awe that wells up within us when we are confronted by God's presence. Praise is the "Hallelujah" that recognizes and acclaims God's presence in the sanctuary. It is for this reason that the gates of God's sanctuary are named Praise (Isa 60:18). Praise is entrance into God's presence.

Thanksgiving, on the other hand, is a recognition that God has blessed us. There are two particularly significant Hebrew words for thanksgiving. *Yadah* means to thank, confess, or witness. Thanksgiving is a recognition of the obligation we have to God because he has blessed us. It is a witness to the world that God has helped us in time of need and a confession of the responsibility which that puts on us. *Barach* is most often translated "bless." Of the very essence of this word is the idea that because God has blessed us we should bless him in return. One could, of course, make the point that the whole of Christian worship could be understood in terms of blessing God for his blessing us. From this standpoint it would be quite logical to begin worship with a benediction just as Paul begins several of his letters with benedictions, but there is another way of looking at it. One can understand the service of worship, particularly the preaching of the Word and the celebration of the sacraments, as God's acts of blessing the congregation. Therefore, we should conclude our service of worship by reflecting that blessing in our blessing of God. It is because of this line of thinking that Protestant worship has put hymns and prayers of thanksgiving toward the end of the service.

In writing prayers of thanksgiving I have returned again and again to one pattern: the prayer of thanksgiving from the Epistle to the Ephesians.

Blessed be the God and Father of our Lord Jesus Christ, who has blessed us in Christ with every spiritual blessing in the heavenly places, even as he chose us in him before the foundation of the world, that we should be holy and blameless before him. He destined us in love to be his sons through Jesus Christ, according to the purpose of his will, to the praise of his glorious grace which he freely bestowed on us in the Beloved. In him we have redemption through his blood, the forgiveness of our trespasses, according to the riches of his grace which he lavished upon us. For he has made known to us in all wisdom and insight the mystery of his will, according to his purpose which he set forth in Christ as a plan for the fulness of time, to unite all things in him, things in heaven and things on earth.   Ephesians 1:3-10

In terms of literary form this prayer is clearly the product of the synagogue even if it is filled with obviously Christian content. Its phrasing is modeled on the best traditions of Jewish doxology used in the synagogue in the two or three centuries immediately before the beginning of the Christian Church.

We find several similar prayers of thanksgiving in Paul's letters. Colossians 1:3-20 is very similar, and the Epistle to the Philippians is filled with admonitions to thanksgiving. "Rejoice in the Lord always; again I will say, Rejoice" (Phil 4:4) is one of those admonitions that fairly demands a prayer of thanksgiving.

More recently it has occurred to me that an even more important pattern for the Prayer of Thanksgiving is found in the Lord's Prayer. The Lord's Prayer is often presented as a pattern of Christian prayer, and in previous chapters we have seen how so many of the characteristic insights of Christian prayer are indeed crystallized in that short prayer. It is in the concluding doxology that the element of thanksgiving is concentrated: "For thine is the kingdom and the power and the glory forever. Amen." This doxology does not appear in the earliest manuscripts of the Gospel of Matthew, but it is often the case that the customary doxologies were considered traditional and therefore were not written out as part of the actual prayer texts. This doxology was taken from the prayer of thanksgiving offered by David at the end of his reign (I Chron 29:11ff.). From that perspective it is clear that this doxology is a true *berakah*, that is, a reflection back to God of the blessing that he has poured out on us. David, at the end of his glorious reign, reflected back to God the kingdom, power, and glory with which he had been so generously blessed. Whoever chose this doxology to conclude the Lord's Prayer was a genius of biblical interpretation. That this genius should have been Jesus himself seems to me, at least, a strong possibility.

A good number of psalms of thanksgiving have served as examples for prayers of thanksgiving. Among the most obvious psalms of thanksgiving are Psalms 9–10, 30, 32, 34, 40, 41, 92, 103, 107, 116, and 138. These are all votive thanksgiving psalms, that is, psalms that were offered at the temple in payment of vows.

It is in relation to these votive thanksgivings that the verb *yadah* ("to thank," "to confess," or "to witness") was used. These prayers are a public witness that God has heard one's prayer and an acknowledgment of the obligation that one therefore owes to God. A person in some kind of trouble or need would make a vow that if God delivered him or her from the situation then he or she would offer to God a sacrifice. This sacrifice was an expression of appreciation and an acknowledgment that one so delivered owed service to the God who had become his or her savior. A detailed description of this ancient prayer discipline is found in the story of Hannah, who after many years of living with her husband had had no children. She went to the temple at Shiloh and vowed that if God would give her a son she would give him to the Lord. Her son Samuel, destined to be one of the great prophets of Israel, was born, and so in fulfillment of her vow she took the boy to the temple to dedicate him to God's service. She also took a sacrificial offering and offered a votive thanksgiving prayer, which is recorded in the second chapter of I Samuel.

Votive thanksgiving psalms are, for the most part, of a much more personal nature than other psalms and were usually offered to God with very particular things in mind — answers to specific requests and help in very specific needs. Sometimes scholars have distinguished between individual thanksgiving psalms and national thanksgiving psalms. The national thanksgiving psalms recounted salvation history and were used to celebrate the major feast days while the individual thanksgiving psalms had to do with specific acts of God's mercy that the worshiper had received.

I have very purposely taken up some of the imagery in these psalms, even though some of it is strange to our ears. It is helpful for us to learn this imagery, because it gives resonance to the language of prayer. Again and again the minister should encourage people to make the Book of Psalms their prayer book. When the congregation begins to do this, then the use of this prayer imagery will become increasingly understandable. The minister's use of this imagery will interpret the psalms. It has particularly been my practice to encourage people to memorize psalms so that they can recite them without having to read them from a book. When they are memorized, their imagery takes its place naturally in our prayers. Part of the leadership that a minister provides for a congregation is, indeed, providing imagery for prayer. The minister needs to teach the congregation the language of prayer. It is not simply a matter of finding a language that everyone will immediately understand. It is much more a matter of providing a richer language than that with which the congregation is already familiar.

Even at this it has to be said that there are limitations to modeling our Christian prayers of thanksgiving on the votive thanksgiving prayers we find in the psalms. While the votive sacrifices give us some of the imagery of thanksgiving, we do not offer sacrifices in Christian worship. It is appropriate to express the obligation we have to God because he has heard our prayers, and it is appropriate to witness to God's grace and mercy in granting our requests, and it is even fitting to give alms to others in expression of our appreciation to God. But beyond that one must be careful. The whole idea of votive prayer has been greatly abused in the history of worship.

From the standpoint of biblical prayer forms, what has seemed appropriate to develop here is a Hebrew *berakah* or benediction. The *berakah* is a very distinct form of prayer found frequently in Scripture. In the days of Jesus the devout Jew filled the whole day and all the things done during it with a series of benedictions. On awakening, there was a benediction of the day: "Blessed art thou, O LORD God, king of the universe, who brings light out of darkness." When one washed one's hands, there was a benediction for that. As one began a meal, the bread was blessed: "Blessed art thou, O LORD God, king of the universe, who bringeth bread from the earth." At the end of the meal a more lengthy benediction was said over the cup of blessing. In the evening there was a blessing of the evening lamp when it was lit.

There were supposed to be a hundred of these benedictions from the beginning of the day to its end. Most of them were very short but some of them were longer and more festive, such as the benediction at the end of a meal or the benedictions before and after the reciting of the *Shema*. The benediction at the end of I Chronicles, in which David thanks God for all his blessings, is, of course, a classic example. These benedictions were such an important part of Jewish life and worship that the first tractate of the Talmud, the tractate *Berakoth*, is devoted to the subject of their use.

One of the best examples of a *berakah* is Psalm 103. Here the traditional themes of this prayer form are unfolded with consummate artistry:

> Bless the LORD, O my soul;
> and all that is within me,
>   bless his holy name!
> Bless the LORD, O my soul,
>   and forget not all his benefits,
> who forgives all your iniquity,
>   who heals all your diseases,
> who redeems your life from the Pit,
>   who crowns you with steadfast love and mercy,
> who satisfies you with good as long as you live
>   so that your youth is renewed like the eagle's.
>
> The LORD works vindication
>   and justice for all who are oppressed.
> He made known his ways to Moses,
>   his acts to the people of Israel.
> The LORD is merciful and gracious,
>   slow to anger and abounding in steadfast love.
> He will not always chide,
>   nor will he keep his anger for ever.
> He does not deal with us according to our sins,
>   nor requite us according to our iniquities.
> For as the heavens are high above the earth,
>   so great is his steadfast love toward those who fear him;
> as far as the east is from the west,
>   so far does he remove our transgressions from us.
> As a father pities his children,
>   so the LORD pities those who fear him.
> For he knows our frame;
>   he remembers that we are dust.

As for man, his days are like grass;
    he flourishes like a flower of the field;
for the wind passes over it, and it is gone,
    and its place knows it no more.
But the steadfast love of the LORD is from everlasting to everlasting
    upon those who fear him,
    and his righteousness to children's children,
to those who keep his covenant
    and remember to do his commandments.

The LORD has established his throne in the heavens,
    and his kingdom rules over all.
Bless the LORD, O you his angels,
    you mighty ones who do his word,
    hearkening to the voice of his word!
Bless the LORD, all his hosts,
    his ministers that do his will!
Bless the LORD, all his works,
    in all places of his dominion.
Bless the LORD, O my soul!

This psalm has a distinct threefold form: an introductory invocation preceding the main body of the psalm, which acknowledges God's blessings, then a concluding doxology to seal the prayer. The invocation (vv. 1-5) calls on God with the tetragrammaton, LORD, then blesses God's holy name. Five relative clauses follow, each blessing God for the blessings that he pours out on his people. The main body of this benediction (vv. 6-18) then blesses God for his characteristic blessings of steadfast love and graciousness toward his people. The whole psalm elaborates this theme: "The LORD is merciful and gracious, slow to anger and abounding in steadfast love" (v. 8). The concluding doxology (vv. 19-22) is noteworthy in that it echoes the introductory invocation. A sense of the spiritual significance of worship is achieved in this doxology by its mention of the heavenly dimension of the blessing of God. It is not only the hearts of the faithful on earth who bless God. The angels, the heavenly host, and all the works of creation bless God as well.

We find in Psalm 103 something quite different from the historical thanksgiving psalms, Psalms 78, 105, and 136, which recount the story of God's mighty acts of redemption. That God "made known his ways to Moses, his acts to the people of Israel" is mentioned in Psalm 103, but those acts are not recounted. We should make the same distinction between the Eucharistic Prayer, that is, the thanksgiving said over the bread and the wine on the Lord's Table, and the thanksgiving that is said at the end of the service. It is of the essence of the Eucharistic Prayer that it recounts the story of God's redemptive work. But the Prayer of Thanksgiving at the end of the service focuses more on the benefits of redemption and is of a more general nature. More like the Prayer of Dedication at the end of the communion service, it draws out the theme of our obligation to give ourselves to God in a life of service.

Still, much that was said in the last chapter about the relation of our communion prayers to our theology of grace can be said about prayers of thanksgiving as well. Especially when such a prayer is offered when we collect our tithes and alms, we need to be sure that our liturgical practice does not contradict our theology. Sad to say, zeal to pump up the collection has all too often corrupted liturgical practice. The collection should be made simply and without ostentation at the end of the service as an act of thanksgiving. Offertory processions should be avoided, as should a ceremonial presentation of what has been collected.

Our prayers of thanksgiving reflect God's glory. When we bless God we reflect his blessing of us. As in Ephesians 1:3, our blessing of "the God and Father of our Lord Jesus Christ" reflects his blessing of us "in Christ with every spiritual blessing." We were, after all, made "to live for the praise of his glory" (v. 12). As we learn in the *Westminster Shorter Catechism,* our "chief end is to glorify God and enjoy him forever." We are glorified in reflecting God's glory. Reformed theology has often spoken of the *ordo salutis,* the steps of salvation — election, justification, sanctification, and glorification. At the end, people will be glorified in the worship celebrated before the throne of God. Our highest glory is to reflect God's glory. That is why we come to worship. It is in worship that the purpose of life is fulfilled. Justified by faith, more and more sanctified by grace, we serve God by reflecting his love toward us in our love toward him and reflecting that same love toward one another. It all comes back to the trinitarian dynamic of worship. God is one, but not in a monolithic way. God's glory is radiant. It always and continuously shines forth and is again and again reflected, and when it is reflected it is magnified.

Ideally, the element of thanksgiving at the end of the service should be generously developed. It is important to unfold at length the doxological tone of our worship so that it is clear that our preaching, our prayer, and our celebration of the sacraments is in the end a matter of serving God's glory; it is a matter of praise and thanksgiving. Some congregations will want to hurry the service and get it over once the sermon has been concluded, but a more mature congregation will set aside ample time for this part of the service. As I see it, a Prayer of Thanksgiving should be accompanied by a hymn of thanksgiving and a collection of tithes and alms.

Giving of alms, as we find it in the New Testament, is one of the disciplines of piety that is supposed to support our prayers. This is especially clear in the Sermon on the Mount, where we find a whole series of teachings of Jesus on the subject of prayer (Matt 6:1-18). It is not as though the Prayer of Thanksgiving were part of the liturgical framing of the collection, or that we are trying to make the collection more solemn by adding a prayer of thanksgiving. If anything, it is much more the case that by giving alms we are trying to make our thanksgiving more concrete. Christians have always understood almsgiving as an expression of joy. Just as we give Christmas presents as a token of our rejoicing, giving gifts to the poor is a way of rejoicing in God's goodness to us. It is in the same spirit that we give our tithes. The Prayer of Thanksgiving, and even more the hymn of thanksgiving, should be given primary attention in the service, and collecting alms and tithes should be a way of supporting this thanksgiving. As Jesus made clear, the giving of alms is not an occasion for sounding a trumpet before us. It should be done unobtrusively, hardly letting the left hand know what the right hand is doing (Matt 6:2-4). It is appropriate, therefore, that a highly ritualized collection should be avoided.

As with praise so also with thanksgiving Protestants have usually tended to make the singing of psalms and hymns the primary means of expressing this facet of our worship. Martin Rinkart's hymn, "Now Thank We All Our God," is a classic expression of thanksgiving. Written in Germany during the Thirty Years War it brings to the service of worship the gratefulness of God's people even in times of trouble.

> Now thank we all our God
>   With heart and hands and voices,
> Who wondrous things hath done,
>   In whom His world rejoices;
> Who, from our mothers' arms,
>   Hath blessed us on our way
> With countless gifts of love,
>   And still is ours today.
>
> O may this bounteous God
>   Through all our life be near us,
> With ever joyful hearts
>   And blessed peace to cheer us;
> And keep us in His grace,
>   And guide us when perplexed,
> And free us from all ills
>   In this world and the next.
>
> All praise and thanks to God
>   The Father now be given,
> The Son, and Him who reigns
>   With Them in highest heaven,
> The one eternal God,
>   Whom earth and heaven adore;
> For thus it was, is now,
>   And shall be evermore.

Singing seems a much more suitable way of expressing our thanksgiving to God than for the minister to offer a prose prayer. But then maybe that is just one of those innate Protestant predilections that others might not feel as strongly about. It is often the case that the last hymn of the service follows the sermon and that the preacher wants to choose a hymn that drives home the point of the sermon. This urge should be indulged only occasionally. The final hymn of the service should above all be a hymn of thanksgiving, particularly a hymn of thanksgiving that blesses God for his redemptive work in Christ. A perfect thanksgiving hymn of this sort would be Charles Wesley's hymn "O for a Thousand Tongues to Sing."

O for a thousand tongues to sing
My great Redeemer's praise,
The glories of my God and King,
The triumphs of His grace.

Jesus, the Name that charms our fears,
That bids our sorrows cease;
'Tis music in the sinner's ears,
'Tis life, and health, and peace.

He breaks the power of canceled sin,
He sets the prisoner free;
His blood can make the foulest clean,
His blood availed for me.

My gracious Master and my God,
Assist me to proclaim,
To spread through all the earth abroad,
The honors of Thy Name.

Glory to God and praise and love
Be ever, ever given
By saints below and saints above,
The Church in earth and heaven.

If there is a good hymn of thanksgiving at the end of the service, a Prayer of Thanksgiving led by the minister is not really necessary. If the congregation feels the need to make things short and perfunctory one can leave out the Prayer of Thanksgiving, being sure to select a final hymn strong in the themes of thanksgiving. If for the sake of brevity one has to make a choice, then the hymn of thanksgiving ought to be given priority. On the other hand, a Prayer of Thanksgiving toward the end of the service is an opportunity to make this important element of prayer very explicit. It helps develop the doxological character of the whole service. We will have more to say about hymnody in the next chapter, but at this point we want to suggest that the congregation's thanksgiving be developed at some length, that there be not only a Prayer of Thanksgiving but also a collection of tithes and alms and a hymn of thanksgiving as well. When this is done then the congregation's thanksgiving is fully developed. Generously dwelling on thanksgiving at the end of the service helps achieve a well balanced diet of prayer.

I have mentioned that the synagogue prayers, Ephesians 1, and the votive psalms have been models for my Prayers of Thanksgiving. Another such source is Isaac Watts's classic manual on leading in prayer, which gives us a number of suggestions for what should be included in prayers of thanksgiving. First, we should give thanks to God for bestowing on us benefits which we have not asked for. "They are the effects of His rich and preventing [i.e., prevenient] mercy." (*Guide to Prayer*, p. 33.) We should praise God for his original design of love to fallen humankind, for the gospel, which he has taken care to have spread throughout the world, for the good news of pardon and peace that he has confirmed by abundant testimonies to raise and establish our faith. We should give thanks that we have been born in a land where the gospel is known and have been raised by godly parents, if that is the case. We should express our gratitude to God for protecting us from unseen dangers and sustaining us with so many of the comforts and conveniences of life and having brought us so near to the means of grace even before we began to know him (*Guide to Prayer*, p. 34). Second, we should give thanks for those benefits that God has poured out on us in answer to our specific prayers. Third, our prayers should bless God by delighting in God's grace and power, majesty, and holiness. "Thus we rejoice and bless the Lord for what He is in Himself, as well as what He has done for us" (p. 35). Watts concludes his thanksgivings by

> wishing the glories of God may for ever continue, and rejoicing at the assurance of it. May the name of God be for ever blest: may the kingdom, and the power, and the glory be for ever ascribed to Him: may all generations call Him honorable, and make His name glorious in the earth. To Thee O Father, Son and Holy Spirit, belong everlasting power and honour. (*Guide to Prayer*, pp. 35-36).

Even more helpful than Watts's remarks on prayers of thanksgiving are some of his hymns and psalm paraphrases. How could a Christian congregation better express its thanksgiving to God than in Watts's version of Psalm 116?

> What shall I render to my God
> For all his kindness shown?
> My feet shall visit thine abode
> My songs address thy throne.
>
> How much is mercy thy delight,
> Thou ever blessed God!
> How dear thy servants in thy sight!
> How precious is their blood!
>
> How happy all thy servants are!
> How great thy grace to me!
> My life which thou hast made thy care,
> Lord, I devote to thee.

Another one of Watts's compositions that so perfectly expresses the evangelical nature of thanksgiving is this hymn:

> When I survey the wondrous cross
>   On which the Prince of Glory died,
> My richest gain I count but loss,
>   And pour contempt on all my pride.

Forbid it, Lord, that I should boast,
    Save in the death of Christ my God:
All the vain things that charm me most,
    I sacrifice them to His blood.

See, from His head, His hands, His feet,
    Sorrow and love flow mingled down;
Did e'er such love and sorrow meet,
    Or thorns compose so rich a crown?

Were the whole realm of nature mine,
    That were a present far too small;
Love so amazing, so divine,
    Demands my soul, my life, my all.

Coming down to our own century, I should also mention a prayer which has influenced my practice considerably. The prayer is found in the *Book of Common Worship* of 1932. If I am correctly informed, the prayer was written by Louis F. Benson:

> Almighty and most merciful Father; From whom cometh every good and perfect gift; We give thee praise and hearty Thanks for all Thy mercies; For Thy goodness that hath created us; Thy Fatherly discipline that hath corrected us; Thy patience that hath borne with us; and Thy love that hath redeemed us.
>
> Grant unto us with Thy gifts a heart to love thee; And enable us to show our Thankfulness for all Thy benefits; By giving up ourselves to Thy services; And delighting in all things to do Thy blessed will; Through Jesus Christ our Lord. *Amen.*

This has always seemed to me a particularly fine prayer. For many years I used it as a unison prayer of thanksgiving at the end of Sunday evening vespers.

Prayer of Thanksgiving 1 ——————

(based on Matthew 6:13)

Blessed you are, O Father,
    to you be all praise and glory.
Blessed be your name,
    O God and Father of our Lord Jesus Christ!

        Yours is the kingdom,
        and the power,
        and the glory.

All the years of our lives,
    you have guided us.

Our needs you have supplied.
Our thirst you have quenched.
Our wounds you have healed.
Our prayers you have heard.

        Yours is the Kingdom,
        and the power,
        and the glory.

We are your people.
We would serve you evermore.
We would claim your name.
We would worship and adore you.

Blessed you are, O Father,
    whom we would serve in your Son,
    to whom with you and the Holy Spirit,
        be glory evermore. *Amen.*

Prayer of Thanksgiving 2 ———————

(based on Ephesians 1)

Blessed you are, God and Father
    of our Lord Jesus Christ!
Blessed you are,
    for you have blessed us
       with every spiritual blessing!

    Before the foundation of the world,
       you chose us to be your people.
    You destined us in love
       to be your sons and daughters.

       Thanks to you we have a destiny,
          an eternal destiny.

    You have given us a Redeemer,
       Christ Jesus our Lord.
    You have provided for the remission
         of our sins
       and the forgiveness of our
         trespasses.

       Thanks to you we are free!

    Freely, therefore,
       we give ourselves to you,
          to serve the praise of your glory.

Blessed Father, eternal God,
       to you be all glory!
Through Jesus Christ, the very incarnation
       of your blessing. *Amen.*

Prayer of Thanksgiving 3 ——————

(based on Daniel 2, 4, and 7)

Blessed be your name, O Most High God,
    forever and ever!
  Your kingdom is an everlasting kingdom
  and your dominion
    is from generation to generation!

You have delivered us
    from the power of darkness,
      from the lion's den
      and the fiery furnace,
    from all the tribulations
      of this life.

You have brought us into your kingdom,
    washed us and clothed us,
    seated us at your table,
    and feasted us with all the goodness
      of your house.

It is to you we belong.
It is you we would serve
    with our praise,
    with our gifts,
    with our selves.

Yours is the kingdom, O Father,
    the power and the glory!
  Through Jesus Christ,
    who has given us the victory. *Amen.*

Prayer of Thanksgiving 4 —————

(based on I Chronicles 29:10-13)

Blessed you are, O God and Father
   of our Lord Jesus Christ!
Blessed you are,
   forever and ever!

   Yours, O Father, is the kingdom,
       and the power,
       and the glory,
       and the victory,
    for all that is in the heavens
      and the earth is yours.

   Yours are all the good things
     of our life,
       home, family, friends,
       food and drink,
       furniture and clothing.

   Yours, O Father, are all things.
    Who are we
      that we should give to you?
   For all things come from you,
     and of your own
     have we given you.

And now we thank you, Our God,
   and praise your glorious name.
In the name of Jesus,
   that name mighty to save,
     that name that is above every name! *Amen.*

Prayer of Thanksgiving 5 ──────────

(based on I Chronicles 29:10-14)

Blessed you are, O God and Father
   of our Lord Jesus Christ!
Blessed you are,
   forever and ever.

   Yours are the greatness,
      and the power,
      and the glory,
      and the victory,
      and the majesty!

   Yours is the mercy and patience,
      the loving kindness, long suffering,
         and covenant faithfulness!

   Yours is the kingdom, O Lord,
      and you are exalted as head above all.

      In your hand are power and might,
         and in your hand it is to make great
            and to give strength to all.

Prosper these gifts
   that we have brought you.
Bless the service
   we would render you,
   that we may be profitable servants,

   That your kingdom come,
      for yours is the kingdom,
      and the power,
      and the glory.

Blessing be to you, O Father.
   Worship and praise be yours evermore.
In the name of your Son, our Savior,
   we would serve you.
         Now and evermore. *Amen.*

Prayer of Thanksgiving 6 —————

(based on I Chronicles 29:10-14)

Blessed you are, O God and Father
    of our Lord, Jesus Christ!
Blessed you are,
    forever and ever!

    Yours, O Father, is the kingdom,
        the power and the glory.

        You have ruled over our lives
            and given order and meaning to them.
        You have empowered us
            by setting us free from sin,
            by arming us with your Spirit,
            and by granting us your peace.

        You are exalted, O Father, above all.
            Both riches and honor come from you,
                and you rule over all.
            Your bounty we have received again
                and again.
            Every imaginable blessing
                you have poured out upon us.

With these gifts we would serve you,
    as you have served us, O Father,
        eternal King,
    in the name of your Son,
        even Jesus, our Savior. *Amen.*

Prayer of Thanksgiving 7 ——————

(based on Psalm 34)

Blessed you are, O Father,
    God and Father of our Lord Jesus Christ!
Blessed you are at all times!
    Your praise shall continually be in our mouths.
    We magnify and exalt your name together!

Thanks be to you.
    We have sought the light
        of your countenance.
    You have answered our prayers.
    You have delivered us from all our fears,
        and our faces are radiant!

Thanks be to you.
    We have tasted your grace,
        and have found that indeed
            you are good.
    We have heard your Word,
        and remembered your covenant promises.

Blessing and honor
    and glory and dominion be to you,
        O Father,
    through Jesus Christ,
        the image of your eternal being,
        the very brightness of your glory.

        Now and forever. *Amen.*

Prayer of Thanksgiving 8 ————————

(based on Psalm 40)

"Great you are, O LORD!"
    May all who seek you rejoice
        and be glad in you.
    May those who love your salvation
        say continually, "Great you are, O LORD!"

We have waited patiently for you, O Lord,
    and you have inclined to us
        and heard our cry.
You have drawn us up from the desolate pit,
    and set our feet upon a rock,
        making our steps secure.
You have put a new song in our mouths,
    a song of praise to you, our God.

"Great you are, O LORD!"
    We rejoice in you and are glad in you.
        We delight in your salvation!
    Sacrifice and offering you do not desire.
    Burnt offering and sin offering
        you have not required.

But ourselves we would give to you.
    We would open our ears to your Word.
    We would have your Law written on our hearts.
    We would have your gospel fill our lives,
        your Spirit anoint our hearts,
            our heads, our hands.

"Great is the LORD!"
    Thanksgiving, honor, and praise be to you,
        O Father.
    Through Jesus Christ,
        to whom be glory now and evermore. *Amen.*

Prayer of Thanksgiving 9 ———————

(based on Psalm 41)

Father,
Most gracious, most blessed Father,
    what love you have given us,
        that we should be called the children of God,
           and so we are.

Blessed you are, O Father above,
    for on our poverty
        you have poured out riches,
    and even more, you have deemed to bless us
        when we consider the poor.

Blessed you are, O Father above.
    You are a protector to the widow,
        a father to the fatherless,
        a friend to the lonely.
    You have blessed us in our poverty,
        and indeed ours is your kingdom.

Blessed you are, O God and Father
    of our Lord Jesus Christ.
    We would dedicate ourselves
        to being your children,
        to reflecting your love,
        to sharing your blessing.

Blessing, thanksgiving, dedication
    and holiness be all yours, O God our Father,
        through Jesus Christ, the righteous,
           the reflection of your eternal glory.
        Our Lord and our God. *Amen* and *Amen.*

Prayer of Thanksgiving 10 ————

(based on Psalm 92)

To you, O Lord,
    it is good to give thanks,
    to declare your steadfast love in the morning
        and your faithfulness by night.
O God Most High! Gracious Lord! Eternal Savior!

By your righteousness
    we have flourished like palm trees
        in the South,
    we have grown like the Cedars of Lebanon.
    We bless you for the fruitfulness of your Spirit,
        and the generosity of your providence.

By your grace,
    we have been planted in your house,
    we have flourished in the courts of our God.
    We bless you for the gift of faith,
        for sowing the seed of your Word
            in our hearts.
    We rejoice in the vision you have given us
        and the promises you have confirmed to us,
        for nourishing our spirits
            in times of disappointment,
        and for your abiding presence
            even until this day.
    Grant that in the image of Christ your Son,
        we might be faithful stewards
            of your blessing.

To you, O Father,
    be all worship and service,
    all praise and thanksgiving.
        Through Jesus Christ,
            the firstborn of all creation,
            your only begotten Son. *Amen.*

Prayer of Thanksgiving 11 ──────────

(based on Psalm 116)

Gracious you are, O Lord,
   righteous and merciful.
      Indeed you have dealt with us bountifully.

We walk before you
   in the land of the living.
Although we have suffered distress and anguish,
   we have kept our faith.
   We are your servants,
      the children of your handmaiden,
      the sons and daughters of your Church.

What shall we render unto you, O Lord,
      for all your bounty to us?
   We will take the cup of salvation
      and call on your name.
   We will pledge to you our lives
      and all that we are.
   We will dedicate ourselves to Christ,
      our crucified and risen Savior.

For it is in his name that we pray,
   and in his name that we glory,
      now and ever more. *Amen.*

Prayer of Thanksgiving 12 ——————

(based on Psalm 138)

We give thanks to you, O Lord,
    with all our hearts,
        for you have exalted above everything
            your name and your Word.

We have cried out to you for help,
    and you have heard us.
We have walked in the midst of trouble
    and you have preserved our lives.
We have hungered and thirsted
        for your higher blessings,
    and you have given us the bread of life,
    and the cup of salvation.
We have lost our sense of purpose,
    and you have fulfilled our lives
        with fresh meaning and new direction.

To you be all blessings,
        all kingdom,
        all power,
        all glory,
    Bountiful God,
    Gracious Savior, one with God,
    Spirit of unity,
        ever three, ever one,
            now and again and yet again. *Amen.*

Prayer of Thanksgiving 13 ——————

(based on Ephesians 1:17)

Blessed you are,
O God and Father of our Lord Jesus Christ,
Father of Glory,
    for your faithfulness to us,
    for our creation in your image,
    for your Law written on our hearts,
    for the faith planted in our souls
        through the preaching
        of the gospel of Christ,
    for the growing of that faith
        by the work of your Holy Spirit
        deep within us.

Blessed you are,
O God of our Lord Jesus Christ,
Father of Glory,
    for the love of Christ,
        which we have experienced from our parents,
            our brothers and sisters,
            our children and grandchildren,
    for the love of Christ,
        which we have experienced in your providential care,
    for the love of Christ,
        which we have experienced in this congregation.

Receive these our gifts, O Lord God,
    for they are but a token of our delight
        in the multitude of your blessings
        and the richness of your gifts.

All blessing be to you, O Father,
    through Jesus Christ our Savior. *Amen.*

Prayer of Thanksgiving 14 ───────

(based on Ephesians 1:11-14)

Blessed you are, O God and Father
   of our Lord Jesus Christ!

You have destined and appointed us
    to live to the praise of your glory.
We have heard the Word of Truth,
   the gospel of our salvation.
   For this we thank you,
     O Lord our God!

We bless you that having heard that gospel,
   we have believed it.
We have been sealed by the Holy Spirit
   and guaranteed the inheritance
    of eternal life,
   and this is to your eternal praise and glory.

Blessed you are, O God and Father
   of our Lord Jesus Christ!

To you we owe all life,
   all that we are,
   and all that we shall be.

Blessing and honor and glory be to you,
   O Father, Son and Holy Spirit,
    One God,
    forever and ever. *Amen.*

Prayer of Thanksgiving 15 ─────────────

(based on Philippians 1:6)

Thanks be to you, O God,
    faithful in your covenant.
    The work that you began in us,
        you are bringing to completion.
    Your Word has called us to a new life,
        inspired in us works of mercy and compassion,
        and brought us into the fellowship of your people.

Thanks be to you, O God,
    for the sign of baptism,
        in which you claimed us for yourself,
    for fulfilling that sign day by day,
        again and again washing us from our sin,
        again and again filling us
           with your Holy Spirit
           and the fruits of your Spirit.

Thanks be to you, O faithful God.
    You have begun a good work in us,
        and you will bring it to completion.
    We are yours and pledge to you
        our service and devotion.

Through Jesus Christ our Lord,
    who with you, O Father,
        and the Holy Spirit,
    we ever worship and adore. *Amen.*

Prayer of Thanksgiving 16 ——————

(based on Philippians 4:4-7)

We rejoice in you always,
>O Lord, our God and Savior,
>>for we know that your coming is at hand,
>>that your kingdom is being established over all.

We rejoice in you always,
>for we have made known to you our requests,
>and you have heard our prayers.
>>You have given us our daily bread,
>>and you have brought us to green pastures.

We rejoice in you always,
>O God and Father of our Lord Jesus Christ,
>>the crucified and risen,
>>>who took on himself our sin
>>>>and the sin of the world,
>>>who suffered all its pangs
>>>>and rose above it.

We rejoice in you always,
>for your peace that passes all understanding,
>which has kept our hearts and minds
>>in Christ Jesus.

For it is in him that we are,
>and in him that we would abide
>>all the days of our lives,
>and it is in him that we would pray,
>>adoring you, O Father, Son, and Holy Spirit.
>>>One God, now and always. *Amen.*

Prayer of Thanksgiving 17 ———————

(based on Colossians 1:3-5)

Thanks be to you,
O God and Father of our Lord Jesus Christ,
 for the faith that your Spirit
  has implanted in our hearts,
 for the love that unites us together
  in the bond of peace,
 for the hope laid up for us in heaven.

Thanks be to you, O God,
 for the Word of Truth,
  the gospel, which has come to us,
  and for the fruit it is bearing in all the world.

 To you we bring these gifts
  because all that we are,
  and all that we have,
   comes from you.

Thanks be to you, O God,
  Almighty, Everlasting, Eternal,
  God and Father of our Lord Jesus Christ.
 To you be all honor,
  all dominion and glory,
  through Jesus Christ our Lord. *Amen.*

Prayer of Thanksgiving 18 —————————

Blessed you are, O Lord God,
 Eternal King.
Blessed you are, O Lord God,
 Our Sovereign,
  now and through all ages yet to come.

We bless you for establishing
 your kingdom among us,
 through the sacrifice
  of our Lord Jesus Christ,
  his sacrificial death,
  his victorious resurrection.

We bless you for the hope that is set before us,
 for the prophetic vision
  of a just society and a peaceful world,
 for the fulfillment
  of our own personal dreams
  and answers to our prayers,
 for the coming of the heavenly Jerusalem,
  and the consummation of all things.

We bless you, O Lord God,
 setting before you our tithes and alms,
  as a token of ourselves,
 dedicating ourselves to your service
  in the world about us,
   among our family and friends,
   among our neighbors,
   and even among strangers.

To you be our service and praise, O Father,
 through Jesus Christ. *Amen.*

Prayer of Thanksgiving 19 ————————

Blessed you are, O God our Creator.
    Indeed you have been bountiful.
Blessed you are, O God our Provider.
    Indeed you have supplied our need,
        our deepest need, with such abundance.

    You have blessed us
        with light and every form of beauty,
        with truth and every form of enlightenment.
    You have blessed us
        with your Word,
        with your call and covenant.
    You have given us
        the hope of eternal life
        and the promise of grace
            in the resurrection of Christ.

Blessed you are, O God our Savior.
    Indeed your gifts to us are without number,
        and all that we give to you comes from you.

Blessed you are, O God our Sanctifier.
    You have given us your Spirit,
        the inner fire,
        the holy glow,
        the bond of peace,
        and the fellowship of the household of faith.

    We present these gifts to you,
        the token of ourselves,
        the dedication of our hearts and lives.

For to you be all blessing, O Father,
    all thanksgiving and praise,
        through Jesus Christ. *Amen.*

Prayer of Thanksgiving 20 —————

Thanks be to you, O God, Gracious Father.

From you we have received every gift,
    the gift of life itself,
    the gift of light and reason,
    the illumination of your Spirit.

From you has come the gift of redemption,
    forgiveness of sin,
    and the healing of our spirits
        by your Holy Spirit.

From you has come the hope of eternal life,
    and all the gifts of grace for this life.
    It is therefore to you that we give ourselves,
    so that you are our God
        and we your people.

Thanks be to you, O God, Gracious Father,
    through Jesus Christ our Lord. *Amen.*

Hymnody

Choosing appropriate hymns is an important part of leading the congregation in prayer. We may not always regard hymnody as prayer, but theologically that is how it makes the best sense. In hymns the people of God pray together with one voice. As Luke puts it in his report of an early Christian prayer meeting, "they lifted their voices together to God" (Acts 4:24). Luke actually says this about psalm singing, but the same is true of hymnody as well. Uniting our voices together is just what we do when we sing.

Hymnody is, in a special way, a spiritual fire that joins our hearts together in a single flame. It is a means of strengthening the corporate nature of our prayer and an aspect of prayer that should constantly come to expression if our prayer is to be full and well balanced. It is important to pray alone, but it is also important to pray together. Strangely enough, for modern Americans praying alone is still much easier than praying together. Yet if we are to have common worship at all, we must learn to pray together, and somehow hymnody eases us into corporate prayer. A good hymn has a way of bringing us into the experience of prayer. The psalmist puts it aptly: "Come into his presence with singing!" (Ps 100:2).

In Germany Protestants often say that their hymnbook is their prayer book. The German hymnbook is a marvelous treasure. What the missal is for the Roman Catholic the hymnbook is for the German Protestant. This great love for hymnody goes back to Martin Luther. Luther was a talented musician, and he liked to sing the gospel as much as preach it. The Reformation produced a great amount of excellent hymnody. Luther left us several superb hymns that we still sing today, but he was not alone; a number of other Reformers did the same. In fact, the Reformation spawned a whole school of hymnodists. Then came the age of Protestant Orthodoxy with the hymns of Paul Gerhardt. With good reason Gerhardt is ranked as the greatest of German hymn writers. Then German Pietism followed with another whole school of Christian hymnody. All the while German composers were supplying the classic hymn tunes of the Lutheran Church. Michael Praetorius, Johann Cruger, and Johann Sebastian Bach all helped shape the hymnbook. Hymn singing is firmly wedded to the very nature of Protestant worship. We Protestants have as great a love for hymn singing as we do for preaching.

John and Charles Wesley deserve the greatest credit for naturalizing

German hymnody for the English-speaking Church. Not only did they translate a number of German hymns into English, they also went on to compose hymns in the German evangelical tradition. In the nineteenth century Catherine Winkworth supplied us with an even larger number of English translations of German hymns. Today the classic German hymns are as much at home in America as in Europe. Many of us would repeat that old German maxim for ourselves: The hymnbook is our prayerbook.

If hymns are indeed an important means of leading the congregation in prayer, then we need to look more carefully at how hymns function as prayer. There are three ways, I would suggest, in which hymns are used to worship God and to serve God's glory: They do so by functioning as Christian psalms, as meditations on God's revelation of himself, and as affirmations of faith.

Hymns as Christian Psalms

Many of the earliest Christian hymns were in fact Christian psalms. Both the *Magnificat* and the *Benedictus,* the two hymns found at the beginning of the Gospel of Luke, are written in the genre and style of the Hebrew psalm.

We find much the same thing in the Revelation of John. There, the hymnody that John heard in the heavenly worship was what might be called elaborated psalmody. That is, it was the psalmody of the ancient temple with Christian themes worked into it. John and the Christians of Asia Minor undoubtedly understood the hymnody of the Church as a more profound and faithful hearing of the heavenly worship. They would have assumed that songs of worship sung here on earth should be copies of the songs sung by the heavenly host, reproductions of the heavenly ideals, faithful copies of heavenly patterns. But the saints of the Old Testament had not heard those songs as clearly as the saints of the New Testament. The Song of Moses was only a foretaste of the Song of the Lamb, and the psalms of David were but a type of the hymns sung by angels and archangels. Just as the plan of the tabernacle and then the temple were attempts to reconstruct on earth the heavenly mansions, so psalmody was an entry into the heavenly praises before the throne of God. The Revelation that John saw and heard on the Isle of Patmos only opened up more fully to human eyes and ears the worship of the heavenly sanctuary. Isaiah did not realize, when he heard the seraphim singing "Holy, holy, holy," that they were singing a hymn to the Trinity, but when John heard the same hymn on Patmos he perceived at least the first strains of its trinitarian implications.

The *Odes of Solomon* are of the greatest possible importance in helping us understand the origins of Christian hymnody. The title of this collection of hymns is emblematic of a distinct theology of worship. The point is that the psalms of David typified or foreshadowed the songs of his son Solomon. Tradition had always maintained that Solomon was a singer just as his father had been. The compiler of the *Odes* has obviously found it very important that the Song of Solomon is a collection of love songs. One type is built on another since the Song of Solomon is also a type of the songs of the heavenly Bridegroom. The Church's hymns are the odes of Solomon because Christ is the spiritual Solomon, the Son of David conceived of the Holy Spirit, the messianic Son of David anointed by the Spirit. In the highest sense the odes are spiritual songs. The typological double play in the title is therefore an argument for the use of Christian hymns and reveals how Christians at the end of the first century understood their hymnody and used it in their worship. Above all, perhaps, the *Odes* shows us what a profoundly important role hymnody played in early Christian worship.

The *Odes* are indeed exquisite Christian hymns. When we read through this collection we find that each piece is an embroidered version of one of the canonical psalms. Rendall-Harris called them "psalm pendants." The term expressed the essence of these hymns very well. But another thing we notice; an air of Christian joy suffuses these hymns. They are from first to last hymns of love. They are the love songs of the heavenly Bridegroom. They resonate with the radiance of the Bride of Christ. Their type is just as clearly the Song of Solomon as it is the Psalms of David. The author so obviously wants to show that the Christian hymn is a song of love. In this respect it is a deeper and fuller act of devotion than were the psalms of David. There is some sense in which the author of these hymns under-stands himself to be inspired. When one reads through the collection, one notices that these odes are Christian hymns, rather than psalm paraphrases, and yet they somehow are a continuation and completion of the psalms.

One has often discussed the distinction between hymnody and psalmody. The discussion has not always been too helpful. It somehow has a way of getting mixed up with defining the nature of the inspiration of Holy Scripture and how that kind of inspiration differs from what we understand by poetic inspiration. Alas, Christian poets have all too often invoked divine inspiration for their compositions in about the same way poets invoked the inspiration of the muses. It was a sort of literary con-vention but it got confounded with the theological doctrine of the inspira-tion of Scripture. On the other hand there have always been those who have been rather too fast in insisting that the psalm settings of one or another poet are psalm paraphrases rather than metrical psalms. Instead of fussing over such matters it seems better to recognize that much Chris-tian hymnody is a Christian meditation on, or appropriation of, the psalms. Not only do we need to recognize it, we need to appreciate it. What could be more appropriate! One might look at it this way: the distinction between psalmody and hymnody is much the same as the distinction between Scripture lesson and sermon. We have no trouble claiming divine inspira-tion for a Christian sermon on an Old Testament text. In fact we quite boldly hold that the preaching of the Word of God is the Word of God. Yet, we still don't imagine that even the best sermons are inspired in quite the same way holy Scripture is inspired.

It is much the same way with Isaac Watts's version of the seventy-second psalm.

Jesus shall reign where'er the sun
Does his successive journeys run;
His Kingdom stretch from shore to shore,
Till moons shall wax and wane no more.

There is a great beauty in the play between the canonical psalm and the Christian interpretation. That is part of the art of Isaac Watts. It is much the same thing as the art of the choral preludes of Johann Sebastian Bach. A musician who can follow the way the variations come from the theme discovers a beauty of artistry and craftsmanship that those who know nothing of the techniques of musical composition miss. My friend and colleague S. T. Kimbrough tells me that the same thing is true of the psalm versions of Charles Wesley. They are filled with profound interpretations of the text of the psalm.

To appreciate the art of a Christian psalm by Isaac Watts or Charles Wesley or even in the *Odes of Solomon,* one has to have the canonical text in mind when one hears the Christian interpretation. The beauty of this form is that in the movement from the text to the interpretation one catches sight of the movement from promise to fulfillment, which is of the essence of prayer. To glimpse this is an exciting experience. Our services of worship should try to make it transparent. It is for that reason that psalmody should be balanced with hymnody and hymnody with psalmody. There is an important dynamic between the two. One might almost say there is a dialectic, a dialectic that the perceptive worshiper should recognize.

There is a sense in which Christian hymnody is the fulfillment of psalmody and should therefore be presented as the culmination of a movement. The service begins with the psalms of ancient Israel and moves to the hymns of heaven. A Christian service of worship should have a heavenly air about it. One should have a sense that eternity stands open before us, assuring us of our place in it. With David we should sing:

> How lovely is thy dwelling place,
>   O LORD of hosts!
> My soul longs, yea, faints
>   for the courts of the LORD;
> my heart and flesh sing for joy
>   to the living God.
>
> Psalm 84:1-2

This longing finally to achieve the goal of our pilgrimage is something universal. We come to Church with that longing, and when we are there we should hear the assurance of the Gospel: "In my Father's house are many mansions. . . . I go to prepare a place for you . . . that where I am there ye may be also. . . . I am the way, the truth, and the life" (John 14:2-6, KJV). It is when we have heard this assurance of God's love toward us in Christ that true Christian hymnody begins:

> Jerusalem the golden,
> With milk and honey blest!
> Beneath thy contemplation
> Sink heart and voice oppressed.
> I know not, O I know not,
> What joys await us there;
> What radiancy of glory,
> What bliss beyond compare.
>
> Bernard of Cluny

Christian hymnody is of its very essence a song of fulfillment. The *Odes of Solomon* have set the pace for true Christian hymnody, which is the outpouring of the joy of fulfillment. It arises from the discovery that the promised salvation has indeed been granted to us. Christ is the type of God's faithfulness. His resurrection and ascension into heaven are the ultimate evidence that God hears the prayer of his people.

When choosing hymns for any particular service, it is important to give a prominent place to a hymn that expresses the Christian joy of fulfillment. Normally for the final hymn of the service I like to choose a hymn that quite explicitly gives thanks for the revelation of God's faithfulness in Christ. At this place in the service a perfect hymn is Charles Wesley's "Rejoice, the Lord is King."

> Rejoice, the Lord is King:
> > Your Lord and King adore!
> Rejoice, give thanks, and sing,
> > And triumph evermore:
> Lift up your heart, lift up your voice!
> Rejoice, again I say, rejoice!
>
> His Kingdom cannot fail,
> > He rules o'er earth and heaven;
> The keys of death and hell
> > Are to our Jesus given:
> Lift up your heart, lift up your voice!
> Rejoice, again I say, rejoice!
>
> He all His foes shall quell,
> > Shall all our sins destroy,
> And every bosom swell
> > With pure seraphic joy:
> Lift up your heart, lift up your voice!
> Rejoice, again I say, rejoice!

Wesley has picked up the liturgical acclamation of Psalms 93, 97, and 99 — "The LORD is King" — and has developed it in a Christian sense just as the book of Revelation has. The psalm is fulfilled in the Christian hymn.

So some hymns function as Christian psalms. I have usually chosen hymns of praise and thanksgiving for both the first and the last hymns of the service, without any particular regard to the subject of the sermon. Sometimes I do this with metrical psalms, sometimes with psalm paraphrases, and sometimes with what I have been speaking of, namely, Christian psalms. This is admittedly something of a departure from what one usually hears on the subject, but one of the primary functions of Christian hymnody is to express our prayers of praise and thanksgiving. For Christians this praise and thanksgiving should be a fulfillment of the worship of Israel. It should be a rejoicing in the way God has heard the cry of his people from all ages. It should be a flowering of the psalms of David.

Hymns as Meditations on God's Word

Christian hymns also function as worship by meditating on God's Word and contemplating the divine Wisdom. The Old Testament Wisdom school had unique insights into the nature of worship that the early Church incorporated into its understanding of worship right from the beginning, as is clear all through the New Testament. At the center of this approach to worship was the belief that by meditating on God's Word, studying Holy Scripture, thinking about these sacred texts, and constantly turning them over in one's mind one entered into communion with God. As the Wisdom school saw it, this was worship at its highest. For Jews in the time of Jesus, the foundation of education was memorization of the biblical text. Higher education went on from there to study the interpretation of the text. It is no surprise, then, that such schools produced a distinct genre of hymnody. The schools were very pious institutions. Alongside the singing of psalms in the temple worship, then, another source of hymnody was the Wisdom hymns produced in the schools.

Probably in the beginning the Wisdom hymns developed as an aid to memorization. Material of special importance was formulated in such a way that it could be sung. This made memorizing a more pleasant task as well as an easier task. Material formulated in this way was retained in the memory and could often be reviewed. Devotional use of these Wisdom hymns no doubt followed closely on pedagogical use of them. In the Wisdom school learning and devotion were closely related.

One of the best known of the hymns produced by the Wisdom school is found in the eighth chapter of Proverbs.

> The LORD created me at the beginning of his work,
>   the first of his acts of old.
> Ages ago I was set up,
>   at the first, before the beginning of the earth.
> When there were no depths I was brought forth,
>   when there were no springs abounding with water.
> Before the mountains had been shaped,
>   before the hills, I was brought forth;
> before he had made the earth with its fields,
>   or the first of the dust of the world.
> When he established the heavens, I was there,
>   when he drew a circle on the face of the deep,
> when he made firm the skies above,
>   when he established the fountains of the deep,
> when he assigned to the sea its limit,
>   so that the waters might not transgress his command,
> when he marked out the foundations of the earth,
>   then I was beside him, like a master workman;
> and I was daily his delight,
>   rejoicing before him always,
> rejoicing in his inhabited world
>   and delighting in the sons of men.
>   Proverbs 8:22-31

Another remarkable Wisdom hymn is found in Job 28. Several of the psalms are Wisdom hymns. One thinks particularly of Psalms 1, 19, and 119. If nothing else these psalms make it clear that meditating on Scripture is worship. We read concerning the righteous:

> His delight is in the law of the LORD,
>> and on his law he meditates day and night.   Psalm 1:2

For those who assume a secularized education, these Wisdom hymns may seem strange, but the Wisdom of ancient Israel saw worship and learning as inevitably linked. Their theme was, "The fear of the LORD is the beginning of wisdom, and the knowledge of the Holy One is insight" (Prov 9:10). That there should be school hymns was to the devout of biblical times quite natural.

Some of the Wisdom hymns are, then, of a distinct philosophical nature. They are meditations on the origins of heavenly Wisdom. Some of the Wisdom hymns, on the other hand, delight in formulating the principles of ethical behavior. Such hymns, as didactic as they undoubtedly are, are clearly understood as worship. The following lines from Psalm 37 are a most obvious example.

> Refrain from anger, and forsake wrath!
>> Fret not yourself; it tends only to evil.
> For the wicked shall be cut off;
>> but those who wait for the LORD shall possess the land.

> Yet a little while, and the wicked will be no more;
>> though you look well at his place, he will not be there.
> But the meek shall possess the land,
>> and delight themselves in abundant prosperity.

> The wicked draw the sword and bend their bows,
>> to bring down the poor and needy,
>> to slay those who walk uprightly;
> their sword shall enter their own heart,
>> and their bows shall be broken.

> The wicked borrows, and cannot pay back,
>> but the righteous is generous and gives;
> for those blessed by the LORD shall possess the land,
>> but those cursed by him shall be cut off.
>>   Psalm 37:8-11, 14-15, 21-22

On the basis of I Peter 3:8-16 some New Testament scholars have suggested that the Wisdom psalms were used as part of the primitive Christian catechism. The Church encouraged new converts to memorize and sing Wisdom psalms such as Psalms 34 and 37 that contained moral teaching. This would certainly explain Paul's admonition: "Let the word of Christ dwell in you richly, as you teach and admonish one another in all wisdom, and as you sing psalms and hymns and spiritual songs with thanksgiving in your hearts to God" (Col 3:16). Both psalmody and hymnody can have a Wisdom dimension. They are a way of having the Word of God dwell in our hearts. This is not just a head trip; it is a heart trip as well. The Apostle makes it clear that singing psalms and hymns is a way of experiencing God's presence.

There is yet another dimension to the hymns of the Wisdom school. The meditation of the Wisdom school can be focused on God's mighty works of creation and redemption, as in Psalm 19:

> The heavens are telling the glory of God;
>   and the firmament proclaims his handiwork.
> Day to day pours forth speech,
>   and night to night declares knowledge.
> There is no speech, nor are there words;
>   their voice is not heard;
> yet their voice goes out through all the earth,
>   and their words to the end of the world.
>
> In them he has set a tent for the sun,
> which comes forth like a bridegroom leaving his chamber,
>   and like a strong man runs its course with joy.
> Its rising is from the end of the heavens,
>   and its circuit to the end of them;
>   and there is nothing hid from its heat.

One has little trouble regarding a psalm like this one as worship. In the same way this splendid hymn of Isaac Watts is easily recognized as a hymn of praise eminently suited for worship:

> I sing th'almighty power of God
>   that made the mountains rise,
> that spread the flowing seas abroad,
>   and built the lofty skies.
> I sing the wisdom that ordained
>   the sun to rule by day;
> the moon shines full at his command,
>   and all the stars obey.
>
> I sing the goodness of the Lord
>   that filled the earth with food;
> he form'd the creatures with his word,
>   and then pronounced them good.
> Lord, how thy wonders are displayed
>   where'er I turn my eye,
> if I survey the ground I tread,
>   or gaze upon the sky!
>
> Creatures, as num'rous as they be,
>   are subject to thy care;

there's not a place where we can flee,
    but God is present there.
His hand is my perpetual guard,
    he keeps me with his eye;
why should I then forget the Lord,
    who is forever nigh?

Meditating on the wonders of creation and providence seems like a natural thing for hymnody to do. It assumes that to some degree God does reveal himself in the making and the governing of the world and that therefore the contemplation of these works of creation and providence leads to worship.

Hymns recounting the history of salvation, on the other hand, might be a bit more difficult to regard as proper hymns, but such hymns are certainly to be found in the Psalter, and they are a distinct type of Wisdom hymn. A number of psalms recount holy history; some of them are clearly liturgical, and would appear to have originated in the temple, as for example, Psalm 136 or even Psalm 105, but others would appear to be school psalms. This is most obvious in the case of Psalm 78, which begins a long recital of holy history with these lines:

Give ear, O my people, to my teaching;
    incline your ears to the words of my mouth!
I will open my mouth in a parable;
    I will utter dark sayings from of old,
things that we have heard and known,
    that our fathers have told us.
We will not hide them from their children,
    but tell to the coming generation
the glorious deeds of the LORD, and his might,
    and the wonders which he has wrought.

He established a testimony in Jacob,
    and appointed a law in Israel,
which he commanded our fathers
    to teach to their children;
that the next generation might know them,
    the children yet unborn,
and arise and tell them to their children,
    so that they should set their hope in God,
and not forget the works of God,
    but keep his commandments.

Anyone who has studied the Wisdom literature of the Old Testament will recognize that these admonitions for children to listen to the teaching of their fathers comes straight from the school Wisdom of ancient Israel. Remembering holy history was the greatest incentive possible to a holy life. True Wisdom learned the parables and sayings of the ancients and passed them on to the next generation. The Wisdom of the younger generation was to learn the sacred history and learn the lessons it taught.

The specifically Christian Wisdom hymn is above all a meditation on the mighty works of God in the death and resurrection of Jesus Christ. The prologue to the Gospel of John might well be considered an example of this. More than one scholar has set up the prologue to the Gospel of John as a Wisdom hymn. Raymond Brown arranges it as follows:

First Strophe
In the beginning was the Word;
the Word was in God's presence,
and the Word was God.
He was present with God in the beginning.

Second Strophe
Through him all things come into being,
and apart from him not a thing came to be.
That which had come to be in him was life,
and this life was the life of men.
The light shines on in the darkness,
for the darkness did not overcome it.

Third Strophe
He was in the world,
and the world was made by him;
yet the world did not recognize him.
To his own he came;
yet his own people did not accept him.
But all those who did accept him
he empowered to become God's children.

Fourth Strophe
And the Word became flesh
and made his dwelling among us.
And we have seen his glory,
the glory of an only Son coming from the Father,
filled with enduring love.
And of his fullness
we have all had a share —
love in place of love.

Still other scholars find a Wisdom hymn in Paul's Epistle to the Philippians 2:5-11, which shows a strong imprint of Wisdom theology and can be set out in lines in this way:

Have this mind among yourselves,
    which is yours in Christ Jesus,
Who, though he was in the form of God
    did not count equality with God a thing to be grasped,
but emptied himself,
    taking the form of a servant,
    being born in the likeness of men.

And being found in human form
 he humbled himself
 and became obedient unto death,
 even death on a cross.

Therefore God has highly exalted him
 and bestowed on him the name
 which is above every name,
that at the name of Jesus
 every knee should bow,
in heaven and on earth and
 under the earth,
and every tongue confess
 that Jesus Christ is Lord,
 to the glory of God the Father.

The hymns of Ephrem the Syrian and Romanos the Melode, though little known in the West, have a special place in the hymnody of Eastern Christianity. They are sermons in poetry. That is enough immediately to spark our interest, but there is something more. Like the *Odes of Solomon,* they originated in the Syriac-speaking regions of Eastern Syria and, like the Hebrew psalms and the prophetic oracles of ancient Israel, are therefore at home in the Semitic world rather than in the civilization of ancient Greece and Rome. While we heirs of Western Civilization may find it difficult to think of preaching and poetry being related, the ancient Orient found this connection quite natural. After all, the classical prophets Amos, Micah, Hosea, Isaiah, and Jeremiah preached in poetry. Syriac hymnody delights in recounting the mighty acts of God and drawing precepts for the Christian life from the accounts of holy history. We may decry this as moralistic or didactic and disqualify it as poetry, but Eastern Orthodoxy looks on it with complete approval.

The sermonic hymns of Ephrem the Syrian were composed in the middle of the fourth century, the grand age of patristic preaching. They are careful and imaginative commentaries on the biblical narrative that attempt to show its ethical implications. It is much the same with the sermonic hymns of Romanos the Melode. While Romanos carried out his ministry in Constantinople during the splendid reign of Justinian, he was a native of eastern Syria, as was Ephrem. His hymns recount the stories of Adam and Eve, Noah and the Flood, the sacrifice of Abraham, the blessing of Jacob, the temptation of Joseph, and so forth. The hymns on the New Testament include several on the Nativity, a hymn on the Wedding of Cana, others on the Good Samaritan, the Prodigal Son, the healing of the ten lepers, the man born blind, and the multiplication of the loaves and, of course, a number of hymns on the Passion and Resurrection of Christ. These hymns are all quite didactic, and some find such subject matter too prosaic and moralistic for proper hymnody, but for those who know the whole tradition of Christian hymnody, there is no impropriety at all. The sermonic hymns of Ephrem and Romanos are classics of Christian doxology.

One of the most striking features of Syriac hymnody is its strong use of typology as meditation on God's revelation. Just as a poet brings together imagery, so the hymnodist brings together types. One hears the rich rhyming of types from beginning to end. Syriac hymnody displays here so clearly an important characteristic of Christian hymnody: It takes delight in the rhythms of creation and redemption, in the patterns in which God again and again brings his people through trial and adversity to the salvation to which he has destined them.

From the Middle Ages we have inherited a profuse treasure of hymns meditating on the mighty works of God for our salvation. Medieval hymnody grew up around the Christian feasts, particularly Christmas and Epiphany, the observances of Holy Week, and the highest of all holidays, the celebration of the Resurrection. The medieval Church unfolded Scripture by means of the festal calendar: For better or worse that is how the Word of God was packaged in those days. The hymns and sermons of medieval Christianity were also organized on the basis of the festal calendar.

Many of our Christmas carols have come down to us from the festal hymns of the Middle Ages. One thinks of this anonymous Latin hymn translated by John Neale:

> O come, O come, Emmanuel,
> And ransom captive Israel,
> That mourns in lonely exile here
> Until the Son of God appear.
>
> Rejoice! Rejoice! Emmanuel
> Shall come to thee, O Israel!
>
> O come, Thou Dayspring, come and cheer
> Our spirits by Thine advent here;
> Disperse the gloomy clouds of night,
> And death's dark shadows put to flight.
>
> Rejoice! Rejoice! Emmanuel
> Shall come to thee, O Israel!
>
> O come, Thou Key of David, come,
> And open wide our heavenly home;
> Make safe the way that leads on high,
> And close the path to misery.
>
> Rejoice! Rejoice! Emmanuel
> Shall come to thee, O Israel!

One notices the rich typology. Israel's release from captivity, the Dayspring, and the key of David were all types of Christ and his redemptive work. Many of these hymns were rich in typology.

Another medieval hymn that develops the Christmas typology is "Lo, How a Rose E'er Blooming." With the coming of the Reformation this hymn was quickly translated into German and in Lutheran Churches particularly became a great favorite.

Lo, how a rose e'er blooming
        from tender stem hath sprung,
of Jesse's lineage coming
        by faithful prophets sung;
it came a flow'ret bright,
amid the cold of winter
        when half spent was the night.

Isaiah 'twas foretold it,
        the rose I have in mind;
with Mary we behold it,
        the virgin mother kind.
To show God's love aright
she bore for us a Savior
        when half spent was the night.

O flow'r whose fragrance tender
        with sweetness fills the air,
dispel in glorious splendor
        our darkness ev'rywhere.
Human, yet very God,
from sin and death now save us
        and share our ev'ry load.

The Christmas rose is a reference to Isaiah 35, which tells us that when the messianic age comes, then the desert will blossom as a rose. This biblical imagery may seem a bit obscure for the modern American congregation, and yet it evokes a beautiful chain of Christian meditation that is recognized by those who have taken the time to familiarize themselves with the classics of devotional literature. The Christmas rose has a well-established place in the iconography of the feast and belongs to the rich deposit of devotional meditation that devout Christians have built up over the centuries. When a Christian congregation sings one of the great historic hymns such as this, it bears witness to the classic nature of Christian faith. The doctrine of the Incarnation is not some newly cooked-up idea. It is rather the condensed wisdom of centuries, an abiding faith that again and again has strengthened countless numbers of Christians, a holy wisdom that has enriched alike the simple and the slow, the profound and the brilliant.

Medieval hymns for the Easter season are likewise numerous. One thinks of this hymn for Palm Sunday by Theodulph of Orleans:

All glory, laud, and honor
To Thee, Redeemer, King,
To whom the lips of children
Made sweet hosannas ring.

Thou art the King of Israel,
Thou David's royal Son,
Who in the Lord's Name comest,
The King and Blessed One.

The company of angels
Are praising Thee on high,
And mortal men, and all things
Created, make reply.

The people of the Hebrews
With palms before Thee went;
Our praise and prayer and anthems
Before Thee we present.

To Thee, before Thy passion,
They sang their hymns of praise;
To Thee, now high exalted,
Our melody we raise.

Thou didst accept their praises;
Accept the prayers we bring,
Who in all good delightest,
Thou good and gracious King.

Christ's suffering on the cross was always the subject of hymnic meditation.
This hymn is ascribed to Bernard of Clairvaux:

O sacred Head, now wounded,
With grief and shame weighed down;
Now scornfully surrounded
With thorns, Thine only crown;
O sacred Head, what glory,
What bliss till now was Thine!
Yet, though despised and gory,
I joy to call Thee mine.

What Thou, my Lord, hast suffered
Was all for sinners' gain:
Mine, mine was the transgression,
But Thine the deadly pain.
Lo, here I fall, my Saviour!
'Tis I deserve Thy place;
Look on me with Thy favor,
Vouchsafe to me Thy grace.

What language shall I borrow
To thank Thee, dearest Friend,
For this Thy dying sorrow,
Thy pity without end?
O make me Thine forever;
And should I fainting be,
Lord, let me never, never
Outlive my love to Thee.

Here, again, the antiquity of the hymn has in no way diminished its popularity. It is a true classic. Every year one hears it sung again and again in all kinds of arrangements. It somehow catches the ears of young and old, the simple and the sophisticated. It has a universal appeal. That, of course, is what makes it a classic.

The Feast of the Resurrection inspired countless hymns. The medieval festal hymnody often simply recounts almost as a ballad the story of the mighty acts of God. This hymn of Jean Tisserand is a good example:

> O sons and daughters, let us sing!
> The King of heaven, the glorious King,
> O'er death today rose triumphing.
> Alleluia! Alleluia!
>
> That Easter morn, at break of day,
> The faithful women went their way
> To seek the tomb where Jesus lay.
> Alleluia! Alleluia!
>
> An angel clad in white they see,
> Who sat, and spake unto the three,
> "Your Lord doth go to Galilee."
> Alleluia! Alleluia!
>
> How blest are they who have not seen,
> And yet whose faith hath constant been;
> For they eternal life shall win.
> Alleluia! Alleluia!
>
> On this most holy day of days,
> Our hearts and voices, Lord, we raise
> To Thee, in jubilee and praise.
> Alleluia! Alleluia!

Other hymns focus on the rich biblical types of the Resurrection, meditating on the inner meaning of the story that each year is faithfully recounted in the Scripture readings and in preaching. Recalling the Easter typology has always been an important means of triggering our meditation. This great hymn of John of Damascus develops at length the Passover typology:

> The day of resurrection!
> Earth, tell it out abroad
> The Passover of gladness,
> The Passover of God.
> From death to life eternal,
> From this world to the sky,
> Our Christ hath brought us over
> with hymns of victory.

Our hearts be pure from evil,
That we may see aright
The Lord in rays eternal
Of resurrection light;
And, listening to his accents,
May hear, so calm and plain,
His own "All hail!" and, hearing,
May raise the victor strain.

Now let the heavens be joyful,
Let earth her song begin;
Let the round world keep triumph,
And all that is therein;
Let all things seen and unseen
Their notes of gladness blend,
For Christ the Lord hath risen,
Our joy that hath no end.

Even today this is one of the most popular hymns of the Greek Church. It permeates the Easter services of the Orthodox Church, constantly bringing the worshipers to meditate on the passage out of Egypt as the type of Christ's passage out of this world to the Father.

Christian hymns give the Church the opportunity to celebrate the mighty acts of God in the long-loved phrases and the traditional types that over the centuries the people of God have come to treasure. Medieval hymnody amply illustrates that a major function of hymnody is to encourage the faithful worshiper to meditate on God's redemptive work in Christ.

While medieval hymnody tended to relate indirectly to Scripture, eighteenth-century Pietists developed a hymnody much more directly related to Scripture. We have already spoken of how Isaac Watts did this with his Christian versions of the Psalms. We find the same thing in Philip Doddridge, John Newton, William Cowper, and above all in Charles Wesley. The Pietists by no means limited themselves to the Psalms. Their meditations on Scripture embrace the whole Bible. One of Charles Wesley's masterpieces is a meditation on the story of Jacob wrestling with the angel:

Come, O thou traveler unknown
    whom still I hold but cannot see;
my company before is gone,
    and I am left alone with thee;
with thee all night I mean to stay
    and wrestle till the break of day.

I need not tell thee who I am,
    my misery and sin declare;
thyself hast called me by my name,
    look on thy hands and read it there;
but who, I ask thee, who art thou?
    Tell me thy name and tell me now.

Yield to me now, for I am weak,
 but confident in self-despair;
speak to my heart, in blessings speak;
 be conquered by my instant prayer;
speak or thou never hence shalt move,
 and tell me if thy name is love.

'Tis love! 'tis love, thou diedst for me;
 I hear thy whisper in my heart;
the morning breaks, the shadows flee,
 pure universal love thou art!
to me, to all, thy mercies move;
 thy nature and thy name is love.

This Christian meditation on the well known Bible story assumes a whole tradition of Christian interpretation. It is typical of a host of eighteenth-century hymns that meditate on a particular text of Scripture.

In the eighteenth century the hymnody of English-speaking Protestantism was closely related to preaching. The hymn meditated on God's mighty acts of redemption as they were interpreted by the sermon. It expressed the reaction of the believer to God's Word. It was an echo of the Word, a meditative echo. It was, to use a figure of speech, like the orchestral accompaniment to the soloist in a piano concerto. It gave resonance to the sermon, or, to put it still another way, it both reflected the Word and reflected *on* the Word.

Often, as we shall see, preachers wrote hymns to accompany their sermons. But in such cases the hymn was not simply another sermon written in poetry instead of in prose. It was, rather, a response to the sermon. It epitomized, sustained, and continued the meditation on Scripture initiated by the sermon. It wrapped the sermon up in a little package so that it could be taken home and appropriated in day-to-day life. These eighteenth-century Pietists, in a way that may be surprising to us but was quite consistent with the very nature of Pietism, made their hymns communal meditations on Scripture.

Sometimes a single biblical phrase or image will inspire a hymn. The Pietists' sermons were often prompted by short biblical texts, and it was the same way with their hymns. Charles Wesley's hymn, "I Know That My Redeemer Lives," is built on the famous text from Job 19:25.

I know that my Redeemer lives,
 And ever prays for me;
A token of his love he gives,
 A pledge of liberty.

I find him lifting up my head;
 He brings salvation near;
His presence makes me free indeed
 And he will soon appear.

He wills that I should holy be:
    Who can withstand his will?
The counsel of his grace in me
    He surely shall fulfil.

Jesus, I hang upon thy Word:
    I steadfastly believe
Thou wilt return and claim me, Lord,
    And to thyself receive.

This is a strongly Christian meditation on the text, but it is a perfectly legitimate appropriation of it that builds on a long tradition of the Christian meaning of the book of Job.

Another example is Wesley's "Christ, Whose Glory Fills the Skies." This hymn meditates on Luke 1:78-79, which speaks of Christ as the Dayspring from on high.

Christ, whose glory fills the skies,
    Christ the true, the only Light,
Sun of Righteousness, arise,
    Triumph o'er the shades of night;
Dayspring from on high, be near;
    Daystar, in my heart appear.

Dark and cheerless is the morn
    Unaccompanied by thee;
Joyless is the day's return
    Till thy mercy's beams I see;
Till they inward light impart,
    Glad my eyes and warm my heart.

Visit, then, this soul of mine;
    Pierce the gloom of sin and grief;
Fill me, Radiancy Divine;
    Scatter all my unbelief;
More and more thyself display,
    Shining to the perfect day.

Still another example of how Wesley's hymns meditate on particular texts is this hymn based on the words of Paul, "Put on the whole armor of God" (Eph 6:11).

Soldiers of Christ, arise,
    And put your armor on,
Strong in the strength which God supplies
    Through his Eternal Son.

Strong in the Lord of hosts,
    And in his mighty pow'r,

Who in the strength of Jesus trusts
    Is more than conqueror.

Stand then in his great might,
    With all his strength endued;
But take, to arm you for the fight,
    The panoply of God.

Leave no unguarded place,
    No weakness of the soul;
Take ev'ry virtue, ev'ry grace,
    And fortify the whole.

To keep your armor bright,
    Attend with constant care;
Still walking in your Captain's sight,
    And watching unto prayer.

From strength to strength go on;
    Wrestle, and fight, and pray;
Tread all the pow'rs of darkness down,
    And win the well-fought day.

If it is true that one of the important liturgical functions of many of our hymns is meditation on Scripture, engaged in by the whole congregation, then this says something very important about the whole nature and uniqueness of hymnody. Hymnody is not, as some people seem to assume, simply religious poetry. It is a separate and distinct art. I have already referred to two biblical texts that are essential to understanding Christian hymnody. The first tells us that the faithful "lifted up their voices together" in their singing (Acts 4:24). Hymnody is essentially congregational singing and so is not simply poetry. With poetry, even lyric poetry, singing is not considered necessary. With hymnody it is quite another matter. Reading hymns in quiet solitude is not a substitute for singing them in church. This is something that Christians of more refined literary tastes have often overlooked in evaluating the Church's hymnody and psalmody. Hymnody needs to be popular. It is more closely related to folk song than to art song. Those who have insisted that good hymnody be good poetry as well have all too often overlooked its popular, congregational nature.

It is because hymnody is, in its very essence, a kind of folk song that we must never close the door to new hymns written in the idiom of our day. Some of these new hymns will inevitably be shallow and without substance. Some may even border on being heretical. Time has a way of selecting the classics. We do not have to worry about that. What is important is that we give each generation its turn at expressing its devotion in the idiom of its day. Christian hymnody is like a great art museum. It has treasures from a great variety of ages and cultures, but it always seems to have room to show the best of contemporary works as well.

A second text that I regard as essential for understanding Christian hymnody is Paul's admonition to the Colossians to "sing psalms and hymns and spiritual songs" so that "the Word of Christ" might dwell in them richly (Col 3:16). This text makes it clear that hymnody is essentially meditation on God's Word. While a particular hymn is not always derived from a particular text of Scripture, the hymn's primary function is to reflect on what Scripture as a whole teaches. Hymnody, unlike poetry, has a canonical orientation. Several generations ago there were those who found this an oppressive and intolerable limitation on artistic freedom. Today we are beginning to appreciate that this is part of the genius of hymnody: It is a mirror for contemplating Scripture.

As the evangelical hymn writers of the eighteenth century realized, hymnody, because it is so closely related to poetry, offers to the worshiping congregation an important means of experiencing the indwelling of God's Word. We, too, need to sing psalms, hymns, and spiritual songs for Christ's Word to have a home in us. Poetry fosters meditation. By using metaphor, rhyme, and imagery, poetry holds impressions in our minds and consciences so that we can appropriate them. Though it is quite different from poetry in other respects, in this respect at least hymnody does the same thing.

The eighteenth-century evangelicals were keenly aware of the beauty of typology. Watts, Doddridge, Wesley, and Newton all recognized its dox-ological quality. They recognized implicitly that it is the poetry of exegesis. With its thought rhyming and parallelism typology has the function that imagery has in poetry. The eighteenth century cultivated poetry extensively, and it is not at all surprising that it should make a rich use of typology. Take, for example, this hymn of John Newton:

> Glorious things of thee are spoken,
> Zion, city of our God;
> He whose word cannot be broken
> Formed thee for His own abode:
> On the Rock of Ages founded,
> What can shake thy sure repose?
> With salvation's walls surrounded,
> Thou mayst smile at all thy foes.
>
> See, the streams of living waters,
> Springing from eternal Love,
> Well supply thy sons and daughters,
> And all fear of want remove:
> Who can faint, while such a river
> Ever flows their thirst to assuage;
> Grace, which, like the Lord the Giver,
> Never fails from age to age?
>
> Round each habitation hovering,
> See the cloud and fire appear
> For a glory and a covering,
> Showing that the Lord is near:
> Thus deriving from their banner
> Light by night and shade by day,

Safe they feed upon the manna
Which He gives them when they pray.

Another classic of this age is the old favorite by Augustus Toplady.

Rock of Ages, cleft for me,
Let me hide myself in Thee;
Let the water and the blood,
From Thy riven side which flowed,
Be of sin the double cure,
Cleanse me from its guilt and power.

Not the labors of my hands
Can fulfill Thy law's demands;
Could my zeal no respite know,
Could my tears forever flow,
All for sin could not atone;
Thou must save, and Thou alone.

Nothing in my hand I bring,
Simply to Thy cross I cling;
Naked, come to Thee for dress,
Helpless, look to Thee for grace;
Foul, I to the fountain fly;
Wash me, Saviour, or I die.

While I draw this fleeting breath,
When my eyelids close in death,
When I soar to worlds unknown,
See Thee on Thy judgment throne,
Rock of Ages, cleft for me,
Let me hide myself in Thee.

Still another we should mention is William Cowper's:

There is a fountain filled with blood
Drawn from Emmanuel's veins;
And sinners, plunged beneath that flood,
Lose all their guilty stains.

The dying thief rejoiced to see
That fountain in his day;
And there may I, as vile as he,
Wash all my sins away.

Dear dying Lamb, Thy precious blood
Shall never lose its power
Till all the ransomed church of God
Be saved, to sin no more.

E'er since by faith I saw the stream
Thy flowing wounds supply,
Redeeming love has been my theme,
And shall be till I die.

When this poor lisping, stammering tongue
Lies silent in the grave,
Then in a nobler, sweeter song
I'll sing Thy power to save.

Admittedly these three hymns with their rich typological meditation on the mighty works of God will be difficult for many people today, but in the eighteenth century they were not considered at all obscure. Those who listened to eighteenth-century sermons would have understood the types very easily. Learned preaching produces a learned hymnody.

The question that naturally arises is whether we should choose hymns for the worship of a modern day congregation that make a strong use of typology. Poetry is not very popular in our society and typology has almost been excommunicated. As I see it this is an incalculable loss! We would do well to learn from the Wisdom tradition of the Bible that God is served by serious and profound thought. One of the greatest dangers that American Christianity has to guard against is shallowness. We have a way of tolerating immaturity and shunning that which is serious and profound. This is a temptation we must resist, especially when it comes to worship.

That some hymnody is best understood as meditation on Scripture or as summarizing the Church's exposition of the Word has a lot to do with what hymns we choose and where we place them in the service of worship. In fact hymnody should fit together with the sermon. Or at least there are certain kinds of hymns that fit together with sermons. One aspect of hymnody is its ability to complement the reading and preaching of Scripture. They should, but this is often too well appreciated nowadays. Most preachers recognize only this aspect of hymnody and think that supporting their preaching is the only value of a hymn. Except on the major feasts, only one hymn at a given service should be chosen for its support of the sermon. The two places in the service where this kind of hymn most naturally fits are after the sermon and between the Scripture lessons and the sermon. The former is more often used, but the latter is sometimes much more effective.

Hymns as Affirmations of Faith

A third function that hymns can serve in worship is to express the faith of the congregation. Hymns can be an affirmation of faith, not only stating what the Church believes but also stirring up that faith, supporting it, and strengthening it. Calvin in his commentary on the Psalms tells us of the value of singing psalms in public worship. What he says about psalms is surely true of hymns as well. Calvin was fond of saying that worship exercises our faith and believed that singing these affirmations of faith does just that. As exercise increases the strength of our physical bodies, so our spirits gain vigor from joining together with other Christians in professing the verities of the Christian faith. From the standpoint of a covenantal understanding of worship, an affirmation of faith is one of the central acts of the worshiping assembly. A hymn can express the covenant vows of the people of God, affirming that God is our God and that we are his people. When this happens God is worshiped.

We read in Exodus 24 the story of that archetypical service of worship at the foot of Mount Sinai, where Moses constituted the twelve tribes of Israel as a royal priesthood, a holy nation, God's own people. After Moses had recited the words of God, the people made a covenant vow to keep the ordinances of the Book of the Covenant. This vow was of the essence of that service of worship. What is reported to us in that story was the beginning of a liturgical tradition that came to be of increasing importance in Israel's worship. Old Testament scholars tell us that services of covenant renewal were fundamental to the liturgical life of the community.

Later, when the synagogue was established, an affirmation of the covenant came to occupy an important place in the service. Surely one of the most ancient prayers of the synagogue is the *Shema*, Deut 6:4-9, a summary of the Law. The *Shema* can be regarded as a recitation of Scripture in capsule form, but from another side, and that is what interests us here, it can be regarded of the creed of the synagogue liturgy:

> Hear, O Israel: The LORD our God is one LORD; and you shall love the LORD your God with all your heart, and with all your soul, and with all your might. And these words which I command you this day shall be upon your heart; and you shall teach them diligently to your children, and shall talk of them when you sit in your house, and when you walk by the way, and when you lie down, and when you rise. And you shall bind them as a sign upon your hand, and they shall be as frontlets between your eyes. And you shall write them on the doorposts of your house and on your gates.

The *Shema* is understood as both Scripture and prayer. As prayer, it is an affirmation of faith. It both expresses the faith of Israel and confirms it.

A particularly fine example of a hymn of affirmation in the New Testament is what has been called a christological hymn in Paul's Epistle to the Colossians, set out here in poetic lines:

> He is the image of the invisible God,
>> the first-born of all creation;
> for in him all things were created,
>> in heaven and on earth,
>> visible and invisible,
> whether thrones or dominions
>> or principalities or authorities —
> all things were created through him
>> and for him.
> He is before all things,
>> and in him all things hold together.
> He is the head of the body,

the church;
he is the beginning,
     the first-born from the dead,
that in everything he might be pre-eminent.
For in him all the fulness of God
     was pleased to dwell,
and through him to reconcile to himself
     all things,
whether on earth or in heaven,
     making peace by the blood of his cross.   Colossians 1:15-20

That this was in fact an early Christian hymn, sung by a worshiping congregation, is, we have to admit, only a supposition. We cannot say which of these lines were actually part of the text of the hymn and which words or phrases may have been the Apostle's commentary. We probably have here either an early Christian hymn or at least something very similar to the hymns sung in early Christian worship. The earliest non-Christian to tell us about Christian worship, the Roman writer Pliny, tells us that in their worship services Christians sang hymns to Christ as God. Hymns affirming the divinity of Christ, one would gather from this, were a fairly conspicuous feature of the worship of the early Church.

While Christian hymnody was used generously in the worship of the earliest Christian Church, it seems to have fallen out of favor in the second century. It is only after the middle of the fourth century that it reappears. Ambrose of Milan is credited with having revived hymnody. He did this with the specific intention of using hymns as a means of affirming orthodox Christian teaching in the face of Arianism. His classic morning hymn is a beautiful example of the way a hymn can be an affirmation of faith.

O Splendor of God's glory bright,
From light eternal bringing light,
Thou Light of light, light's living Spring,
True Day, all days illumining:

Come, very Sun of heaven's love,
In lasting radiance from above,
And pour the Holy Spirit's ray
On all we think or do today.

Confirm our will to do the right,
And keep our hearts from envy's blight;
Let faith her eager fires renew
And hate the false, and love the true.

Dawn's glory gilds the earth and skies,
Let Him, our perfect Morn, arise,
The Word in God the Father One,
The Father imaged in the Son.

When we come to the Reformation we find that the whole spirit of Luther's hymnody was affirmative. One of his most popular hymns was a metrical version of the Nicene Creed, "We All Believe in One God." We find the same thing with Calvin. The *Genevan Psalter* of 1542 has a French version of the Apostles' Creed provided by the French lyric poet Clément Marot. For the Reformers it is clear that one of the reasons we sing Christian hymns is to affirm our faith.

This dimension of Christian hymnody is also characteristic of the hymnody of Pietism. Pietism, contrary to what we have so often been told, has century after century both vitalized and edified Christian worship. This is true of both Protestant Pietism and Catholic Pietism. The Protestant Pietism of the eighteenth century, as we have seen, inspired what can truly be called a golden age of hymnody. We have mentioned among English hymnodists Watts, Doddridge, the Wesleys, Newton, and Cowper. We should not forget their forerunners among the German Pietists, Joachim Neander, Nikolaus von Zinzendorf, August Hermann Franke, and Gerhard Tersteegen. An American hymn writer of the period was Samuel Davies, the "apostle of the Great Awakening" in Virginia. He had a gift for writing verse just as he had a gift for oratory. He began to compose hymns to conclude his sermons. This was, in fact, the beginning of Presbyterian hymnody.

In the English-speaking world it was these Pietists of the eighteenth century who recovered hymnody for us. Neither the Anglicans nor the Puritans would allow anything but psalmody until well into the eighteenth century. The Anglicans, particularly the High Church Anglicans, did not really reconcile themselves to hymnody until John Mason Neale began translating the hymns of the Middle Ages in the middle of the nineteenth century. It was really Pietism, therefore, that gave us a hymnody for English-speaking people, though we should qualify that by saying that in the strictest sense neither Watts nor Doddridge were Pietists and that it would be more proper to call Newton and Cowper evangelicals. One might insist that evangelical would be a better word for all these hymn writers and use the word Pietist only for eighteenth-century German Protestants influenced by Philipp Spener. But Pietism was a very broad international and interconfessional movement. Even if one feels that such distinctions are necessary, it is still true that it is due to the religious revivals of the eighteenth century that English-speaking Christianity recovered the hymnal.

As I have mentioned, it became a common practice in the mid-1700s for a preacher to compose sermons and hymns together. In a service of worship, after the sermon, the minister or precentor would line out the freshly composed hymn. Congregations were accustomed to having psalms lined out and therefore found nothing novel about having hymns lined out the same way. When the sermon was published, as it often was, the hymn would be published with it. This was the origin of the Methodist hymnal and then the Presbyterian hymnal. Needless to say, not every minister had the gifts needed to compose a fresh hymn for every sermon. As time went on, the hymns of those who did were collected, and the average minister was expected to conclude the sermon with an appropriate hymn.

One might imagine that what one meant by an appropriate hymn to follow the sermon was a hymn that supported the sermon's theme. But this does not really explain the devotional fire of Pietist hymnody. A careful reading of such hymns shows something much more profound. The central thrust of this school of hymnody is that the hymn is a profession of faith. It functions as a covenant vow by means of which the congregation engages itself to be the people of God. Just as Israel, having heard Moses recite the Law at the foot of Mount Sinai, answered with one voice, "All the words which the LORD has spoken we will do" (Exod 24:3), so the Christian congregation hearing the gospel of Christ proclaimed in the sermon responds by singing a hymn in which it pledges itself to be a Christian people serving Christ as Lord and Savior.

When one sees its essential devotional function, one realizes why hymnody was so essential to the revivals of the eighteenth century. The whole point of Pietism was to recover the personal relationship between Christ and Christians. One entered into this personal relationship by surrendering oneself to Christ, and this was done in the singing of a hymn that expressed the covenant vows of faith. Countless examples could be quoted, but one classic hymn of Charles Wesley expresses the whole thing perfectly:

> Come, let us use the grace divine,
>   And all with one accord,
> In a perpetual covenant join
>   Ourselves to Christ the Lord.
>
> Give up ourselves, through Jesu's power,
>   His name to glorify;
> And promise in this sacred hour
>   For God to live and die.
>
> The covenant we this moment make
>   Be ever kept in mind!
> We will no more our God forsake,
>   Or cast his words behind.
>
> We never will throw off his fear
>   Who hears our solemn vow;
> And if thou art well pleased to hear,
>   Come down, and meet us now!
>
> Thee, Father, Son, and Holy Ghost,
>   Let all our hearts receive!
> Present with the celestial host,
>   The peaceful answer give!
>
> To each the covenant-blood apply
>   Which takes our sins away;
> And register our names on high,
>   And keep us to that day!

This approach to hymnody should frequently guide our selection of hymns. The point is obvious enough when our preaching has an evangelistic emphasis, but even when the sermon is not explicitly evangelistic in focus it still holds true. There should always be a place in worship for the whole congregation to express its faith. In fact one should probably say that in every service of worship Christ should be exalted as Lord and confessed as Lord. What more important liturgical function could a hymn serve? To witness to our common faith that Christ is Lord is, after all, one of the reasons we come together each Lord's Day.

Benedictions and Doxologies

Benedictions

Giving a benediction at the end of the service of worship is one of the oldest traditions of biblical worship. In the worship of the temple it was one of the high points of the service. When the sacrifice had been made the high priest would raise his hands in blessing and pronounce the Aaronic Benediction:

> The LORD bless you and keep you:
> The LORD make his face to shine upon you, and be gracious to you:
> The LORD lift up his countenance upon you, and give you peace.
>
> Numbers 6:24-26

This form of prayer was already ancient when Jesus ben Sirach mentioned its use (Sirach 45:15), and it was greatly beloved and a high point of the synagogue liturgy, even in the days of Jesus. There it was used as the conclusion of the Prayers of the Eighteen Benedictions.

Even in the synagogue, reciting the Benediction was still considered the prerogative of the descendants of the Aaronic priesthood. It is interesting that according to the Gospel of Luke, when Jesus had finished his ministry just before his ascension, his final prayer for his disciples was a benediction. He led his disciples out to the Mount of Olives and blessed them, with his hands lifted up (Luke 24:50).

In the worship of the ancient Church, there was evidently some form of benediction at the end of the service, but it must have gradually lost its importance during the Middle Ages. Evidences of it appear in a number of different places, though it does not seem that any one particular text was used. Since I have written about the Benediction in detail in my book *The Patristic Roots of Reformed Worship*, I will not go into it at any length here, except to say that by the time of the Reformation the restored Benediction became an obvious feature of Protestant worship.

Martin Luther was responsible for the importance of the Benediction in Protestant worship. He suggested that it was the Aaronic Benediction that Jesus gave when he blessed the disciples (Luke 24:50). To contemporary biblical scholarship this seems a bit fanciful, but it does seem to be what Luke intends to convey, and Luther may well have understood the text better than exegetes of today. However we understand the passage today, the other Reformers were convinced by Luther's explanation and saw a certain theological appropriateness in it. No doubt it made a great deal of sense as more and more they began to understand their worship in terms of covenant theology.

Ever since, it has been the custom of Protestant ministers to conclude the service by lifting up their hands and blessing the congregation with the Aaronic Benediction. Gradually other biblical benedictions were introduced. The Apostolic Benediction from the end of II Corinthians is heard on occasion, as well as several others.

In more recent times, some ministers have replaced the Benediction with a prayer asking God's blessing on the congregation because the classical Protestant practice has seemed to contradict their theology of the ministry. They figured that Luther must have temporarily forgotten his doctrine of the priesthood of all believers. Some churches have even gone so far as to insist that someone besides the minister give the Benediction.

While this fits in much better with contemporary ideology than the older tradition, it misses the central theological significance of the Benediction as it has been understood in the classical Protestant tradition. When one of the biblical benedictions is used, particularly the Aaronic Benediction, then the covenant blessing of the patriarchs, which Abraham passed on to Isaac, and Isaac to Jacob, and Jacob to his descendants, is passed on to the congregation, and thus from generation to generation. It is the blessing that was given for a thousand years in the temple, that Simeon gave to the baby Jesus when he came to the temple, and that Jesus in turn gave to his disciples. It is the blessing that even Gentiles have come to receive: "that in Christ Jesus the blessing of Abraham might come upon the Gentiles, that we might receive the promise of the Spirit through faith" (Gal 3:14; cf. Eph 1:3). The Reformers understood the Benediction not as one Christian's prayer for other Christians, a prayer that they might receive God's blessing, but rather as the conferring of the covenant blessing, the blessing that God gave Abraham and that we as the descendants of Abraham by faith have received through faith.

But what about our theology of the ministry? Do we contradict our doctrine of the priesthood of all believers when we reserve to a minister the giving of the Benediction? One of the things one notices in the various stories we find in the Bible about the giving of a benediction is that quite often those giving the benediction were particularly called or qualified for that task. This is most obviously the case in the story of Balaam. Balaam was specially called to give that benediction. He really did not want to do it, but, as we read in the book of Numbers, God sent him out to give that prophetic oracle of benediction to God's people and to no one else. God made it so obvious that even Balaam's ass understood. A special person was sent with a special and prophetic benediction. Balaam, as the minister of the benediction, was responsible for delivering the benediction to those to whom God had sent him and to no others, a profoundly prophetic act.

Scripture makes it clear that the Aaronic priesthood was supposed to give the Aaronic Benediction in the temple. As Luke tells the story, there was something prophetic about the arrival of Simeon in the temple at just the right time to bless the infant Jesus and thus deliver the message that would fulfill his own life. It was for that very purpose that his whole life had been lived. For Luke, at least, the benediction given to Jesus when he entered this world must have been the benediction that Jesus gave his disciples when he left this world. It is not explicitly said in the third Gospel, and Jesus was not a member of the priestly tribe, but throughout the New Testament Jesus is the high priest of the new covenant and therefore the one qualified to pass on the benediction. That today a minister of the Gospel should give the Benediction makes good biblical sense.

This practice also makes good theological sense, for in some ways the ministry of the Church of the new covenant succeeds to the priesthood, the ministry of the old covenant. To prove this point the Reformers cited Paul's argument that just as the ministry of the old covenant was paid, so the ministry of the new covenant should receive financial support from the faithful (I Cor 9:13-14). In the *Second Helvetic Confession* it is pointed out that the new covenant Church has a distinct ministry of Word and sacrament charged with preaching the gospel and administering the sacraments. All Christians may take part in the common priesthood of the people of God, but priesthood and ministry are not the same thing. All Christians may be priests performing the service of the royal priesthood, but not all Christians are ministers of Word and sacrament. It is as a ministry of the Word that ministers of the new covenant pronounce the Benediction. It used to be an old Presbyterian custom that at the ordination of a new minister the whole service was conducted by the other ministers of presbytery. After prayer and the laying on of hands, however, the newly ordained minister was conducted to the pulpit by his colleagues and for the first time raised his hands and gave the Benediction. The theological significance of this was more than clear.

It has been my practice to use the Aaronic Benediction on most Sunday mornings. At Sunday vespers, I use the benediction in Phil 4:7, "The peace of God, which passes all understanding, . . ." On Sunday mornings from Christmas to Palm Sunday, I use the Apostolic Benediction from II Corinthians. From Easter Sunday to Pentecost I use "May the God of peace who brought again from the dead our Lord Jesus Christ, the great shepherd of the sheep . . ." (Heb 13:20-21). For weddings I use several other benedictions, at the baptismal service I use a benediction from Isa 43:1b-3a to bless the newly baptized child, and I use several others for other occasions. There is no reason why it should be done this way rather than some other way or why other biblical benedictions should not be used. This system does, however, allow for a full unfolding of the word of blessing as it is found in Scripture.

Let us look at these classic benediction texts, making a few remarks about each in turn. We have already quoted the Aaronic Benediction, which is found in Num 6:24-26. It is the classic benediction text of which others are but expansions and interpretations. Why it has been preferred over all others is probably due to its beauty. The story goes that Francis of Assisi was particularly fond of using it. I have never found textual evidence for this. On the other hand it seems completely appropriate to that altogether miraculous man. This benediction, like the person of Francis himself, seems to breathe an air of peace wherever it is heard. The whole text sets up the word "peace." *Shalom,* that great Hebrew word, sums up the whole thing. Even as a single word it is the blessing beyond all others. Set in this liturgical text, it is the classical benediction, which is therefore the benediction that we should hear most often.

Second, let us look at the benediction commonly called the Apostolic Benediction:

> The grace of the Lord Jesus Christ and the love of God and the fellowship of the Holy Spirit be with you all.
>
> II Corinthians 13:14

This, like the other biblical benedictions, might well be considered an expansion or elaboration of the Aaronic Benediction. From very early times Christians must have detected in the use of the Aaronic Benediction, with its threefold repetition of God's name, a foreshadowing or at least an intimation of the Trinity. Scholars can be very critical about these tendencies, but that was how the pious understood things when Christian worship was first taking shape.

The Apostolic Benediction, when considered in its context in II Corinthians, is not so much a benediction as a valediction. It is the sort of final greeting with which the letters of classical antiquity closed. The question is whether it was ever used formally in a service of worship as a benediction. A number of New Testament scholars, notably Gerhard Delling, feel that there is good evidence for thinking it was. Though it seems to have been understood as a sort of supplement to the Aaronic Benediction, the evidence suggests that the wording of such elaborations of the traditional benediction was quite fluid. Sometimes we find simply "The grace of our Lord Jesus Christ be with you" (I Thess 5:28) or even just "Grace be with you." Perhaps what we are seeing here is Paul's tendency to supplement the typically Hebrew blessing, *shalom*, with something a bit more significant to his Greek converts, namely *charis*, "grace." We find this in the salutations of several of his epistles: "Grace to you and peace" or "Grace, mercy, and peace. . . ."

"Peace" was the word of both salutation and valediction in ordinary Jewish social life and the word of blessing bestowed in the worship of both the temple and the synagogue. We find this in a number of the psalms. That basic word of blessing was often expanded as we find it in Psalm 67. No doubt "peace" remained the word of blessing in the worship of the New Testament Church, but it, too, was expanded. Here in II Corinthians we find it expanded into "grace," "love," and "fellowship."

A third benediction is one that was frequently used during the Second World War:

> The peace of God, which passeth all understanding, keep your hearts and minds in the knowledge and love of God, and of His Son Jesus Christ our Lord; and the blessing of God Almighty, the Father, the Son, and the Holy Spirit, be amongst you, and remain with you always.
>
> *The Book of Common Worship* (1932)

One might possibly call this the Peace Benediction. There are several other New Testament passages that expand this basic word of blessing. For example,

Peace I leave with you;
my peace I give to you;
not as the world gives do I give to you.
Let not your hearts be troubled,
neither let them be afraid.   John 14:27

Paul also gives a benediction simply using "peace," as in Rom 15:33, "The God of peace be with you all," or again at the end of Ephesians,

Peace be to the brethren,
    and love with faith,
from God the Father
    and the Lord Jesus Christ.   Ephesians 6:23

Here "peace" is supplemented by "love" and "faith," and yet the basic word "peace" is still the benediction's key word. The text of this benediction is particularly interesting because it makes clear that Paul, the minister of this particular benediction, understands himself to be imparting the peace of God in the name of Christ. That is, the Apostle understands giving the benediction as a ministerial act.

Another blessing that we hear from time to time might appropriately be called the Covenantal Benediction:

Now may the God of peace who brought again from the dead our Lord Jesus, the great shepherd of the sheep, by the blood of the eternal covenant, equip you with everything good that you may do his will, working in you that which is pleasing in his sight, through Jesus Christ; to whom be glory for ever and ever. *Amen.*   Hebrews 13:20-21

This benediction, as the whole Epistle to the Hebrews, has a rich sonority to it that makes it particularly appropriate to a very solemn occasion. It is very clearly an unfolding of the basic word of benediction, peace. It is the God of peace who is called on to bestow his blessing. The blessing that is bestowed is clearly the covenant blessing. It is the covenant blessing given by the patriarchs to their descendants, but even more it is the blessing of the new and eternal covenant established in the blood of Christ. The blessing that is bestowed is a sanctifying blessing. When God grants us peace he grants us the sanctifying graces that enable us to live the life of the people of God. Of all the Christian expansions of the Aaronic Benediction this is surely the most profound. It gives a clear basis for a Christian understanding and use of the ancient Levitical benediction.

Doxologies

In the worship of American Protestant churches the Benediction is often followed by some sort of doxology sung either by the congregation or the choir. There are, of course, many different doxologies, even if for most of us *the* doxology is the one sung to Old 100th,

Praise God from whom all blessings flow,
Praise Him all creatures here below,
Praise Him above ye heavenly hosts,
Praise Father, Son, and Holy Ghost. *Amen.*

Somehow that one doxology has become such a favorite that in popular usage it has pretty much monopolized the term. But there are many other doxologies. One thinks of the doxology that concludes the reading of the Psalter, popularly called the *Gloria patri.*

Glory be to the Father,
    and to the Son and to the Holy Ghost,
As it was in the beginning,
    is now, and ever shall be,
    world without end. *Amen. Amen.*

This, too, is a doxology. Then there are the doxologies found at the end of prayers. A formal public prayer almost always concludes with a doxology. The first that comes to mind is at the end of the Lord's Prayer: "For thine is the kingdom and the power and the glory, for ever. Amen." A well known closing like "This we ask in the name of Christ, our Lord, to whom with you, O Father, and the Holy Spirit, be all honor and glory, now and evermore, Amen" is a doxology. There is also the doxology that in American Protestant Churches so traditionally follows the reading of the Scripture lesson:

May the LORD bless this reading
    of His holy Word,
And to His name be the honor
    and the glory. *Amen.*

A doxology might be defined as a short ascription of praise in the service of worship. The word "doxology" can also quite properly be used to speak of the theology of worship. Here, however, we are speaking of doxologies as those short ascriptions of praise used so often in Christian worship. From ancient times doxologies have laced both public and private worship. Again and again throughout the whole service they serve to draw the congregation back to the fundamental fact that worship is doxological. It is the work of the Holy Spirit in the body of Christ to the glory of the Father.

When I was a boy, it was *the* doxology that posed for me the first theological mystery. The solemnity of those words, set to that music, always said to me, in the most profound manner possible, "This is worship." Until I was about twelve there were three churches that I attended with regularity. In New Jersey I went to the Presbyterian Church with my Grandmother Oliphant, and in California I went to the Congregational Church with my parents. In both places every service began with *the* doxology. Whenever I was in Missouri with my Grandmother Old, I went to the Southern Methodist Church. There every service *ended* with *the* doxology. It was one of those inexplicable denominational differences, like saying "debts" or "trespasses" in the Lord's Prayer. I finally decided that in the Congregational Church and in the Presbyterian Church *the* doxology meant "Now let us worship God," while in the Methodist Church it meant, "Now we have worshiped God." I explained this to my father one Sunday on the way home from Church, and he advised me not to trouble myself with the mysteries of religion, which were quite beyond human understanding. As I have grown older and become a bit more initiated in liturgical history, I have decided that both practices are to be commended. Singing a doxology is a good way to begin a service and a good way to close a service as well. Doxologies should salt the whole service. Or, putting it another way, doxologies are a biblical way of framing worship. Just as pictures have frames around them to bring them into perspective, so doxologies serve as a sort of framing to our worship, setting it apart for the glory of God.

Let us look at a number of biblical doxologies. Very early in the Bible we read that when Melchizedek blessed Abraham he followed his benediction with a doxology:

> Blessed be Abram by God Most High,
>   maker of heaven and earth;
> and blessed be God Most High,
>   who has delivered your enemies into your hand!

Genesis 14:19-20

This act of worship was given great significance by the author of the Epistle to the Hebrews (ch. 7). Melchizedek, the priest of Salem, is understood there as a type of the priesthood of Christ, and his use of a benediction followed by a doxology cannot help but be of particular interest to Christians. The story suggests the utter graciousness of God's benediction: God is ultimately gracious and our doxology is, at its most profound, a reflection of that wondrous and amazing grace.

Doxologies play a particularly important role in the Book of Psalms. Many of the psalms end with doxologies. There is a very short and simple doxology at the end of Psalm 68: "Blessed be God!" Another doxology is found at the end of Psalm 145:

> My mouth will speak the praise of the LORD,
>   and let all flesh bless his holy name for ever and ever.

Then there is the doxology that both begins and ends the eighth Psalm:

> O LORD, our Lord,
>   how majestic is thy name in all the earth!

At the end of Psalm 135 a more elaborate doxology calls on all Israel, the Levites, the priests, and even the God-fearers among the Gentiles to bless God:

> O house of Israel, bless the LORD!
>   O house of Aaron, bless the LORD!
> O house of Levi, bless the LORD!

You that fear the Lord, bless the Lord!
Blessed be the Lord from Zion,
    he who dwells in Jerusalem!
Praise the Lord!   Psalm 135:19-21

As we shall see, this emphasis on the universality of godly praise is characteristic of biblical doxologies.

Psalm 100 is a fully developed doxology. It may have originally been used as the doxology to follow the Sabbath psalms, Psalms 93 and 96–99, which were used at the beginning of the Sabbath service.

Make a joyful noise to the Lord, all the lands!
    Serve the Lord with gladness!
    Come into his presence with singing!

Know that the Lord is God!
    It is he that made us, and we are his;
    we are his people, and the sheep of his pasture.

Enter his gates with thanksgiving,
    and his courts with praise!
    Give thanks to him, bless his name!

For the Lord is good;
    his steadfast love endures for ever,
    and his faithfulness to all generations.

The universalism of this psalm, fully expressed already in the psalms that preceded it, is seen in the first line, "All people that on earth do dwell," as the *Anglo-Genevan Psalter* so exuberantly expressed it. The missionary imperative of a covenantal theology of worship is of the essence of doxology.

Another example of the same thing is Ps 103:20-22:

Bless the Lord, O you his angels,
    you mighty ones who do his word,
    hearkening to the voice of his word!
Bless the Lord, all his hosts,
    his ministers that do his will!
Bless the Lord, all his works,
    in all places of his dominion.
Bless the Lord, O my soul!

Evidently at some time before the canonization of the Psalms it became the practice to end the liturgical recitation of the Psalter with a doxology. This probably explains why each of the five books that comprise the collection of canonical psalms ends with a doxology. The first of these is found at the end of Psalm 41:

Blessed be the Lord, the God of Israel,
    from everlasting to everlasting! *Amen* and *Amen.*

This doxology, like several of the other psalter doxologies, emphasizes that the praise given in the psalms is directed to the God of Israel, and yet the praise of God is eternal, "from everlasting to everlasting."

A similar doxology is found at the end of the second book of psalms.

Blessed be the LORD, the God of Israel,
　　who alone does wondrous things.
Blessed be his glorious name for ever;
　　may his glory fill the whole earth! *Amen* and *Amen!*

Psalm 72:18-19

In this doxology we find a development. The praise of God is not only eternal but also worldwide. God enters into our experience by his works of creation and providence, but he does this in such a way that his name is renowned throughout the whole earth.

Then finally at the end of the Psalms we find a long, comprehensive doxology that is numbered as Psalm 150, but is in reality the doxology for the whole collection:

Praise the LORD!
Praise God in his sanctuary;
　　praise him in his mighty firmament!
Praise him for his mighty deeds;
　　praise him according to his exceeding greatness!

Praise him with trumpet sound;
　　praise him with lute and harp!
Praise him with timbrel and dance;
　　praise him with strings and pipe!
Praise him with sounding cymbals;
　　praise him with loud clashing cymbals!
Let everything that breathes praise the LORD!
Praise the LORD!

Once again we notice a development in the scope of this doxology. God's praise is universal. All peoples are summoned to the temple in Jerusalem to enter into this universal symphony of praise. It is of the essence of a doxology to witness both to the eternity and the universality of God's praise. God is praised by the ministers of the temple, by the whole people of Israel, by all nations over the face of the earth, by every living, breathing thing, and finally by all the host of heaven.

The custom of concluding the public recitation of the Psalter with a doxology, in both the temple and the synagogue, must have passed into the Church at an early date. We learn, for example, from John Cassian that when the monks of the Egyptian desert had finished chanting a group of psalms they sang a trinitarian doxology. The early Church felt it was important to unfold the biblical doxologies in a trinitarian sense. Basil of Caesarea, toward the end of the fourth century, discusses the doxology that concludes a recitation from the Psalter with penetrating thoroughness in his essay on the Holy Spirit. As he understands it, this doxology was a means of making it quite clear that the divinely inspired praises of the Psalter were from the very beginning intended to be sung to the triune God revealed in Christ. The Church is to sing the psalms just as Israel did. Even more, Basil assures us, the meaning of the psalms is fully expressed only when they are sung by those who recognize how they have been fulfilled in Christ. Basil made a great point of insisting that the doxology is a hymn of praise addressed equally to the Father, to the Son, and to the Holy Spirit, and that the praise of God's people had always been just that.

The cultivation of doxologies in our worship has always seemed to me one way of emphasizing the doxological character of worship as a whole. A number of years ago I discovered in the *Scottish Psalter* a little collection of doxologies that can be sung to a great variety of tunes. Apparently the purpose for this collection is to provide a doxology for each meter used in that psalter. To tell the truth, I have never used these doxologies in quite the way the psalter intended. Instead, I have used them at the end of the service following the Benediction. One I have been particularly fond of using is the doxology that is offered for Psalm 124 sung to Old 124th:

> Glory to God the Father, God the Son,
>   And unto God the Spirit, three in One.
> From age to age let saints his name adore,
>   His power and love proclaim from shore to shore,
> And spread his fame, till time shall be no more. *Amen.*

In many ways this is the most complete of these doxologies, for it mentions both the eternity and the universality of the praise of God. The tune is one of the classics of Protestant church music. It was the favorite hymn of the French Huguenots, who sang it as an affirmation of their faith in God's steadfast help during their years of pilgrimage. The music itself seems to convey a sense of God's everlasting faithfulness. Somewhat like singing the doxology to Old 100th, singing this doxology to Old 124th affirms our faith in the universality and eternity of God's glory.

The Book of Revelation reports several doxologies that may have been used in the earliest Christian services of worship. In fact one of the interesting features of these doxologies is the way they appear repeatedly through the whole of the book from beginning to end. This would certainly suggest that the whole service of worship as it was celebrated toward the end of the first century was generously sprinkled with doxologies.

The Revelation opens with a superb doxology:

> To him who loves us
>   and has freed us from our sins by his blood
> and made us a kingdom,
>   priests to his God and Father,
> to him be glory and dominion
>   for ever and ever. *Amen.*

Revelation 1:5b-6

In my first Church the choir director found a marvelous choral setting of this by Ralph Vaughn Williams, and we often sang it following the Benediction. Perhaps some would insist that we should have used it as an opening doxology rather than a closing doxology. That never occurred to me at the time. What did occur to me was that a doxology from the Revelation was a very appropriate way to end a service of worship. It helps us to lift our eyes to the consummation of the Kingdom, to those glorious things above. It brings to mind, if only very briefly, the ultimate conclusion.

Another doxology that I have often used after the Benediction is the one that John heard as part of the celestial liturgy sung before the throne of God. It must have been a mighty chorus since it rose from every creature in heaven, on earth, and under the earth and from the creatures on the sea and under the sea:

> To him who sits upon the throne
> > and to the Lamb
> be blessing and honor and glory and might
> > for ever and ever!   Revelation 5:13

There are two well-known settings of this doxology, one by Isaac Watts:

> To Him who sits upon the throne,
> > The God whom we adore,
> And to the Lamb that once was slain,
> > Be glory ever more.

The other is by Horatius Bonar:

> Blessing and honor and glory and power,
> > Wisdom and riches and strength evermore
> Give ye to Him who our battle hath won,
> > Whose are the Kingdom, the crown, and the throne.
>
> Soundeth the heaven of the heavens with His Name;
> > Ringeth the earth with His glory and fame;
> Ocean and mountain, stream, forest, and flower
> > Echo His praises and tell of his power.
>
> Ever ascendeth the song and the joy;
> > Ever descendeth the love from on high;
> Blessing and honor and glory and praise —
> > This is the theme of the hymns that we raise.
>
> Give we the glory and praise to the Lamb;
> > Take we the robe and the harp and the palm;
> Sing we the song of the Lamb that was slain,
> > Dying in weakness, but rising to reign.

Whenever I have used these doxologies from the worship before the throne of God as John saw and heard it in his ecstatic vision on the Island of Patmos, it opens up for me the holiness and solemnity of true worship. Our worship here on Earth, plain and simple as it may be, by the secret working of the Holy Spirit is joined to that worship that is heavenly.

Finally I want to say something about the often repeated Amens and Hallelujahs that resound through the heavenly worship. Worship in the temple in Jerusalem was punctuated with doxologies. Hallelujahs and Amens constantly echoed faith. As John saw and heard the heavenly worship it was the same way: The Hallelujahs, Doxologies, and Amens poured forth like the sound of many waters. It was a cascade of praise. The early Church's worship must have been the same way.

There have been times when these constantly repeated ejaculations of praise troubled me, particularly when I was in college. I went to Centre College of Kentucky, and the chapel services there in Danville's old First Presbyterian Church were observed with great care and devotion. The chapel choir was directed by a master. After the Benediction the choir would sing a series of Amens that went on and on, repeating that one word several dozen times. It was beautiful, but I could not understand the sense of it. I resolved it by remembering that the ways of heaven are not always understood here on earth. After all, the ways of worship are heavenly ways.

It was only years later in a Romanian Orthodox monastery high in the Carpathian Alps that I began to perceive what it was all about. I was there with a group of students from the socialist world. We had one thing in common: We had left our own modern up-to-date worlds far behind. I was about as far away from the traditions of American Protestantism as I could be. Somehow up there in the snow-covered mountains of eastern Europe I did not feel that I absolutely had to make everything relevant and applicable to the world in which I lived. The Orthodox liturgy, too, is punctuated with doxologies. It constantly resounds with ejaculations of praise, just like the heavenly worship. As the Amens, Hallelujahs, and Doxologies rolled through that monastery chapel I let myself flow in its rhythm. I began to realize what was happening. The prayer of the congregation was soaring. It was entering into heavenly delights. There we were, a group of young men who had left the world behind and had begun to catch sight of the transcendent. What a marvelously exotic experience.

And yet it was not really exotic. When at Easter or at Christmas here at home in America we sing the Hallelujah Chorus, we experience something of the same thing. When David Brainerd back in colonial days knelt in the woods of New Jersey ecstatically repeating "Holy, holy, holy," he was also doing the same thing. Sometimes prayer takes wings and begins to soar in the bounteous winds of the Spirit. This kind of soaring can be a very private experience, but it can also be something we do together as I was doing it back in college chapel and had done it with so much more understanding in that Orthodox monastery. Public prayer should always give the congregation opportunity to do this, to stretch out the wings of prayer and to mount up as eagles and soar in the Spirit. To do this is both to glorify God and to enjoy him together.

The Ordering of
Public Prayer

Finally we need to say something about putting it all together. How is it that public prayer should be ordered in a typical American Protestant Church, be it Dutch Reformed or Congregational, Baptist or Methodist, Presbyterian or any one of a number of other churches that to one degree or another shares the Reformed heritage?

Here we have to be very realistic. If public prayer is to be recovered as a meaningful part of the Christian life, considerably more time, thought, and preparation needs to be given to it. I think many will agree that today, in the usual sort of American Protestant church, prayer is not one of the more engaging elements in the service. The old Wednesday evening prayer meeting has all but disappeared. At the Sunday morning service less and less time is devoted to prayer. What little there is tends to be formal and perfunctory. Charismatic churches are the great exception. Once we non-charismatics get past the speaking in tongues, we often discover that what is most valuable in the charismatic movement is its life of prayer. In churches where the charismatic movement has not been influential, the experience of public prayer tends to be rather stereotyped. Some congregations have been able to maintain small, more intimate prayer groups, and this is certainly encouraging, but it is not quite the same thing as public prayer, that is, the prayer of the whole congregation.

For at least a generation we have experienced a sort of atrophy in public prayer. It has just dried up. This has had a disastrous effect on the vitality of our worship. If we have a lot of dysfunctional churches today, it is because we have been spiritually starved for a long time, and one of the places this starvation is most evident is public prayer. We ministers have a challenging task in this regard. Teaching a congregation to pray together as a congregation takes time and patience on the part of the minister, and on the part of the congregation.

The place to start is with what I like to call a balanced diet of prayer, but one must start slowly. Look at it this way: Those who have been suffering from starvation should not suddenly have a nine course gourmet feast set before them. They could not get it all down, and it would make them sick if they tried. It is the same way with those who have lived on a starvation diet of prayer for a long time. We need to start out with small amounts of simple, honest prayer and gradually work up to a fuller and more varied diet. It is important, however, that the diet be well balanced. There should be praise and there should be lamentation, petition and intercession, confession, and thanksgiving. Just as good nutrition requires that our bodies get a good balance of green vegetables, meats, dairy products, cereals, and fruits, so our spiritual health needs a good balance of all the varieties of prayer.

The Protestant Reformation had a great deal to say on the matter of a full diet of prayer. The *Strasbourg Psalter* of 1537 was a masterpiece in this regard. The pastors, poets, and musicians of Strasbourg worked on it for more than a decade, producing its corporate prayers, its orders for the celebration of the sacraments, its preaching services, its hymns, and above all its psalms, which could be sung in German to popular folk tunes. There were the regular Lord's Day services, vesper services, the daily services of morning and evening prayer, and the feast day celebrations at the cathedral. Martin Bucer guided the development of this psalter and wrote a good number of the prayers, but others produced the psalms and the music.

Calvin followed the example of Strasbourg quite closely in providing a psalter for Geneva particularly in its recognition of the various genre of Christian prayer. He himself spoke of a number of different genre: praise, invocation, confession, supplication, intercession, thanksgiving, and benediction. He also allowed for a variety of ways that public prayer could be exercised. In the *Genevan Psalter* he provided set prayers but he also encouraged spontaneous prayers. He particularly emphasized congregational singing of psalms and canticles.

In the following century, the Puritans in England, the Huguenots in France, the Presbyterians in Scotland, and the Calvinists in the Netherlands developed the idea of the various genre of prayer at considerable depth. This fivefold schema of praise, confession, petition, intercession, and thanksgiving, with certain additions or variations, was used in the eighteenth century by such masters as Isaac Watts and Matthew Henry, who refined and elaborated this approach with much sensitivity.

Generally speaking, the Reformers were much more interested in the content of the service, in whether all these biblical genre of prayer were included, than they were in the order of the various parts of the service. They did not understand the liturgy as a sacred drama unfolding some sort of Neoplatonic ascent to divine reality. During the Middle Ages, the Church had gone to extremes in explaining the Mass as a recapitulation of the history of redemption. It had become a passion play in which the devout could follow the drama of the incarnation, and the altar had become a stage on which the story of Christ's humiliation and exaltation was reenacted in the movements and gestures of the liturgy. The Reformation found this artificial and contrived. It became characteristic of Protestants that they took Acts 2:42 to mean that worship should consist of gathering together for the reading and preaching of the Scriptures, the celebration of the sacraments, the service of prayer, and the giving of alms. And they believed that the prayers of the Church should include those five elements: praises, confessions, petitions, intercessions, and thanksgivings.

They did recognize that both logically and theologically there ought to be a certain succession of the different parts of the service, though that was not a primary consideration. Calvin, for instance, found a certain theological significance in following the sermon with the major prayer of the service, the Prayer of Intercession. The Word calls us to prayer, shapes our prayer, and opens up the proper concerns of our prayer. Prayer should be our first reaction to the challenges that the study of Scripture opens up to us. To hear the Word of God must inevitably bring us to our knees. "Put off your shoes from your feet, for the place on which you are standing is holy ground" (Exod 3:5). In Strasbourg it was for very theological reasons that the offertory was removed from the place it occupied in the Mass, at the beginning of the communion service, and replaced by a collection of alms at the end of the service. The Reformers considered the placement of the offertory, as it is found in the Roman Mass, thoroughly Pelagian, a dramatic contradiction of the Pauline doctrine of grace. They sought to make it clear that our gifts are not offered to God so that we might come into communion with him, but rather collected at the end of the service as an act of thanksgiving for the gracious gift of communion.

Some of these logical or theological arrangements were even suggested by Scripture. As we will see, Protestants more and more began to place their prayers of adoration and psalms of praise at the beginning of the service, followed closely by a Prayer of Confession. This apparently was the way worship was begun in the temple, as can be gathered from a number of different passages in the Old Testament. That Scripture lessons should first be read and then preached has an obvious logic to it, but it is also clear from a number of passages of Scripture that this is the way it has always been done. It is the same way with the liturgical framing of certain elements in the service. The Prayer for Illumination has a definite theological appropriateness but, as we learn from the eighth chapter of Nehemiah, it goes back to the practice of the synagogue. So also with following the Scripture reading with a doxology. The liturgical framing of both the major elements of the service and the service as a whole was the standard procedure of pious Jews in the days of Christ and the Apostles, and there are many traces of this in the New Testament.

The Reformers were quite willing to accept certain traditional orders for their worship. This is particularly clear in Strasbourg, where Bucer and his colleagues did in fact maintain the general outline of the service of worship as they inherited it from the Middle Ages. They recognized, of course, that the Roman Mass as they knew it had undergone quite a bit of change and development from the way worship had been celebrated in the patristic age. But as they saw it, even in the patristic age things had gotten away from the example set by Christ and the Apostles. But still the tradition was basically sound. (In my book *The Patristic Roots of Reformed Worship* I have gone into this subject at some length.)

The important question here is how public prayer might be ordered so as to include the full diet of prayer. A full diet of prayer not only makes use of all the genre of prayer, it also uses all the occasions of prayer as well. There is prayer done "in the courts of the Lord," and there is the prayer in secret, "in your closet," as Jesus put it. There is the prayer of the Lord's Day service, and the prayer of the weekday, the "continual sacrifice," offered up each morning and evening. There is the prayer of the feast days, when we pray with rejoicing, and there is the prayer for days of humiliation. To be sure, a healthy congregation, in addition to its ministry of public prayer on Sunday morning, should foster a ministry of daily prayer. There should be a number of more intimate prayer groups, and there should also be more fully developed prayer services such as a Sunday evening vespers or a Wednesday evening prayer meeting. With careful cultivation these things all come in time, but here I want to zero in on the ordering of prayer at the Lord's Day service. How can this be done so that God is truly served?

My pastoral experience makes me very much aware that deepening and broadening the prayer life of a congregation does not happen overnight. A rookie preacher would be ill advised to spring all the prayer forms found in this book on a torpid village church within a few months of arriving. For this reason I will suggest here two orders of service, one simpler, the other more fully developed. The simpler order recognizes that some members of our congregations are not willing to give much more than an hour to the service of worship. In my experience this is particularly true of the older generation. Older people have their ways of doing things, and they can get quite upset by an enthusiastic young pastor who challenges them to something more than that to which they have been accustomed. This is particularly the case with the generation born in the first three decades of our century. One might refer to it as the *Reader's Digest* generation. Everything had to be condensed, and consequently it all became very bland. Everything worth saying could be said in twenty minutes. Once over lightly was always good enough because the modern world could not wait for anything that took any longer. On the other hand those whose spiritual lives were shaped before the invention of the automobile, that is, the horse and buggy generation, seemed to have a much deeper perception of things. It is almost as though the sudden burst of speed achieved by automation threw everybody's sense of timing off. More recent generations tend to recognize the need to take more time to center in on the more profound matters of life. It is strange how different generations can be so far apart in spiritual things, but that is the way it is, and a mature pastor will recognize the needs of the older generation as well as those of younger people.

At the beginning one has to work within the accustomed structure. This is particularly the case with the time structure. Here is where the other prayer services during the week can be helpful. What you do not have time to do on Sunday morning, you might be able to do at a service some other time during the week. One cannot, however, let the more truculent members of the congregation keep everyone else from moving ahead. There is a coming younger generation, yearning for spiritual depth. This generation is learning how to cope with the speed of modern life and beginning to discover that timesaving and laborsaving devices can be used to free one up to give more time to the things of the spirit. It is this generation that needs to be engaged. When that happens a Church will grow. For a Church to mature and flourish it needs to challenge the most creative members of the community. It needs to speak to the aspirations of those who are yearning for meaning in life and are willing to devote themselves and spend their energy for the high purposes of the Kingdom of God. It is these people who must be allowed to set the tone of our worship.

It is not the order of service that is at the heart of the reform that needs to be made. It is rather the content of the service. The minister's job is to help the congregation discover the true nature of praise, to lead the congregation into that experience, and to recognize what it is that is happening. The same is true with confession and supplication. This is a particular kind of prayer experience, and it comes to us very naturally if the hangups of our humanist culture do not hold us back. Sometimes it can be a tricky job to show a congregation how to cry to the Lord. Simply introducing a unison Prayer of Confession is not enough. Ever since the Greek philosophers began to taunt the pious with the unseemliness of sniveling over their frustrations in front of the unmoved mover, good humanists have been a bit backward about prayers of confession and supplication. Solid biblical preaching can do much to overcome this reticence, but so can the well thought-out prayers of the minister. It is the same way with intercession, thanksgiving, and the other genre of prayer.

What we are really concerned about is deepening the experience of prayer. When we make some progress with this, then the ordering of our prayers will come quite easily. When our congregations discover that prayer is genuine rather than merely ceremonial, they will be happy to give it more than an hour.

With a certain pragmatism, then, I suggest this first order. It can be done in not much more than an hour, allowing half an hour, or a bit more, for a sermon. (When the Lord's Supper is celebrated one has to allow more time, but we have already spoken of the ordering of the Lord's Supper.) My proposed order, even in this shorter time, allows for the full diet of prayer.

    Prelude

    Doxology

INVOCATION

HYMN OF PRAISE
> *(This hymn should be a metrical Psalm or paraphrase. It could be followed by an anthem.)*

PSALTER

    Gloria patri

Prayer of Illumination

SCRIPTURE LESSON

HYMN

(This should be a hymn or anthem appropriate to the Lesson and the Sermon.)

SERMON

HYMN

(This hymn should be one of affirmation or dedication. Any necessary announcements are best made after this hymn and before the choral preface to prayer.)

———————————————

Choral Preface to Prayer

PRAYERS OF INTERCESSION
    for the Church
    for the ministry
    for all people
    for the civil authority
    for those who suffer

    Lord's Prayer

———————————————

COLLECTION OF TITHES AND ALMS

HYMN OF THANKSGIVING

(This could be replaced by an anthem sung while the collection is being received. A single stanza of a thanksgiving hymn might then be sung at the conclusion of the collection.)

BENEDICTION

    Doxology

    Postlude

Several remarks need to be made about this suggested service. The elements of praise, intercession, and thanksgiving are prominent in it for two reasons. First, I think these genre are the easiest to start with because they are easiest to explain. That we should offer our praise and thanksgiving to God is a fairly simple concept to make clear to people. It is also easy to get across that an important part of public worship is to pray for the public concerns of a Christian people. What could be more logical? We pray for each other when we pray with each other. It is easy to explain that we come together to continue the ministry of intercession begun by Christ. I have often put it this way: One of the reasons we come together as a Christian people each Lord's Day is to pray for the work of the Kingdom of God throughout the world, for our country and its leaders, and for any in our own community who are in special need. People readily understand that this is a legitimate function of public prayer.

The second reason that I emphasize praise, intercession, and thanksgiving in this service is that these types of prayer are particularly appropriate to public worship. Praise and thanksgiving are magnified when done in fellowship with other Christians. We build our praises on the praises of others. Calvin comments that our praises are warmed, encouraged, and made more fervent when we offer them in the company of a whole congregation. It is the same way with intercession. The very gathering of the community presses us to pray for each other.

There is no Prayer of Confession and Supplication here. I wish it were not the case, but somehow the whole idea of confession waves a red flag for a lot of people. Happily, there are churches that already have a unison Prayer of Confession and Assurance of Pardon. So much the better! If there is nothing of this sort already in the service, it can be made up for in other ways. One might introduce a Prayer of Confession at an evening service, or one might select psalms of lamentation and confession fairly regularly for the responsive reading of the psalter. Another way of compensating for the omission of a Prayer of Confession is to build the elements of lamentation, confession, and a humble approach to God into the Invocation. Ultimately, however, a prayer of confession is an indispensable element in Christian prayer.

The service I have just outlined also does not have a separate Prayer of Thanksgiving. One might compensate for this in similar ways. Singing a hymn of thanksgiving at the end of the service is a possibility. Or perhaps, if one does not have time to sing a full hymn, one could regularly conclude the taking of the collection with the first stanza of a hymn such as "Now Thank We All Our God." In my first church it had long been the custom at that point in the service to sing those well known lines from Solomon's prayer of dedication:

All things are thine:
    no gift have we,
Lord of all gifts,
    to offer Thee;
And hence with grateful
    hearts today,
Thine own before
    Thy feet we lay.

Another possibility would be for the choir to sing an anthem of praise and thanksgiving while the collection is being received.

It is important for the minister to recognize the value of the elements of prayer with which the congregation is already familiar. As the minister teaches and preaches about prayer, these things need to be interpreted. In this way one makes solid the foundations that have already been laid. Then, as time goes on, one can build on them further. This is all part of what is involved in the pastoral ministry of leading a congregation in prayer.

This briefer order of service also has only one Scripture lesson. This I regret. If a congregation has a tradition of both an Old Testament Lesson and a New Testament Lesson, I would certainly not change it. I have always felt that one needed both an Old Testament Lesson and a New Testament Lesson. I also find the public reading of Scripture a very worthwhile part of the service, but when pressed for time, it seems more important to allow plenty of time for proper expository preaching and for a more fully developed service of prayer. This brief order of service allows for quite a bit of hymnody, psalmody, choral anthems, and responses. Such things are done best in public worship. They are rather hard to do in small prayer groups and in private prayer, except by accomplished musicians. The reading of Scripture on the other hand can be done easily when one is praying alone or with a small group. A way of making up for this is to give more time to the public reading of Scripture in the special services at Christmas, during Holy Week, or at Thanksgiving. Here again, I think it is important for the minister to make such decisions with pastoral sensitivity. Different ministers have different gifts. Sometimes a Church has a strong choir; sometimes no choir at all. Sometimes the congregation sings well; sometimes it does not. The minister has to be realistic about what can, practically speaking, be effective. That realism is an important part of leading in prayer.

This short service has quite a bit of liturgical framing. This liturgical framing, which we find so often in Scripture, delights in setting up the service of worship with solemn admonitions to prayer and declarations of praise. The service I have laid out begins with a Prelude and a Doxology and ends with a Doxology and a Postlude. There is an Invocation at the beginning and a Benediction at the end. The Psalter is concluded by the *Gloria patri*, and the Scripture lesson is introduced by a Prayer for Illumination. The major prayers are introduced by admonitions to prayer or perhaps a choral preface or an organ prelude. In the chapter on benedictions and doxologies I had quite a bit to say about this, but now all I need to say is that one finds quite a bit of this sort of thing even in smaller churches today. It is poorly understood, but it is there. What the perceptive pastor needs to do is help the members of the Church understand what it is they are really doing.

Without a doubt the most difficult aspect of this service is having the main prayer follow the sermon and the collection at the end of the service. There will be considerable objection to this. As it has been put to me so many times, "I just think that the sermon is the main part of the service. It gives me a boost and that is what I want to leave church with." For many people, especially elderly people, that is the conclusive argument and no amount of theological considerations or historical evidence is going to change it. The fact that all the historical evidence shows that the ancient Church had the main prayer after the sermon or that the Reformers and especially Calvin made a big point of having the sermon lead into the prayers of intercession will carry no weight at all against this kind of argument. It begins with the unfortunate assumption that the sermon is all that really matters in the service and concludes by imagining that the purpose of worship is to make people feel good. We can expect this kind of argument from a Church that has forgotten how to pray, especially when it has forgotten how to pray together. Only when one has succeeded in teaching quite a bit about the ministry of prayer, especially about the ministry of intercession, can one make major changes like this. When people begin to perceive that there is more to prayer than polite liturgical form and when they begin to recognize that the minister is a trustworthy guide in this rugged high country, then and only then will they tolerate significant changes in the service of worship. One can formulate it as a principle: Liturgical reform depends on spiritual growth.

In the meantime there is one thing the pastor can easily do toward developing a sense of intercessory prayer in the congregation. By long tradition the minister is expected to conclude the sermon with a short prayer driving home the point of the sermon. This is, in fact, the vestige of the older practice. It has survived from the days when the sermon was regularly followed by the prayers of intercession. This short prayer as we now have it could be cultivated into a proper Prayer of Intercession. Instead of using the prayer as a way of concluding the sermon, the minister could develop themes of intercession suggested by the sermon in the way I have suggested in the chapter on the Prayer of Intercession.

As one begins to be aware that a congregation is learning to pray together, then one can move toward a more fully developed service of worship. Such a service might go something like this:

Prelude

Doxology

INVOCATION

HYMN OF PRAISE
(A metrical psalm or paraphrase. This could be followed by an anthem of praise.)

PSALTER

Gloria patri

_____

PRAYERS OF CONFESSION AND SUPPLICATION
Confession (in unison)
Petitions and Supplications
Assurance of Pardon
Doxology

_____

Prayer for Illumination

OLD TESTAMENT LESSON

NEW TESTAMENT LESSON

HYMN

*(A hymn or anthem appropriate to the lessons and the sermon. An
appropriate anthem could be sung between the lessons and an
appropriate hymn before the sermon.)*

SERMON

HYMN OF DEDICATON

Choral Preface to Prayer

PRAYERS OF INTERCESSION
for the Church
for the ministry
for all peoples
for the civil authority
for those who suffer

Lord's Prayer

COLLECTION OF TITHES AND ALMS

*(An anthem of thanksgiving might be sung during the taking up of the
collection.)*

PRAYER OF THANKSGIVING

HYMN OF THANKSGIVING

BENEDICTION

Doxology

Postlude

All this, it must be admitted, assumes a rather fervent congregation.
But as we are beginning to discover, it is the more fervent congregations
that at the end of the twentieth century are beginning to grow. The Church
of the future, as I see it, is interested in more prayer rather than less prayer,
and it is for those who want to lead the Church in this direction that these
pages have been written.